Leadership:
Tidbits and Treasures

Chris Brady and Orrin Woodward

Leadership: Tidbits and Treasures

By Chris Brady and Orrin Woodward

First Edition, July 2008

Published by:

Obstacles Press, Inc.
4072 Market Place Dr
Flint, MI 48507

Cover design and layout by Norm Williams

Printed in the United States of America

www.the-team.biz
www.chrisbrady.typepad.com
www.orrinwoodward.blogharbor.com

Dedication

This book is dedicated to all the leaders who have the courage to take a stand and make a difference.

Acknowledgements

Nearly a year ago (at the time of this writing) we found a strange need to communicate "from the grave" you could say. It was almost as if we were in enemy territory (figuratively, of course) and all lines of communication had been severed. We knew we had to communicate with the rest of the troops or victory indeed would be jeopardized. (slightly melodramatic but we LOVE military examples!) If only we had a way to transmit and receive information without the use of phones, radios, letter carriers…etc. Just then, it dawned on us. There was a way, created years ago for just such a scenario…the internet! And so this book was born, well, at least indirectly. Orrin and I began a blistering assault of information into the blogosphere (a fancy way to say, we started typing words on a web log!) and we received so much feedback from y'all (southern term for "yous guys", which is an east coast term for "all of the wonderful people who read our blog"), that we decided to make a book from the leadership articles in cyberspace. So, the first acknowledgement goes to you, the readers and leaders that necessitated this kind of information in the first place, because without you and your insatiable appetite for learning, this book would not exist.

Next, we need to give a hearty tip of the hat to the many writers, leaders, speakers and world changers, both contemporary and deceased from which we draw our examples and our inspiration. One such world changer, mentor and friend is Pastor Robert Dickie. Without his wisdom, spiritual guidance and unconditional love we would not have the capacity or the insight to have even begun a project like this. We would also like to thank our wives, Terri Brady and Laurie Woodward whose beauty, love, flexibility and encouragement pale only in comparison to their loyalty and love for others. Without their support over the last year we are certain this book would not be a reality. Special thanks go to our fellow Policy Council members whom we look up to and respect. Your insights and actions in perilous times have inspired us to become better ourselves. We would like to thank our parents, Jim and Gayle Brady, and Bud (deceased) and Kathy Woodward, for their constant belief and encouragement. Norm Williams, our graphic designer and artist, deserves special recognition. His talent, creativity and patience have made a bunch of words on a page come to life. We would also like to give a literary high-five to Bob Dickie III and his staff, Tom Maguire and Doug and Tiffany Huber, who have faithfully served in various capacities behind the scenes.

Most importantly, we wish to give all the glory to our Lord and Savior, Jesus Christ. Everything we have and will ever accomplish is by His Grace.

Contents

TABLE ONE

NOTE: This map has been divided into categories so you can search specifically for the Treasure you're most lookin' for!

BIOGRAPHY

Joe DiMaggio: A Quest for Excellence................21
Abraham Lincoln 202
Benjamin Franklin's Leadership Example 109
Billy Durant: Creator of General Motors 263
Booker T. Washington: Bitter or Better 149
Walt Disney: Creative Leadership 224
Dwight Eisenhower: Power of Perseverance 98
George Washington: Centurion Principles 33
John Wooden: Quotes & Stories 64
Patrick Henry: Part One 135
Patrick Henry: Part Two 177
Robert E. Lee: Self Denial 218
Ronald Reagan: A Great American 251
Edward Deming: Success Process 282
Tom Brady: The Cumulative Effect of
Incremental Change 76
Mark Twain: Surprising Leadership Example 157
William "Billy" Mitchell: Courageous Leadership ... 192

PEOPLE SKILLS

People Do Not Care How Much You Know, Until
They Know You Care 31
Predictability Through Emotional Intelligence 62
The Loyalty Effect 138
We Grow When We Serve 133

TABLE TWO

SUCCESS THINKING

A Couple of Fish Stories 40
Blessings in Disguise 143
Charles Swindoll: Attitude 38
Circle of Concern vs. Circle of Influence 81
Doesn't Matter, Doesn't Matter, Doesn't Matter . . . 128
Do Not Survive: Thrive 175
Giving 51
If You Are Dumb, You Had Better Be Tough 119
It is How You Think That Counts 154
It is Not Enough to be Busy 172
Leadership is Character in Motion 211
Life is Too Short to be Little 106
Lincoln Quote 58
Obstacles 130
Purpose Transcends Pleasure 93
Self Deception 239
Taking Stock of Accomplishments 291
The Only Way to be Happy, is to Give Happy 275
The Power of a Dream 17
The Right Information 247
Two Important Questions 73
Urgency: The Press of Time 156
We Have Been Taught How to do. But Have
We Learned How to Be? 122
You Don't Know What You Don't Know 24
You Only Get What You Picture 88
Mortimer Adler: Reading Great Books 83

TABLE THREE

NOTE: Look for the special boxes with Quotes, Facts and Trivia at the bottom of many articles!

HISTORY

Captain Pellew and the Indefatigable 125
Character Under Fire 277
Goals In Stone 90
Historical Example: Captain Samuel C. Reid 235
Leaders Get Results: The Battle for America 215
Level Four Leadership: Every Captain Was
a Nelson 273
Mental Toughness 28
Separation of Religion and State 267
The American Creed 169
The Great Awakening 195
The Underground Railroad 56
Today's The Day! 152

SPIRITUAL

Competing Views of Success 26
Eternity is a Long Time to Be Wrong 74
People Skills 184
Quiet Strength 209
Standing on Conviction 248
The Leadership of Proverbs: Part One 44
The Leadership of Proverbs: Part Two 140
The Leadership of Proverbs: Part Three 167
The Leadership of Proverbs: Part Four 198
The Leadership of Proverbs: Part Five 286

BUSINESS/POLITICS

Counter Productive Compassion 187
Economics 162
The Tipping Point 59
Wolf at the Door 164

TABLE FOUR

LEADERSHIP/CULTURE WAR

A List of Principles. 121
A Walk on the Wild Side 71
America's Culture War:
Ideas Have Consequences 46
Ideas Have Consequences -
Economic Thought and Karl Marx 228
Character 86
Courage of Your Convictions. 145
Creative Destruction 204
Developing Heroic Value 284
Four Common Myths About Leadership 79
Fruit on the Tree 96
Initiative: The Not-So-Secret Secret to Leadership . . 289
Leaders Are Learners 19
Leaders Carry an Unfair Load 181
Leaders Make Others Feel Important 241
Leaders Under Managers 221
Leadership Begins and Ends With Hunger 54
Leadership is an Inside Job 190
Leadership Perspectives 100
Levels of Influence 103
On Becoming a Leader 118
Real Leaders Take 100% Responsibility 69
Social Capital and Leadership 258
Struggle 245
The Main Thing 36
The Ripple Effect 148
Three Steps For Leaders in the Fog of the Battle . . 207
When All is Said and Done 254

Forward

As I write this, the United States finds itself in the midst of an election season where political leaders are desperately vying for their party's nomination and a chance to be the future president. The jaded masses crowd into union halls, coffee shops, hotel lobbies, and outdoor market places to catch a glimpse of these leaders in hopes that a positive vision of the future will be cast, igniting a passion within them. With the ever present television commentators and political pundits pouring over data in the background, the real debate begins as families wade through the rhetoric to make their decision. People are no longer preoccupied with political parties, mud slinging, and the volatile Washington banter that has numbed most as they ask the question: who can best lead our country and deal with the many difficult issues that we all must face together? Do we have a trustworthy leader who can inspire and lead us?

In my opinion, the authors of this book embody the very essence of what the American people are searching for in a leader. All successful leaders have developed a set of core leadership traits that have helped them rise to prominence. Orrin Woodward and Chris Brady strongly believe that these principles transcend time, background, and industry. It can take a lifetime of trial and error to learn these principles. Orrin and Chris have taken the time to draw upon their incredible backgrounds of lifetime experiences and distilled these into this book.

From their humble backgrounds beginning in Flint, Michigan, they first entered the professional world as engineering students at General Motors Institute, now Kettering University. Orrin and Chris quickly climbed the corporate ladder of success. At the tender age of twenty four, Orrin had already impressed the engineering world as the holder of four recognized US patents and as the winner of a prestigious national benchmarking award. His success led him to start a lucrative career as a pri-

vate consultant in the automotive industry. Chris Brady's mete-
oric rise as a young man is equally impressive. After graduating
with honors from GMI, he was offered multiple full ride scholarships to study engineering. Turning down Stanford's graduate
school to attend Carnegie Mellon, Chris once again graduated at
the top of his class.

Not content with past success and the comforts it brought
them, Orrin and Chris continued to develop their leadership
abilities and decided to leave their lucrative careers as engineers for General Motors to enter the private sector and become
entrepreneurs. They have continued to be successful in every
endeavor they have led.

Wanting to make a difference in the lives of others by sharing what they learned about success
and leadership, Orrin and Chris decided to author their first book for national publication,
Launching a Leadership Revolution. This book
provided a ground breaking analysis of these
principles and how aspiring leaders could
grow in their leadership influence and ability
over time. Complete with historical examples
woven throughout insightful leadership development techniques, the book became a *New York Times*
and *Wall Street Journal Best Seller* in less than two months and
was ranked as the number one business book on multiple lists
including *USAToday*!

As I have worked with Orrin Woodward and Chris Brady for
the past three and a half years, my respect and admiration for
them as leaders has grown every day. Prior to this, I served as
an officer in the United States Air Force where I had the opportunity to work for several generals and other great leaders in the
military along with a host of high ranking government officials
from around the world. This opportunity allowed me to observe
high-level leaders in various industries around the globe and
I am convinced that Orrin and Chris are in the top echelon of
leaders in the United States today.

The more time I get to spend with Orrin and Chris, the higher
regard I have for these men and their leadership ability. More
importantly, however, is the moral character displayed by them
and their deep desire to help others and make a difference in
the world. I admire Orrin and Chris because they are not only

teachers of leadership principles but students and practitioners as well. They teach timeless biblical principles and display them in their lives each and every day.

Orrin Woodward and Chris Brady aspire to help you expand your leadership abilities so you can lead wherever God calls. Whether you are a leader in your church, school, job, community, or in your home, the leadership traits and principles taught in this book will help you realize your full potential. Truly understanding these principles and putting them into practice will enable you to be the most effective in making a positive difference in the world. I believe you will be blessed by reading this book and I know the success principles discussed in the following pages are timeless and will help you be successful in every endeavor you may choose to pursue. The deep desire of Orrin and Chris is that this book will make a difference in your life and that you in turn will be able to make a difference in the lives of many more.

Robert Dickie III
CEO, Team

Leadership: Tidbits and Treasures

This leadership book, filled with tidbits and treasures, will give you a priceless liberal (old meaning of liberal, meaning well rounded in classic literature and thought) education, including many prescriptions for successful living. Here is a book that will stimulate your thinking and help you to be successful in your work, your study, and in your every day living. Our prayer is that it will also educate the reader in the areas of history, politics, economics and the culture war that is currently upon us. The articles and illustrations from great thinkers and doers throughout history outlined on these pages, will, if studied and applied to your life, help develop your inner qualities, and that is where your real wealth is.

"Employ your time in improving yourself by other men's writings so that you shall come easily by what others have labored hard for." – Socrates

This book is compiled and written for the express purpose of condensing some of the best thoughts, experiences and illustrations of the greatest men and women in history in the hope that this distilled wisdom will be a guide to inspire you to build a solid bedrock foundation for a better, nobler life. This leadership book contains some of the most powerful and persuasive utterances of man—words that will inspire, help and delight you.

"If I have seen farther than others, it is because I have stood on the shoulders of giants." -- Sir Isaac Newton

Through the centuries great men and women have stood out

like the beacons of a lighthouse to guide and enrich their fellows. The examples of these greats live on through the years; everyone can benefit by the trails they have blazed toward a better life. No person is great in and of themselves; they must touch the lives of other great beings that will inspire them, lift them, and push them forward.

"The short sayings of wise and good men are of great value. They are like the dust of gold or the sparkle of the diamond." – Tolstoy

"Those who cannot learn from history are doomed to repeat it" – George Santayana

This leadership book of wise principles was undertaken in the belief that there was a need for a book of practical, every day, usable sayings, thoughts and articles, that would help people develop their full potential. If we are to be highly successful in life, we must look backward to learn from the experience of the greatest minds of the past, and then apply this wisdom to the greatest fulfillment of our every day living. The experience of the sages, coupled with our own, gives us an unbeatable combination. Let us develop and apply wisdom together, so we can make a difference.

The Power of a Dream

Carl Sandburg said, "Nothing happens unless first a dream." A dream is the root of vision. A leader has a concept of a better future, situation, or outcome, and dreams of the day when it becomes reality. The vision of the dream creates a tension on today, and that tension produces the hunger that drives a leader onward.

The concept of dreaming is imperative, and it is actually an exercise in discipline. It is quite easy to slip into complacency and lose track of the dream we are chasing. "Oh, I can work toward that tomorrow," or "I don't really need to accomplish that, I guess, it was just a crazy dream," or "I don't know what I was thinking, it all looks so unrealistic to me now." These and many other phrases I have heard from people who were once infused with a dream only to have it fade with either the passing of time or when facing delays or challenges. Or maybe the 'pressure' of the chase

> *Dream no small dreams for they have no power to move the hearts of men.*
> – Goethe

was too great for them. There is a kind of tension around a leader's vision, a healthy anxiety deep down that says, "We aren't finished yet. Remember the dream? Remember the vision? We should be doing something about it!" Oh, those irritating inner voices! Just like a child, they seem never to forget a promise or goal! Losing one's grip on a dream, I suspect, is quite natural. Considering all the people that are out there, only a small percentage really engage in the chase of a dream. Of those, an even smaller percentage musters the courage to persevere *no matter what*. To hang tough to the vision requires courage and mental toughness. It also requires one to stay in close contact with one's dream.

How is this done? By refreshing the dream in our minds

17

on a regular basis. What was it that you saw when you first got that hint of what could be? What did you want to accomplish? Whom did you want to help? What rewards inspired your soul? What made you 'come alive' in the first place? Answer these questions, and then get around that original source of inspiration on a regular basis to keep it fresh. Refresh your dreams, and do it often. Stoke the flames that ignite the hunger deep inside. Then, look out world, because not only is it true that "Nothing happens unless first a dream", but it is also true that "nothing can stop a leader with a dream!"

Learning is not attained by chance, it must be sought for with ardor and diligence.
–Abigail Adams

The knack of flying is learning how to throw yourself at the ground and miss.
–Douglas Adams

Life is about learning; when you stop learning, you die.
–Tom Clancy

Leadership and learning are indispensable to each other.
–John F. Kennedy

Leaders are Learners

Leaders are hungry to assault the status quo. And one of the biggest commonalities you will find among leaders of different colors and stripes is their hunger to learn, to equip themselves with what they will need to make their vision a reality.
Here are some key questions for any would-be leader:

1. **Are you reading good books on a regular basis? Is reading a habit in your life?** Remember, as the saying goes: Leaders are Readers.
2. **What are you reading...and why?** There is only so much time in life, and we cannot do it all. Frankly, there just will not be time to read and learn everything we would like, so we had best make our choices carefully.
3. **With whom are you mentoring?** Without mentorship, leaders drift like a sailboat without a keel. Mentors provide perspective, wisdom, correction, reframing, encouragement, experience, and honest feedback. Your leadership journey will take you farther and make more of an impact if you find and follow a great mentor.
4. **Where are you in your spiritual life? You may have your beliefs, but are you sure about what you believe? Where did you get those beliefs?** The reason spirituality plays such an important role in leadership is that leadership will test you. When pushed against the wall because of your courageous assault on the status quo, where will you turn for internal strength? A leader is guided by his or her belief in a higher calling and purpose, and it is really difficult to understand this without addressing the spiritual questions.

5. **In what areas are you currently holding yourself accountable for personal growth?** In other words, what are you trying to improve about yourself? Additionally, what new skills are you currently seeking to acquire? Sustained, quality leadership requires this kind of commitment to personal growth.

There are many more questions of this nature you can explore, but these five should give you a good start toward learning as a leader. And do not forget: learning is a lot of fun!

A Quest for Excellence

In today's highly competitive market there are fewer and fewer ways to separate your company and your products from the competition. All products offer the latest features and all companies offer guarantees. What keeps some companies and some individuals always near the top of the pack? I would say the biggest differentiator in the New Economy is a constant and never-ending quest for excellence. The Japanese have a word for this called *kaizen*. Do you practice kaizen in your personal and professional life? If you were hiring a doctor, lawyer, builder or accountant—(you would hope they were practicing constant and never-ending improvement in their personal and professional lives) If you discovered they were not interested in excellence, would you think of hiring someone else? I am shocked by how many people accept the mediocrity in their own lives and yet expect excellence in others. We would be upset if the server does not refill our water when it is empty, but, at the same time think nothing of giving less than 100% on our own job or business. Why the double standard?

Let us decide today to live our lives, in all areas, to a standard of excellence. Anyone desiring to live a life of excellence must declare war on average. If you can do better, then it is time to start giving the world your better, on the way to your best. How can we possibly change others if we will not do the hard work of changing our own average habits? The world will flock to a man or woman who is focused on giving their absolute best to their chosen profession. If you wish to get more—you must begin by giving more! In fact, I would tell you to give more even if you never get more. Success is an inside job and the satisfaction obtained from knowing you did your personal best is the ultimate reward. My attitude anytime I speak, write, or mentor is to give my personal best.

Regardless of whether anyone recognizes it or not—I still feel great because I know I did my personal best.

There is a story told of Joe DiMaggio, of New York Yankee fame, that exemplifies this principle. Joe was one of the greatest hitters of all time and a Hall of Famer. In a spring training game that did not count in the standing or statistics, Joe drove a ball down the first base line. Instead of jogging to first with a single, Joe sprinted around first and dove head first into second just ahead of the outfielder's throw. Joe hit a double in a meaningless game that did not count in the record book. It looked like Joe was playing in a World Series game instead of a spring training exhibition. Why did Joe do that? A reporter after the game asked just that. Joe's answer ought to be taught to every person in every profession. Joe said he could not help but think that some mother or father had brought their young child to the game. Maybe this was the only time that child would ever see Joe DiMaggio play the game of baseball. He wanted to be sure to give them something to remember. Wow! That gives me goose bumps just thinking about it! In your life, are you giving people something to remember? Are customers raving about your quest for excellence in all that you do? Many people remember watching Joe play the game because he was in a quest for excellence in his chosen field. Joe understood that success was from the inside out, and if he played baseball he would play it at his high standards.

I encourage you to live a life in a quest for excellence. Listen to your customers and seek ways to improve their satisfaction with your service. The more you have them raving about what you do, the easier it is to market your profession. A satisfied customer is the best advertisement for what you do. An unhappy customer is the worst advertisement for what you do. You will never make everyone happy, but you must start by making yourself happy with your efforts. If you are not happy, then it is no surprise that others are not. Today is the day to make your life a quest for excellence and live kaizen as a habit. I volunteer to be your coach and I expect nothing less than your personal best. Together we can change your habits and then teach what we have learned to world.

What are we waiting for?

- Nicknamed *"Joltin' Joe"* and *"The Yankee Clipper"*, DiMaggio was a Major League Baseball center fielder who played his entire career (1936–1951) for the New York Yankees.
- He was a three-time MVP winner and 13-time All-Star.
- Widely hailed for his accomplishment on both offense and defense, as well as for the grace with which he played the game.
- When he retired at age 36, he had the fifth-most career home runs (361) and sixth-highest slugging percentage (.579) in history.
- He is also the only player in baseball history to be selected for the All-Star Game in every season he played.
- A "picture-perfect" player, DiMaggio achieved a 56-game hitting streak (May 15 – July 16, 1941) that has been called the top American sport feat of all time
- In total, DiMaggio led the Yankees to nine titles in thirteen years.

You Don't Know What You Don't Know

Learning starts when we realize that we still have more to learn. As the saying goes, "The more I learn, the more I realize how much more I still have to learn." In fact, I am continually surprised at how often I have to re-learn something. I did not realize I had to re-learn it, until I actually did re-learn it, at which time I realized I had known it before but somehow forgotten it!

Confused? A better way to say it might be, "You don't know what you don't know." And, not only do we not know what we don't know, but we are forgetting what we used to know! So if we don't know what we don't know, and we are forgetting what we do know, it kind of makes you wonder what we DO know, you know?

The point is that the human mind is an organism that requires constant care and feeding in order to stay healthy. And the more you feed it, the more you learn, the better it does and the better you feel. Staying hungry for learning is one of the healthiest things anyone can do in life.

Those who do not spend any time learning are usually not very much fun to be around. Ignorance is normally louder than wisdom! I was thinking about this one day, and wondered why more people do not take an active approach to learning and growing. They buy food constantly to feed their physical hunger. Why would they not they invest just as readily in their mind? Then it occurred to me; when we are hungry our stomachs are empty, our stomachs actually make a growling noise! Perhaps it would be good if our brains made a noise when we start getting ignorant! (Some people would need earplugs before going in to work). But actually, ignorance has a way of getting heard. It may not be "growling" per se, but our tongues normally convey our ignorance loudly enough! Let us all avoid the "brain growl" that a lack of learning promotes. Embrace learning at least as much as you embrace that turkey dinner on Thanksgiving! A few audios, a good book or two, a stimulating conversation with someone that can teach you something, travel to a new place, etc.: these are the delicacies of knowledge. Bon appetite!

Wisdom from children

When your mother is mad and asks you, "Do I look stupid?" it's best not to answer her. Megham, age 13

When you complain about doing the dishes, you usually get stuck doing them more often. Nichole, age 14

When your mom is mad at your dad, don't let her brush your hair. Morgan, age 11

You should not be the first one to fall asleep at a slumber party. Katie, age 12

Reading what people write on desks can teach you a lot. Tiffany, age 13

If you put a frog in a girl's desk, you're going to hear some screaming. Nicholas, age 9

Competing Views of Success

There are competing views of success in our world. Achieving success in your life will depend largely on how you define success in the first place. I must admit, my own personal definition of success has changed drastically over the years.

One view of success in the world is measured by victory. We will call this the Victory School of Thought. If you are in sports or business or any type of competition, success is defined by winning. Interestingly, though, some of the most successful in this category, such as legendary coach John Wooden of the UCLA basketball team, defined success as doing one's personal best and giving full effort toward that end. In his view, winning was a natural by-product of this philosophy. It certainly worked for Wooden. He remains the most successful coach on record in nearly any sport at any level. However, Wooden, even though he was so successful, is still rare in his philosophy. Most consider winning as the true measure of success.

Another view of success involves "capturing" things; weather it be titles, status, recognition, fame, or material possessions. We will call this the Attainment School of Thought. This is the "He who dies with the most toys wins" philosophy. This view is a close cousin to the Victory School of Thought.

While these two schools certainly have their good points, and victory and some of the trappings of success are not wrong in and of themselves, they do both come with a fundamental flaw. That flaw relates to the real way we human beings are wired and what truly gives us satisfaction. The flaw in the thinking of both the Victory School of Thought and the Attainment School of Thought is that the things of this world can please us, that they are worthy as an end-goal in our lives.

The third and final School of Thought, I believe, is the Eternal School of Thought. Here true success is found. While it is okay to pursue victory in our professional endeavors (and who among us does not like to win once in a while?), and it is okay to enjoy the rewards of hard work and prosperity, real success is found in filling what one author called "The God-shaped void in our hearts." You see, humans scratch around on the earth, busy about all kinds of things, pursuing all sorts of pleasures and objects designed to bring satisfaction, when the whole time what they are really searching for is a relationship with their Creator. How do I know this? It is what the Bible is all about, and it is what has happened in my own life.

After reading Indianapolis Colts Head Coach Tony Dungy's book, *Quiet Strength*, I would recommend it to anyone. And I will pull one piece from that book to illustrate what I am talking about here. According to Dungy,

"God's Word . . . presents a different definition of success - one centered on a relationship with Jesus Christ and a love for God that allows us to love and serve others. God gives each one of us unique gifts, abilities, and passions. How well we use those qualities to have an impact on the world around us determines how 'successful' we really are."

I love Dungy's definition of success. It focuses on God's grace and what He has done through Christ on the cross, and shows that our grateful response should be one of service to others and sacrifices for God's glory. That is true success. If the other, worldly definitions also happen here and there, so be it. The world's definition of success by itself is hollow and leads to increased depravity as people strive for more and more, hoping to fill that "God shaped vacuum" that no amount of "the world" will fill. Real success comes from that relationship with God through His son Jesus Christ, and living out our days fulfilling, to the limits of our ability, the calling He places on our lives.

Mental Toughness

Marcus Luttrell, a U.S. Navy SEAL, was the lone survivor of Operation Redwing in Afghanistan, in which just four Navy SEALS held off and/or killed a large group of Taliban fighters, wrote about the difficulty of the SEAL program training. At one critical point in the grueling routine, in which all but the most resolute fail out or resign, Luttrell's mentor gave him some advice:

"Marcus, the body can take damn near anything. It's the mind that needs training. Can you handle such injustice? Can you cope with that kind of unfairness, that much of a setback? And still come back with your jaw set, still determined, swearing you will never quit? That's what we're looking for!"

In the book, *Lone Survivor*, Luttrell explains in great detail the unbelievably harsh training all SEALS must go through in order to call themselves by that name of honor. Just reading about it is exhausting. One instructor told Luttrell, "You're going to hurt while you're here. That's our job, to induce pain; not permanent injury, of course, but we need to make you hurt. That's a big part of becoming a SEAL. We need proof you can take the punishment. The way out of that is mental, in your mind." Luttrell explains why some men just could not make it through the training:

"Judging by the one guy I knew, I did not think any of the ones who quit were in much worse shape than they had been twelve hours before. They might have been a bit more tired, but we had done nothing new, it was all part of our tried-and-tested routines. In my view, they had acted in total defiance of the advice handed to us by Captain

Maguire. They were not completing each task as it came, living for the day. They had allowed themselves to live in dread of the pain and anguish to come. And he had told us never to do that, just to take it hour by hour and forget the future. Keep going until you are secured. You get a guy like that, a legendary U.S. Navy SEAL and war hero; I think you ought to pay attention to his words. He earned the right to say them, and he is giving you his experience. Like Billy Shelton [the other mentor mentioned above] told me, even the merest suggestion [should be listened to]."

Point #1: Both comments were from instructors who were also SEALS, who had been through it before, who knew what they were talking about. For advice givers, this should be the only kind we listen to; those with fruit on the tree. Luttrell did listen to those men, realizing that every little thing they said was important and for a reason.

Point #2: Success is more a matter of mental toughness than physical strength or intellectual prowess. Battles are always first won in the mind.

Point #3: The only way to make it through difficult circumstances is to take each blow as it comes, to focus upon the day at hand and not worry or be overcome by the burden of the days still ahead. One step at a time, you can get through almost anything.

These three points are very important. They apply not just to the incredibly tough life of a United States Special Forces Officer, but to any of us who want to achieve significance in our lives. There will always be difficulty, opposition, and obstacles. Getting through them is a game of mental toughness, forcing the mind to take things one at a time, and listening and adhering to the best advice available from qualified mentors.

During Operation Redwing, Luttrell and three other of America's finest, most highly trained, tough-as-nails, fighting machines were betrayed by an act of kindness they showed to three goat herders. Within about an hour of having their lives spared, the goat herders alerted an entire Taliban army to the presence of Marcus Luttrell, Matthew Axelson, Michael Murphy, and Danny Dietz. Although the odds were overwhelming, four men held their own against an army of over a hundred whom were armed with explosives and RPGs. Mental toughness was on hand to even the tables. Far away from home, cut off from any back-up, on unfamiliar terrain, surrounded by enemies, and always concerned about the "liberal press" back home in America which would crucify them for their tiniest error, these four young men used every ounce of their training and combat experience. For hours and hours they kept up a continuous fire-fight, three times falling off cliffs to establish new defensive positions. Wounded and dying, the American guns continued to eliminate their enemy.

How could it be possible that with odds of 35 to 1, the Taliban could not even kill one of the American soldiers for hours and hours? How did these fine young men stand up to such terrifying horror? What was the substance they summoned deep from within that pushed them to fight even when mortally wounded? The answers are many, and worth taking a quiet moment to ponder.

The valor, patriotism, honor, courage, and mental toughness of these men are a credit to the country they represented. I salute them. I admire them. I thank them and I am committed to learning from their example. We should all learn from their example.

It's the least we can do.

People Do Not Care How Much You Know Until They Know How Much You Care

There is a famous saying that, "People don't care how much you know until they know how much you care." Although there are many important aspects to leading people, such as the need for leaders to learn, to grow, to discipline themselves, to carry heavy burdens, and to serve others, it can never be forgotten that leadership is made up of the substance of *caring*.

Many, many leaders throughout history have started well but finished poorly. Studying their lives, it quickly becomes evident that they lost touch with their roots. Somehow, in the process of gaining ascendance and advancement, they became corrupted by their power gain. They became a little too focused on themselves. Along the way, they forgot who they were and what they were about. Somewhere on the journey they stopped caring about the cause or the individuals involved and became engulfed by self-interest. One author called this phenomenon becoming "unmoored," as when a sailboat drifts away from its anchorage.

Caring is an interesting concept. Of course a leader cares about his or her cause. Of course a leader cares about the attainment of the vision. Of course a leader cares about his or her legacy and what is left behind. But does the leader care about the people? More importantly, does the leader care about individuals? And most importantly, does the leader care about you?

Insincerity does not work for those who truly want to lead. There is no "fake it 'till you make it" in true leadership. Phonies are easy to spot. True caring is a heart thing. It can be felt. We know that someone cares for us and about us instinctively. And my experience has been that the biggest

31

leaders are the ones who, along with all the other great traits we have been discussing here, can also connect on a heart-level of caring with the people they influence.

The questions to ask yourself about your leadership are these: Do my people know how much I care about them? Do they know what I respect about them the most? Have I told them lately or made sure they know this? Am I actively adding value to their lives?

Let people know that you care. Play with your heart on your sleeve. Give yourself to your people as much as you give yourself to your cause, and you will see the cause advanced much quicker. And most importantly, you will be loving people all along the journey, which is the point of the journey in the first place.

George Washington: Centurion Principles

Author Jeff O'Leary has hit a homerun with his book *Centurion Principles*. Former Colonel O'Leary's views of world changing leadership are right in line. This is an inspiring read from a man who has walked his talk. He has a section on George Washington about Leadership that Serves Greater Ends. George Washington took an incredible risk to be part of the Revolutionary War. He had plenty of land and was doing "pretty well." Why would someone get involved in a conflict in which they were severe underdogs? I think the answer is: George lived by certain principles and he would rather sacrifice his wealth than those principles. There was many times during the war when it was Washington's convictions and character that held the army together. Compromising on your core convictions is cowardice. In the end, George Washington and his principles overcame England, and a new country was formed. We need more men and women with the courage of George Washington. Allow me to quote from the Centurion Principles:

"The greatest leaders were also great risk takers. Stop for a moment and decide if you are willing to become that kind of leader. If not, move on to the next chapter. This risking is costly. If it wasn't everyone would be doing it. Who wouldn't want to leave a legacy like Washington's behind him?

The key to getting beyond the illusions of fame, money and power is to take the long view. It is paradoxically both simple and difficult. Take the long view—not the quarterly, monthly, or daily view of your business or calling.

When you finish your race and look back at the footsteps of your life, what are you going to see, and what are you going to be proud of?

Near the end, I was offered the opportunity to continue my service and be promoted to brigadier general within a few years. I politely declined and turned in my papers for retirement at the same time my book was released. This infuriated my superiors, and I was quickly moved from my special status of "golden boy" to untouchable leper. But I believed then, as I do now, that we are created for a destiny greater than accumulating power, money, or fame. (Certainly, being a general could be a high calling for someone if that was his or her destiny. It just wasn't mine.)"

This is some incredibly courageous thinking! A Colonel that is offered an opportunity to be a general turns it down to follow his destiny. Very few people will do that. Most settle for the immediate and give up the long term. Leaders must stay focused on the long term even through the inevitable criticism. How is your legacy coming together? Have you even considered a legacy before? I was 25 years old and had never thought about it. That is why I am so thankful for mentorship. I heard a speaker when I was 26 and he said, "You must be willing to give up everything you have to accomplish everything you want." This thought resonated with me and I realized I had been playing it safe with my life. Why are we playing it safe? Have we not we all figured out that we are not making it out of life alive? So if we are all going to die—the only question is—are we going to truly live?

When you make long term decisions in your life you will be criticized. The myopic thinkers cannot see what you see or think what you are thinking. They will see your choices as foolish, self-serving or worse. You can take heart that George Washington was criticized greatly in England for his choices. Abraham Lincoln was criticized horribly from people in the North and South during the Civil War. Winston Churchill was a pariah for his thoughts on Nazi Germany before World War II. Albert Einstein said, *"The biggest people with the biggest ideas will be criticized by the smallest people with the smallest ideas."* Colonel O'Leary was offered a promotion and when he refused, he was criticized by the same people who loved him minutes before. The old saying, *"Everyone wants you to get by, just not by them"* is appropriate here. To Mr. O'Leary's credit, he followed his destiny. Sometimes you have to take the road less traveled.

Follow your dreams! Follow your destiny! Leave a legacy! If it hurts—then you know you are right on track. What is your Legacy?

Words of Wisdom from George Washington:

Be courteous to all, but intimate with few, and let those few be well tried before you give them your confidence."

"Discipline is the soul of an army. It makes small numbers formidable; procures success to the weak, and esteem to all."

"Few men have virtue to withstand the highest bidder."

"Firearms are second only to the Constitution in importance; they are the peoples' liberty's teeth."

"If the freedom of speech is taken away then dumb and silent we may be led, like sheep to the slaughter."

The Main Thing

One of my favorite Pat Riley quotes is, *"The main thing is to keep the main thing the main thing."* Success is largely a result of the leader's ability to focus, and to maintain that focus over time.

There are so many GOOD things that we can do in our lives, and these opportunities plead for our attention all the time. But there are few and sometimes only one GREAT thing that we should be doing. As the saying goes, GOOD is the enemy of GREAT.

For most people, maintaining focus is a major challenge. They have plenty of talent, they are extremely motivated, they are impassioned by a cause, but they fall victim to their own lack of focus. Distractions are like shiny objects on the side of the road, and some leaders never reach their potential because they are always scampering off to investigate some new fancy. When comparing two equally capable leaders, the one who maintains his or her focus the longest and most consistently will post results far in excess of the one who could not.

There is another point in Riley's quote: *"not only is it important to keep the main thing the main thing, but it is fundamental that we have a main thing."* How many people do you know who don't really have a main thing? There is nothing about their life anyone could point to and say, "That is what they stand for," or, "This is what their life is all about." Sadly, this is true for a majority of people. In most cases, the main thing worthy of comment in a person's life is insignificant at best. "Video games, fantasy football, golf, washing his sports car, etc." are the types of answers

> *If you chase two rabbits, both will escape.*
> —Chinese proverb

one might hear. How about Mother Theresa? Ministering to the poor. George Washington? Winning independence for the colonies. Frederick Douglass? Freeing the slaves. Notice the contrast?

One of our main goals in life should be to discover what God has built us to do, and then get about doing it with all our heart. This will require pruning away some of the GOOD things to do, and focusing on the GREAT things. We must discover what our main thing is. Then we must work to make sure it remains our main thing. Then when someone brings up our name, and inquires as to what our main thing is, let us make sure there is an answer. And let us be sure that the answer is a main thing worthy of the blessing we've been given!

Charles Swindoll: Attitude

A proper leadership attitude is the difference maker in relationships, leadership and results. To be a person of influence you must be like the North Star to others—always pointing in the right direction. If your attitude is constantly changing based on victories or losses—you are making it very hard for others to follow you. Having a positive attitude does not mean ignoring the facts. A positive attitude is a confidence that regardless of the facts, you will plan and work to overcome and win. I have watched many incredibly talented people fail. The "failure" itself is not fatal; as everyone "fails" at some point. The attitude you take after a "failure" is crucial to your long term success. If you label yourself a loser because of a loss, this will have more long term negative affect than the loss itself. I love the statement, "It is not what happens to you, but how you handle it that counts!" Here is my all time favorite attitude quote from Charles Swindoll. Charles is an excellent pastor and author. His books have made a huge impact in my life!

"The longer I live, the more I realize the impact of attitude on life. Attitude, to me, is more important than facts. It is more important than the past, than education, than money, than circumstances, than failures, than successes, than what other people think or say or do. It is more important than appearance, giftedness, or skill. It will make or break a company ... a church ... a home.

The remarkable thing is we have a choice every day regarding the attitude we will embrace for that day. We cannot change our past. We cannot change the fact that people will act in a certain way. We cannot change the inevitable.

38

The only thing we can do is play on the one string we have, and that is our attitude ... I am convinced that life is 10% what happens to me, and 90% how I react to it. And so it is with you ... we are in charge of our Attitudes. "

I could not possibly say it better than Swindoll has in this passage. Do you have an attitude of gratitude? When challenges hit you, how do you respond? Leaders must guard and nurture the proper attitudes. Your team must know that you are a principle centered person and follow the North Star of your principles. A ship following the North Star is not carried away by the latest winds or currents. The captain of the ship stays focused on the North Star and guides the ship to this absolute. In the same way, leaders must stay focused on the North Star of their absolute principles and not be blown by the latest victory, loss, or setback. Are you that type of leader to your team? How do you protect and nurture your attitude? Do you encourage others in your team by your positive example? I have decided to live my life by principles, period. My personal responsibility to God is to follow the right principles and I will leave the consequences of following the right principles to God Himself! As moral agents, we are responsible for the choices we make, and God is responsible for the consequences of our choices. Attitude does make the difference and it starts with you.

Attitude is the difference maker.
– John Maxwell

Assignment: Ask yourself: Are you a thermometer or a thermostat when it comes to attitude? When people need encouragement, do they come to you?

A Couple of Fish Stories

We were fishing near the Northwest Channel, just outside the boundaries of the Dry Tortugas. As we bobbed around on the mild chop, the Woodward's *Dreambuilder* yacht nicely handling the waves, we not only encountered new fishing stories, but we heard some old ones as well.

Shark fishing is what we were supposed to be doing. Only the sharks did not seem to know that. So instead we caught Yellow Tail Snapper, Mangrove Snapper, Blue Runners, and a bunch of other fish that ended up getting immediately re-hooked and sent squirming to the bottom as bait for sharks. At one point (apparently thinking he was a shark) a thirty pound Black Grouper hooked himself on Tim Mark's line and found his way into our cooler. Later, with much effort by Orrin, a fifty pound Goliath Grouper (also playing the part of a shark) made his way to the transom platform of our boat. Only the Goliath Grouper did not know that it was illegal for him to bite our line, so we had to let him go with a warning. What happened next was a fish story and a half.

Tim's rod bent violently downward and one of the best fights of the day had begun. The rod tip dipped and swerved from side to side with Tim expertly maneuvering in counterattack to keep the feisty fish on the line. It swam under the boat and tried to get the line hooked on the props. Then it darted from one side of the boat to the other. Next it dove straight down, then came jiggling back up. Finally Tim's superior angling brought the mighty opponent exhausted to the surface. Gaffed and dragged aboard, we were quickly informed by "Captain Bill" that the worthy opponent was a Horse Eye Jack. "About thirty pounds," he said. We nodded. In seconds, Tim chopped the Jack into sections and used it to bait his shark rigs for another try at the elusive species. After a few moments, I wandered inside the living room of the Dreambuilder (isn't it cool when a boat has a "living room"?) and retrieved the Florida fish guide book we had brought along. Curious, I looked up the Horse Eye Jack. There on the page was a magnificent picture of a fish exactly like the one Tim had just caught. Exactly like it, except it was smaller and the size was different. Then I noticed it. The part about the world-record size Horse Eye Jack ever caught, that is: a mere twenty four pounds, eight ounces!

At first Tim was all right with it. After all, he was at that moment hoping for a shark to bite his chopped up trophy fish. It was not too late to save face. But as the night wore on, and the trophy fish parts became soggy, stringy trophy fish parts, and the sharks continued to stay away from our boat by the thousands, Tim's smirk changed slightly. We had gotten so focused on catching sharks we missed a world-record fish!

I immediately saw a lesson in our little caper. We were out there on that ocean to catch sharks, sure enough. But we were also out there to catch fish, have fun, enjoy each other's company, and yes, generate some fish stories. It was probably every bit as exciting catching that Horse Eye Jack as it would have been to catch a shark (maybe), but we were focused beyond the Jack, and we missed a unique piece of scenery along the way (but we did get a good story). We should never lose site of the blessings we get along the way. Sure we want to achieve greatness, sure we want to get our goals and dreams, but we should never be so focused that we lose site of the many blessings life delivers, on the journey.

So much for the new fish story: now on to the old one. "Captain Bill" had many to tell, but the best was about a shipwreck somewhere in our vicinity that day. Apparently the wreck is a favorite among scuba divers (so we will be sure to double back and do that soon). Apparently, a large Goliath Grouper, of the variety that Orrin caught, swam into the old wheelhouse of the sunken ship. It was very cozy in there, and a good supply of small reef fish swam through it on a regular basis, providing a constant and easy source of food. Also, the Goliath Grouper was relatively safe from predators in his little wheelhouse. But gradually he grew in size, as

Goliaths do. And he grew, and he grew, and he grew (sounds like a children's story). You see, Goliath Grouper can get up to over eight hundred pounds, and apparently this one did. In fact, he grew so big in his little habitat, that he got too big to get out. So for the rest of his days he is sentenced to swim in little circles around an old sunken wheelhouse wondering why so many scuba divers come to look at him!

Again, the lesson for us is a compelling one (I guess I never thought about what value fish stories can have in our lives. I think I will pay more attention to them in the future)! That Grouper became imprisoned by his desire for comfort. Born into the beautiful, vast ocean, he was free to swim and eat where he pleased. But comfort and complacency lured him into an easy existence that at first didn't appear dangerous. I am sure in the early days he swam out whenever he wanted. Then, gradually, he began scraping his scales off getting into and out of the wheelhouse. Finally, it was just too late. His lifestyle had imprisoned him. How often do we see that happening in people's lives? At first, our cubicles are merely comfortable, safe places to earn a living. But then, slight increases in salary and status begin the imprisonment until it is too late. Dreams and goals become regrets and missed opportunities. We switch from living in the vast ocean of possibility thinking and become trapped in the wheelhouse of "If only I had have...". It is no longer "what am I going to do," it is "what I wish I had done." We surrender what we want in the future for what we can have in the moment. We give up the long-term GREAT to get the short-term GOOD.

Do not get me wrong. I am not saying anything derogatory about anyone's position or career in life. I'm talking about individual choices and decisions. What may make one fish happy may not make another happy. Perhaps that Grouper in the wheelhouse is just as satisfied and content as he can be. Maybe all the other Grouper are envious of his easy existence. But I think somewhere in the very back of his little Grouper brain, that big fish wishes he could swim free, out among the depths and currents with other free fish.

I for one will choose to stay out of the wheelhouses of comfort. I prefer to take my chances among the predators and currents of the open sea. And I hope you do too.

TEST YOUR FISH KNOWLEDGE!

1. Approximately how many species of fish are there worldwide?
   A: 9,000, **B:** 27,000, **C:** 56,000, **D:** 72,000

2. What species of fish produces the most eggs?
   A: Ocean sunfish, **B:** Squirrelfish, **C:** Redtooth triggerfish, **D:** Salmon

3. How many different varieties of goldfish are there?
   A: 20, **B:** 50, **C:** 100, **D:** 250

4. What is the fastest fish?
   A: Swordfish, **B:** Racing Shark, **C:** Mako Shark, **D:** Sailfish

5. What is the most poisonous fish?
   A: Needle fish, **B:** Rice fish, **C:** Puffer fish, **D:** Snail fish

6. What is the largest species of fish?
   A: Giant Gourami, **B:** Bluefin Tuna, **C:** Whale Shark, **D:** Blue Whale

7. What is the smallest species of fish?
   A: Dwarf goby fish, **B:** Stout infantfish, **C:** Tadpole cod, **D:** Stargazer

8. How many teeth can a shark grow during its lifetime?
   A: 500, **B:** 5,000, **C:** 50,000, **D:** 500,000

Answers: See pages 293-294

The Leadership of Proverbs: Part One

I would like to start a series on the wisdom and leadership of the Proverbs. My goal will be to review verses of the Proverbs and discuss what they mean to leaders and people of faith. Proverbs is a collection of wisdom quotes written over the centuries by the Jewish nation. Solomon was responsible for many of them, but other authors added to the collection as God deemed necessary. There is much wisdom to be gleaned from the Proverbs about wisdom, leadership, association, worship, money, relationships, etc. A hungry student should devour the Proverbs and practice their precepts. Let's get started with the first Proverb and discuss verse five.

Proverbs 1:5 - A wise man will hear, and will increase learning; and a man of understanding shall attain unto wise counsels:

This verse of Scripture is teaching that a wise person is hungry to learn and understand. This goes right along with the concept that hunger is the first qualification of leadership. Without hunger there is no drive to understand and people will remain ignorant of their ignorance. The Delphic oracle stated that Socrates was the wisest Greek because he was the only one who knew he did not know all the answers. We are all ignorant in different areas, the key is to continue to learn and gain understanding from the generations of wise men and women who have come before us. Human nature has not changed over the centuries and that is why we can learn so much from history. Are you listening, reading and learning to obtain wisdom for your own life and your community? Any leader worthy of their calling is constantly striving to improve; to be able to serve with more wisdom and under-standing. As a person seeking wisdom, you have a lifetime assignment ahead of you! Charlie "Tremendous" Jones em-phasizes, "In five years, you will be the person you are from the books you read and the people you associate with." I personally associate with great ideas through books, CD's, partners and mentors. I encourage you to do the same!

America's Culture War –
Ideas Have Consequences

I wanted to let all of you know that I have been reading extensively in the scientific arena seeking to better understand micro-biology. I know, I can hear you already…"Orrin, Why would you, a former engineer who now is a leadership consultant, bother reading about micro-structures and the cell?" There is a method to my madness. I have news for those who have missed it. America is involved in a culture war. Whether people believe it, have decided to remain neutral, or just do not care – it is still a reality. If you do not believe it you are just not informed. If you wish to remain neutral, you will soon realize that neutrality is impossible. If you just do not care – I will attempt to explain why you should. I love this country and all that it was founded upon. We have been the most blessed country the world has ever known. The United States and Canada stand in the historic flow of Western Civilization and enjoy the benefits of its gathered wisdom. The founders created our country on Judeo-Christian principles from the Bible that resulted in the blessings of America. Then what is going so wrong and why? A wise statement from G.K. Chesterton sums up much of our current crisis: "Never remove a fence until you determine why it was there in the first place." How many fences have been torn up in America by judicial activists or well-meaning but unwise politicians? It is time to retrace our footsteps back to the principles that are timeless and proven.

Human nature has not and will

not change regardless of what the evolutionist will tell you. Technology has changed the way we live, but has not changed who we are. We still struggle with our emotions overcoming our reason. We still ask who are we and why are we here? How you answer the questions will have a radical impact on the way you live. Yes: Ideas do have consequences. Rabbi Daniel Lapin is the author of *America's Real War*. He has a perceptive message to America today:

> One of the most profound truths about America as we approach the end of the twentieth century is that we are no longer one nation under God. We are really two separate nations with two distinct and incompatible moral visions.

> For the purpose of trying to clarify the cultural tug-of-war, we need only ask the question: Did we get here by a process of unaided materialistic evolution or did God arrange it? Do we come from a Creator or from apes?

Are human beings purposefully created or here by chance? The answer to this question changes the role of leadership, does is not? We must understand the foundational principles of who we are and what our purpose is, in order to lead people properly. Understanding who we are and why we are here will have a huge effect on the culture of America also. This is why I read Michael Behe's incredible book, *Darwin's Black Box*. Michael Behe is Professor of Biological Sciences at Lehigh University. He received his PhD in Biochemistry from the University of Pennsylvania in 1978. The book is a biochemical challenge to evolution and is still un-refuted (albeit much discussed) a decade later. According to Behe,

> Biochemistry is the study of the very basis of life: the molecules that make up cells and tissues that catalyze the chemical reactions of digestion, photosynthesis, immunity, and more. . . . . .

> In its full throated, biological sense, however, evolution means a process whereby life arose from non-living matter

and subsequently developed entirely by natural means. . .

The cumulative results show with piercing clarity that life is based on machines—machines made of molecules! Molecular machines haul cargo from one place in the cell to another along "highways" made of other molecules, while still others act as cables, ropes, and pulleys to hold the cell in shape. Machines turn cellular switches on and off, sometimes killing the cell or causing it to grow. Solar-powered machines capture the energy of photons and store it in chemicals. Electrical machines allow current to flow through nerves. Manufacturing machines build other molecular machines, as well as themselves. Cells swim using machines, copy themselves with machinery, and ingest food with machinery. In short, highly sophisticated molecular machines control every cellular process. Thus the details of life are finely calibrated, and the machinery of life enormously complex. . . . .

If you search the scientific literature on evolution, and if you focus your search on the question of how molecular machines—the basis of life—developed, you find an eerie and complete silence. The complexity of life's foundation has paralyzed science's attempt to account for it; molecular machines raise an as-yet-impenetrable barrier to Darwinism's universal reach.

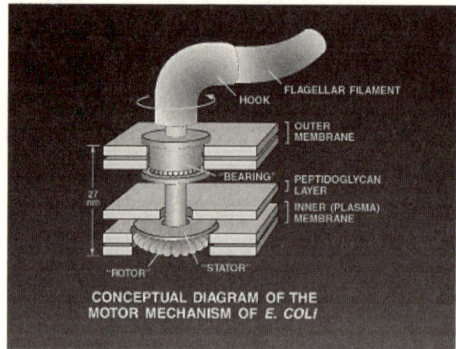

CONCEPTUAL DIAGRAM OF THE MOTOR MECHANISM OF *E. COLI*

Do you understand what Professor Behe is saying? As an engineer - I walked through miles of factories with specifically designed processes to start from raw materials to finished assemblies. When I observed an intricately designed process, I was inspired to be a better engineer and sought to find the person who designed the machines to learn from him or her. Professor Behe is telling us the design of cells is more intricate than the best process any human engineer has ever designed. Are we really suggesting that a level of complexity beyond any engineer's ability was created by chance outcomes? This sounds like an incredible leap of faith to me! What I appreciate so much about Professor Behe is that he is intellectually honest and lets the data speak to him without bias. Professor Behe is one of the early originators of a growing movement known as Intelligent Design. Intelligent Design does not claim to know who designed the system, but claims evolutionary theory or chance could not generate the level of complexity discovered in micro-biology.

Darwin himself stated, "If it could be demonstrated that any complex organ existed which could not possibly have been formed by numerous, successive, slight modifications, my theory would absolutely break down."

What type of biological system could not be formed by "numerous, successive, slight modifications"? Professor Behe has an answer.

Well for starters a system that is irreducibly complex. By irreducibly complex I mean a single system composed of several well-matched, interacting parts that contribute to the basic function, wherein the removal of any one of the parts cause the system to effectively cease functioning. An irreducible complex system cannot be produced directly (that is, by continuously improving the initial function, which continues to work by the same mechanism) by slight, successive modifications of a precursor system, because any precursor to an irreducibly complex system that is missing a part is by definition nonfunctional.

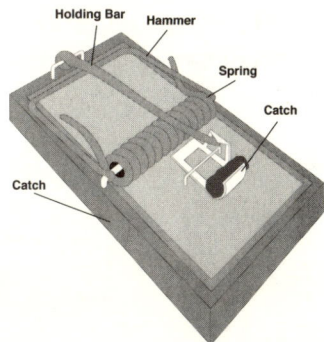

Microbiology is full of irreducibly complex systems and Professor Behe displays several examples in all their intricate details in his fabulous book. My personal favorite is the bacterial flagellum. It has a rotor, stator, bearings, etc. I was stunned when I read about the flagellum because it looks so similar to the fuel pumps I designed. The fuel pumps had commutators, rotors, bearings, and pumps. The motor mechanism in the flagellum is an ingenious design by an incredible Engineer!

A good example of a simple irreducible system is the mousetrap. If it is missing one of its irreducible parts— it will never catch the mouse. The mousetrap needs all of its parts to work and is worthless unless all the required components are functional. This makes it irreducibly complex because any part taken away eliminates the function of catching mice. This is a sure sign that someone designed the mousetrap because it could not have happened through steps of smaller to greater complexity as each step would be non-function and thus not retained. There is not a functioning "half a mousetrap".

What does this have to do with leadership and America's culture war? I believe plenty! If a person is created, then leaders must help the individual fulfill the purpose he or she was created for. If a person is here by chance, then any authority figure can manipulate people for the authority's purpose. This is what the culture war is about. Are leaders leading people to fulfill the individual's Godly purpose or are leaders manipulating people for the leader's self interest? If there is no God, then the leader must decide what the purpose of the people is. This is a scary thought! True leadership of people and God's plan for someone's life are intricately linked—like the irreducible complex systems. We will finish this discussion in part two. How we view man and his creation has a huge impact on how we view America and our roles as leaders.....

Giving

The concept of generosity is rarely discussed these days, and I dare say it should be included in the pantheon of leadership principles. In a world riddled with selfishness, "me-first" mentality, and "every-man-for-himself" behavior, it certainly is refreshing to run across people who have a generous spirit.

Pastor Robert L. Dickie is one of the most generous men with whom I have ever had the privilege of associating. His sweet spirit and others-first focus is refreshing, inspiring, and a great example for any budding leader to follow. It seems that every time I am with him, I feel lifted, encouraged, and valued. He is always first to inquire about me, my family, our health, and our general well-being. He is quick to ask about people who need help and prayer, and he is very slow to talk about himself or complain about anything.

Why is it that generosity is in such short supply today? Should it not follow that when we talk about servant leadership, generosity should automatically be included? But I have noticed that many mistake "serving others" for "serving themselves." What do I mean? I believe it is very easy, as in so many aspects of leadership, to become self-deceived. We may think we are serving others as we should, but if we find we are doing it for motives which are designed to serve ourselves, the serving cannot be labeled as generosity. It may be calculated sharing, but it is calculated nonetheless.

Generosity knows no calculation. It knows nothing about "self." It is the gracious outpouring of the heart that results in material aid, spiritual assistance, caring, and love freely given to someone else who is in no position to repay the favor in any way. True generosity is the hallmark of a mature leader's heart.

I believe that we can get far on the leadership journey by

serving others in ways that also serve ourselves. In and of itself, there is nothing wrong with this approach, as far as it goes. Win-win relationships are absolutely fine, and preferred to win-lose or lose-win, and certainly to lose-lose. But I also believe that we will not maximize our potential, and our impact on others, until we strive to develop our generosity. Great leaders do not rise to greatness alone. They have been helped, inspired, guided, and gifted to achieve what they have achieved. In the spirit of thankfulness, great leaders become generous as they realize the full extent of the measure of their blessings and the role others have played in their lives. And this generosity is measured by their giving. I was struck recently when reading a biography of a famous

We make a living by what we get. We make a life by what we give.
–Winston Churchill

industrial giant from the nineteenth century. While he was generous in his dealings and negotiations with fellow businessmen, and he was apparently often concerned to make sure his business partners prospered in their affairs with him (the embodiment of win-win), in his personal giving and generosity he was no better than a scrooge. On millions of dollars of income, he had donated less than a few hundred dollars to worthy causes, including churches and charities. No matter what else he accomplished in his life, I felt that this one fact alone tarnished his legacy.

Others give very publicly. In some ways, this unsettles me, too. When every dollar given must be accompanied with the donor's name emblazoned across the building (for example), it seems that, as the Bible says, "They already have their reward" (meaning here on earth).

What if we as leaders could develop our generosity? What if we grew our heart for others? What if we, as Pastor Dickie in my example above always says, could "die to self" and learn to serve others without calculating how it might also serve our interests? Do you think the world would be a better place? Do you think we might make a bigger difference in the world, in Christ's name (instead of our own)? Do you think it might mean more for our individual legacies (even

52

if it remained anonymous among men, and remained solely between God and ourselves)?

I like thinking these thoughts. I like thinking about the difference we could all make. And I like thinking that each of us can hold ourselves accountable to grow in this area and truly become generous, avoiding the pitfall that appears to have ensnared the industrialist I mentioned above. People may forget our leadership, they may forget our achievements, but I doubt they will ever forget our generosity!

Leadership Begins and Ends With Hunger

The genesis of our book, *Launching a Leadership Revolution,* was a late night discussion Orrin Woodward and I had about the essence of leadership. It seems everybody has a general concept about leadership, and there are innumerable misconceptions out there. But when it comes to analyzing the subject and really understanding it, the topic of leadership becomes somewhat elusive.

What Orrin and I finally struck upon, and what became the opening salvo in our book, was that leadership begins and ends with hunger. The willingness of an individual to risk his or her own personal peace and affluence and attack the status quo is not only the initiation of leadership, but its sustaining force. Hunger, it should be noted, is slightly different from ambition. Where ambition is largely about self-aggrandizement, hunger is more about service and significance. This type of leader, the truly authentic kind, is unable to leave "well enough" alone. They must assault what they observe to be an unacceptable status quo, and they often do this at great risk to self. Such leaders are more willing to compromise their comfort than their principles. This is precisely why leadership is so inspiring. By definition, however, when a person's hunger wanes his or her leadership wanes along with it. When the status quo becomes increasingly acceptable, a leader's influence diminishes correspondingly. That is why Orrin and I put such a heavy emphasis on the hunger of a leader in the book.

It is not enough to gain this insight, it must be applied. Armed with this knowledge, a leader can take charge of his or her personal hunger and work it like a muscle to keep it healthy and make it stronger. Hunger actually becomes a discipline and must be nurtured by the leader. In fact, history shows that throughout ages, great accomplishments were made by the hungriest individuals. It was hunger that drove them to take a risk to change the world in the first place. It was hunger that drove them on in the face of criticism. And it was hunger that propelled them to persevere when things got tougher than anticipated. History is also replete with events that illustrate what happens when hunger dries up and complacency replaces it.

May you find the source of your hunger to grow, change and influence, and may you stoke its flames without ceasing. Why? Not only does the world need you to come alive and maximize your potential by embracing your hunger for significance, but when you live such a life, it is the most exhilarating ride imaginable. And that, perhaps, is leadership's most valuable hidden treasure.

The Underground Railroad

If leadership is about attacking the status quo and railing against injustice, then the unsung and often unnamed heroes of what came to be known as the "Underground Railroad" are a great example.

A loose network of sorts, committed to aiding escaped slaves reach freedom, existed in the North American colonies at least as far back as George Washington's time. The "brethren" of the Quaker sect had long been involved in procuring freedom for slaves, and found mention in one of the first President's correspondences. Eventually, the affiliation would come to be called the Underground Railroad, and would consist of a highly developed process of shared responsibility. Certain participants would be responsible for getting slaves off a plantation. Others would be involved in concealing them secretly in their homes. Still others would be responsible for transport.

No matter the share of the load, each step in the process was extremely dangerous. This was especially true for the large number of former slaves working within the Railroad. Whites caught assisting runaway slaves would be convicted of breaking the law. Blacks would be returned to bondage, and, regarding their efforts at "stealing property", could expect harsh and likely even fatal, punishment. Further, the Fugitive Slave Act was passed in Congress forcing northern states to assist southerners in the recapturing of their "property." This meant that upon reaching the north, after an arduous and dangerous journey, an escaped slave could never really be free. They were, at best, only free for the moment. Fortunately, as the Civil War drew nearer, northern states were less and less likely to participate in the returning of slaves to the south.

Harriet Tubman, an escaped slave herself, was one of the

most active participants in the Underground Railroad, responsible for the freedom of more than three hundred slaves. It is approximated that she made nineteen trips into the Deep South, risking her life for the freedom of others.

It would be almost impossible in our era of peace, comfort, education, and tolerance to really comprehend just what it was like for the heroes of the Railroad. Their risk of injury, punishment, torture, and death were enormous. Their allies were few. Their next journey into the deep, dark south could be their last. Preachers in pulpits strained the scriptures to try and find Biblical evidence that slavery was acceptable. Lawyers across of the land argued for its legality. It is hard for us to even imagine the concept that one human being could consider another to be their "property." Heroes like Tubman and thousands of others involved in the Underground Railroad embodied the true spirit of leadership. They confronted a brutal reality with fierce determination, massive risk to personal peace and affluence, and with unrelenting perseverance. This is what leaders do. They cannot stand idle when they are needed. They cannot hide behind their peace and affluence, nor take the easy way out, nor sell out to comfort, when confronted with injustice. Leaders do not calculate the cost when it comes to doing what is right: they simply do it.

In a day when it is hard to get people to leave their couch, put down their video games, and live a real life, it is incredible to consider that just a few short years ago people were willing to risk their entire lives, fortunes, and reputations in the name of freedom for others. May that spirit of justice still live on in our society. May that streak of leadership courage still find its way into the hearts of many amongst us today. Our countries need it more than ever. Slavery in the United States may be gone, but injustice still reigns in a thousand different forums in our world, and if good people do nothing, evil wins. But if leaders can be aroused across the land to stand up and lead, to fight for what they believe in, to rail against injustice, to protect and free others less fortunate, then the spirit of Harriet Tubman and the operators of the Underground Railroad lives on.

Abraham Lincoln Quote

"Whenever I hear anyone arguing for slavery, I feel a strong impulse to see it tried on him personally."

This quote is appealing even beyond the historical significance of slavery in our society. It speaks to anyone and everyone who will tell you what you should and should not do, who will represent facts as though they have experienced them, who will give advice when they have not experienced what they describe, and who will dare to make the rules for a game they have not played nor intend to play. As another quote says, "Talk is cheap; it takes money to buy whiskey." Those who are "doing" should never be at the mercy of those who are "managing." The best leaders are always those who can, and have, performed well at the endeavor.

Slavery was propagated for years in our country because good people listened for too long to those who painted it with colors other than the truth. Lincoln cut through all that with one elegant sentence. As a matter of fact, his quote is timeless and can apply to anything we might consider. Try this. Substitute anything for the word "slavery" and see how the quote works. If thinking is asking questions to ourselves and then working out the answers, and quality thinking is the asking of quality questions, then this little trick ought to elevate the quality of our thinking just a bit!

Think.

Act.

Lead...

...Then think some more.

The Tipping Point:
Mavens, Connectors, Salesmen

There is a fantastic book worth reading that I read several years back called *The Tipping Point* by Malcolm Gladwell. Gladwell calls a community tipping point a social epidemic and states that there is only a small percentage (5%) that can create it. Gladwell documents three traits that cause an epidemic: contagiousness, little causes having big effects, and changes happening not gradually but at one dramatic moment. The third trait is called a tipping point. There are three types of people involved in a social epidemic: Connectors, Mavens and Salesmen. Any business that expects to grow must focus on serving these three crucial catalysts. No business will survive long-term that mistreats these irreplaceable community influencers. Malcolm states:

"In a social epidemic, Mavens are data banks. They provide the message. Connectors are social glue: they spread it. But there is also a select group of people—Salesmen—with skills to persuade us when we are unconvinced of what we are hearing, and they are critical to the tipping of word-of-mouth epidemics as the other two groups."

To create a tipping point we need the thinking and actions of all three groups. Not long ago, I attended a conference in

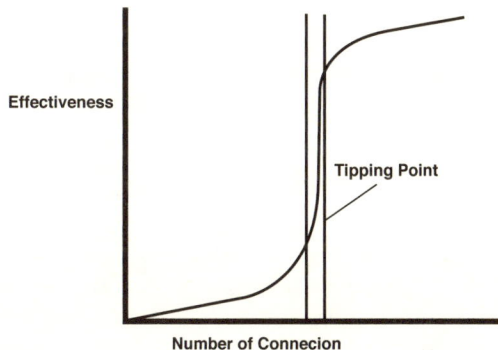

Effectiveness

Tipping Point

Number of Connecion

Hawaii where I heard Mr. Gladwell speak. His concepts of the tipping point are mind-expanding and ought to be read and understood by any company expecting to grow its market share. Let us read what Gladwell has to say about the three categories of people involved in tipping points.

Connectors

"What makes someone a Connector? The first—and most obvious—criterion is that Connectors know a lot of people. . . Six degrees of freedom does not mean everyone is linked to everyone else in just six steps. It means that a very small number of people are linked to everyone else in a few steps, and the rest of us are linked to the world through those special few.

In the graph below, notice how Louise connects almost every other person.

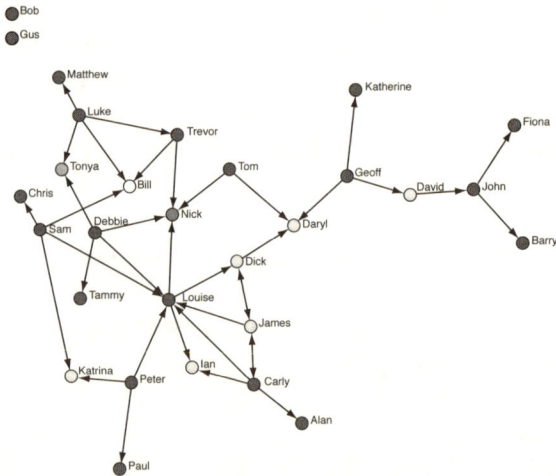

Mavens

"The word Maven comes from the Yiddish and it means one who accumulates knowledge. In recent years, economists have spent a great deal of time studying Mavens, for the obvious reason that if marketplaces depend on information, the people with the most information must be the most important.

Salesmen

"Part of what it means to have a powerful or persuasive personality, then, is that you was becoming synchronized with him. . . . But the essence of the Salesmen is that, on some level, they cannot be resisted.

I believe we are on the verge of the tipping point, and with a leadership community made up of Connectors, Mavens and Salespeople we can win the culture war that is raging! Our communities deserve the best and it is our responsibility to develop our gifts and skills. We all have roles to play and promises to keep!

What role will you play in the tipping point of the leadership community?

Are you a Connector, Maven or Salesmen/Saleswomen?

Predictability through Emotional Intelligence

I finished another book on relationships and personal development the other day. There were some points where I strongly agreed and others where I disagreed. We should come to all books with the idea of being stretched. The old saying, "Iron sharpens Iron" comes to mind and this book sharpened me. The book was *You Inc.* by Harry and Christine Beckwith. (Not the *You Inc.* from Burke Hedges) Let me quote a snippet from the book:

"....she asks him, 'From your work, what do you consider the key to successful relationships?'

'Predictability,' he answers, 'We are most comfortable with people whose behavior we can predict.'"

Being predictable means you are the same person in all situations. Are you an inner directed person whose values are developed through your reading and faith? Or are you outer directed and take on the values of the group you are with at the moment? You cannot possibly be predictable if your core values change depending on which group you are with. Live an authentic life and be predictable (consistent). Many people are afraid to be themselves for fear of rejection. My thoughts are, if you are rejected for believing in virtuous principles, then so be it. I would rather be rejected by a thousand people than have my conscience rejecting me for not being true. Who are you? Are you the same you in all situations? No one is perfect but the key is to close the gap between what you say you are and what you really are. This makes your character predictable which creates security in the group, team or family you are leading.

We are most comfortable with people who are in emotional control of their life. If the ups and downs of life cause you to emotionally respond then others cannot predict your behavior. If they cannot predict your behavior they will avoid spending time with you. The reverse of this is true also. No matter what is going on in your personal life, focus on serving others. When you see someone, focus on encouraging them. Life can be discouraging at times and we must choose to be an encourager and not a discourager. If I were to add one trait to every person I know it would be the trait of encouragement. I know what a difference a kind word has made to me at times in my life. God has blessed me with an association of incredible friends and leaders. I have been blessed to speak across the world on leadership principles. But to this day, when someone pays me a sincere compliment it is appreciated and motivates me to improve further. I try to remember that if kind words have that affect on me after all these years of speaking, then they have an even greater effect on a new potential leader. Think of the people who have had the greatest impact in your life. Were they not all encouragers who expected more from you? If they had an impact in your life, why not become that kind of person in someone else's life? The choice is yours, because leadership is a choice.

Emotional intelligence, more than any other factor, more than I.Q. or expertise, accounts for 85% to 90% of success at work... I.Q. is a threshold competence. You need it, but it doesn't make you a star. Emotional intelligence can.
– Warren Bennis

John Wooden: Quotes and Stories

John Wooden through his books and interviews has been one of the most influential leaders and mentors in my life. His books have resonated in my mind and heart and forced me to rethink some of my leadership actions. Let me share a few of my favorite quotes and what they mean to me.

"Never try to be better than anyone else, but never cease trying to be the best you can be. You have control over that. Not the other."

This is so important in life. You do not control the other person or their performance, but you are responsible for your performance. Focusing on what you cannot control is not empowering and creates a helplessness-hopelessness situation. Addressing areas you can control empowers and motivates you to improve. John Wooden has nailed a key success principle here.

"Success is the peace of mind which is a direct result of self-satisfaction in knowing you made the effort to become the best you are capable of becoming."

This is a radical philosophy change from the current culture's love affair with winning and loathing of losing. I was of this mindset myself and felt that if I lost, it did not matter how hard I had worked. I was wrong. I learned that losing is the major stepping stone to success. Effort and preparation bring an internal peace that communicates you have done all you can do. In fact, I would say you win or lose before the competition begins depending on how you prepared mentally, physically and spiritually. I love when people count me out. People say, "Orrin lost this" or "Orrin failed at that", when I know that I have had another learning experience and did all I could do with what I knew at the time. On the other side of the coin, someone can be winning and receiving the awards and yet be losing. How is that possible? If they are not giving 100% effort then they are not honoring God with their abilities. Do we all enjoy winning? Absolutely, but winning is only the icing on the cake and not the main meal. The main meal is your personal best. Everyone can give their personal best and only you truly know when you are giving it. My questions to you are these:

1. Are you giving your personal best?
2. Are you successful using John Wooden's definition of success?

My third John Wooden example is not a quote, but a true story of his grade school basketball coach. Coach Earl Warriner taught John Wooden two important leadership principles.

No individual is more important than the team. Coach Warriner benched John Wooden even though he was the star of the grade school team. John had tried to use his position as the team's best player to get a teammate to do what he should have done himself—get his jersey which he had inadvertently left at home. When John explained to the coach that they would lose with him, Mr. Warriner said, "Johnny, there are some things more important than winning."

I love this story! Coach Warriner knew that winning by violating your core principles is not winning at all. It is a catastrophic loss of character and conscience to violate principles in an effort to "win." There are principles more important than winning or losing and John Wooden learned a valuable lesson he would carry with him throughout his coaching career.

Be willing to suffer the consequences of standing up for

your beliefs. Mr. Warriner was the principal of a local grade school in Indiana and expelled a student who had done something very bad. The boy's father was on the school board and demanded his son be reinstated immediately. The father told Principal Warriner he would have his job if his son was not allowed back in school. Mr. Warriner stuck to his convictions and was "fired" by the school. A year later the father was off the school board and Mr. Warriner was rehired. I believe there is a justice in the world and the truth will come out. It has been said, "The wheels of justice grind slowly, but they do grind finally."

John Wooden states about his former coach, "Earl Warriner would not compromise on principle to save his own skin. He would not kneel at the altar of expedience as so many others do. He was a man of fine character."

Are you a person of this type of character? Without principle centered leadership, you will blow with the winds of convenience and never inspire loyalty to your cause. Would you risk your job or business like Mr. Warriner did for your deeply held principles? We have one life to live and it begins by knowing what principles we are willing to die for.

AMAZING FACTS ABOUT JOHN WOODEN

- The only athlete to be honored in the basketball Hall of Fame as both player and coach, he was named Player of the Year at Purdue Univ. in 1932.
- Born in Hall, Indiana, as a high school student Wooden played in Indiana where he led the Martinsville High School team to the state championship finals for three consecutive years, winning the tournament in 1927. He was a three time All-State selection. After graduating in 1928 he entered Purdue University, where he was a three-time All-American guard and a member of Purdue's 1932 national championship team.

- Wooden was nicknamed "The Indiana Rubber Man" for his suicidal dives on the hard court.
- During one 46 game stretch he made 134 consecutive free throws.
- In 1942 he enlisted in the Navy where he gained the rank of lieutenant during World War II.
- Wooden coached at Indiana State University in Terre Haute, Indiana from 1946 to 1948... In 1947, Wooden's basketball team won the conference title and received an invitation to the NAIB National Tournament in Kansas City. Wooden refused the invitation citing the NAIB's policy banning African American players. A member on the Indiana State Sycamores' team was Clarence Walker, an African-American athlete from East Chicago, Indiana. In 1948 the NAIB changed this policy and Wooden guided his team to the NAIB final, losing to Louisville. That year, Walker became the first African-American to play in any post-season intercollegiate basketball tournament.
- During his tenure with the Bruins, Wooden became known as the "Wizard of Westwood" and gained lasting fame with UCLA by winning 665 games in 27 seasons and 10 NCAA titles during his last 12 seasons, including 7 in a row from 1967 to 1973. His UCLA teams also had a record winning streak of 88 games, four perfect 30-0 seasons, and won 38 straight games in NCAA Tournaments.
- Since 1977, one of the four college basketball player of the year awards has been named the John R. Wooden Award.
- Two annual doubleheader men's basketball events called the "John R. Wooden Classic" and "The Wooden Tradition" are held in Wooden's honor.
- In 2003, UCLA dedicated the basketball court in Pauley Pavilion in honor of John and Nell Wooden. Wooden also has the gym at Martinsville High School and the student recreation center at UCLA named in his honor. Named the "Nell & John Wooden Court," Wooden asked for the change from the original proposal of the "John & Nell Wooden Court," insisting that his wife's name should come first.

- December 18, 2005, Congressman Brad Sherman introduced a legislation that would rename a San Fernando Valley post office in honor of Wooden. On August 17, 2006, it was announced that President George W. Bush had signed the legislation enacting Sherman's proposal into law. The post office at 7320 Reseda Boulevard was named the Coach John Wooden Post Office on October 14, 2006 - Wooden's 96th birthday.
- To this day, Wooden retains the title Head Men's Basketball Coach Emeritus at UCLA, and attends most home games.
- On November 17, 2006, Wooden was recognized for his impact on college basketball as a member of the founding class of the National Collegiate Basketball Hall of Fame. He was one of five, along with Oscar Robertson, Bill Russell, Dean Smith and Dr. James Naismith, selected to represent the inaugural class.
- UCLA had actually been Wooden's second choice for a coaching position in 1948. He had also been pursued for the head coaching position at the University of Minnesota, and it was his and wife Nell's (to whom he was married for 53 years until her death in 1985) desire to remain in the Midwest. But inclement weather in Minnesota prevented Wooden from receiving the scheduled phone offer from the Golden Gophers. Thinking they had lost interest, Wooden accepted the head coaching job with the Bruins instead. Officials from the University of Minnesota contacted Wooden right after he accepted the position at UCLA, but he declined their offer because he had given his word to the Bruins.

REAL LEADERS Take 100 Percent Responsibility

One of the major things to understand, if you are going to be a leader, is that you must take responsibility for your results in life. One of my favorite quotes goes something like this, "You are where you are because of the sum total of your actions to this point in your life." That is tough advice, but in my experience it is totally true.

What I run into a lot are people who would like to lead, or people who think they are leading, or people who have lead in the past, who refuse to take responsibility for their situation. Maybe they missed a goal, or maybe they did not do as well with their finances as they had planned, or maybe a business venture did not go so well, or maybe they have messed up relationships, or maybe they have trouble at home, but the ONE THING they will not even CONSIDER as a possibility is that THEY ARE THE PROBLEM.

Contrast this condition with REAL LEADERS. Real leaders take stock of a situation, take a look at themselves, and as Jim Collins says, they confront the brutal reality as it really is. Then they TAKE the RESPONSIBILITY to make the changes necessary to move on and fix the situation.

I do not know why this is so rare. But what I have witnessed time and again are people who decide that their circumstances are to blame, or their mentor is to blame, or their spouse is to blame, or any number of things that safely keep THEM out of blame's way.

Do you want to become a leader? Do you want all the benefits of success, admiration, recognition, contribution in the lives of others, and everything else that comes from striving as a leader? Do you want respect from those who should be following you? Do you really want this? I hope you do. And

I will share a secret with you about how to accomplish it... Are you ready?...Here it is:

The secret to becoming a leader and enjoying all the benefits of leadership is:

LEAD!...What?...You have got it...LEAD.

You are not a leader if you are not leading. In my opinion, anyone who is daring to become a leader ought to wake up each morning and command themselves to do just that, to "LEAD."

This is silly. This is dumb. It seems so redundant. "Of course," you might say, "If I want to be a leader I have got to lead. Who would not have THAT figured out already?" Well, believe it or not, hundreds, if not thousands of people.

People want all the trappings of leadership without accepting any of the responsibility. People want the success without the struggle. And they want the respect without the battle.

If you ever feel as though you are failing in your leadership journey, the solution is simple. Go out and lead. Get active. Take command. Begin performing right now, right where you are, with what you have. Take responsibility for your results and DO something about it. Get off your couch. Throw away the excuses. Go out the door. Lead. There is no faking it in leadership. You are either leading or you are not.

We all have a choice. We can either lead, or we can try to explain why we are not.

A Walk on the Wild Side

I would like to take a quote from author Dan Allender in the book *Leading with a Limp:*

> *"God does call every one of us to lead. Again, a leader is anyone who is moved to influence others to engage a problem or an opportunity for good."*

And perhaps my favorite quote from Allender:

> *"Leadership is a walk on the wild side . . . moving toward a goal while confronting significant obstacles with limited resources in the midst of uncertainly and with people who may or may not come through in a pinch. Leadership is about whether we will grow in maturity in the extremity of crisis."*

I especially like the last part of that last line: "grow in maturity in the extremity of crisis." Leadership is really a strange art. Whereas most people in the midst of crisis shrink from it, complain about it, or wish it away, leaders use it to come alive. Conflict, crisis, confusion and uncertainty bring a leader to life. Challenge presents an opportunity for change, not pain. That is why so many of history's best known stories of leadership come from times of grave crisis. Difficult times reveal people for who they really are. When others cower, leaders stand tall. When others shrink, leaders rise to the challenge.

Understand: the world is full of fakers and posers. Anyone can beat their chest and say tough words. But watch who performs when the guns start firing and the ammunition is real, and you'll have your leader.

71

Use the crises in your life as agents for change and growth, and pray that God will strengthen you to utilize your gifts mightily. One of life's biggest regrets is to look back over it and wish it would have counted for something. Do not let that happen. Take a walk on the wild side! Lead! Right where you are with what you've got!

OBSTACLES
Go ahead, Wimpify! You know you want to!

Two Important Questions

There are two important questions we should each ask ourselves on a regular basis:

1. Ten years from now, what will I wish I had done today?
2. If I knew I could not fail; what would I be working on?

Life is complicated. No matter who you are, you will encounter problems and challenges. There are endless tasks to complete, and there is always something around the next corner to challenge your resolve. Keeping yourself grounded in the bigger picture is a good guard against distraction, discouragement, and ineffectiveness. These two questions help keep the bigger picture of what you are trying to accomplish at the forefront of your mind.

Eternity Is a Long Time to Be Wrong

The first time I heard the saying, "Eternity is a long time to be wrong", it was my friend and co-author Orrin Woodward saying it. I was immediately struck by the truth of it.

Life is interesting how it blinds us. We can cruise along through days, weeks and even months somehow ignoring our own mortality. We know deep down in our hearts that we are only here for a moment; that our lives will end in death, and that everything we see, feel and do will be gone. But somehow, the glitter and complications of life keep us occupied, and keep our minds far away from thoughts about our reason for living, our purpose here on earth, and our destination afterward.

I would encourage everyone to figure out what they believe about these great truths, and to clearly examine why and how they have these beliefs. Getting the "eternity" part of your existence into proper framework is absolutely critical. What is this life all about? What happens when it is over?

The Bible holds the answers to these questions. I am not talking about "religiosity" or "churchianity" here (two terms that describe how turned off I was about any "religion talk" from people). What I am talking about is the truth. Man was created by God, fell into sin, and therefore separated himself from God. Jesus Christ came into the world as a man, lived the perfect life none of us could live, died the death of punishment (the spiritual punishment from God the father on the cross was infinitely more severe than the physical suffering) that we should have received, then rose again from the dead, proving he was the only begotten Son of God.

Heard it all before? Turned off by people who profess to

74

believe in Christ, but do not glorify Him with their lives? I know how you feel, I was there myself.

But just because I had heard it all before did not make it any less true. And just because God's people struggle with sin and some profess him falsely, does not make his saving grace on the cross on my behalf any less true!

What I could not deny is how I knew beyond a shadow of a doubt that I was a sinner. I also knew I was powerless to do anything about it on my own. And I knew that at the end of the struggle with sin I would die in my sins. Only Christ has the power to save me from this dead end street. His finished work on the cross is salvation.

During the early days of my spiritual journey, I was given great spiritual guidance by Pastor Robert L. Dickie and Orrin Woodward. I was also fortunate enough to be handed some incredible books, in addition to the Bible, of course, that helped me tremendously. I would like to recommend a couple of them to you:

1. *Studies in the Sermon on the Mount,* by Martyn Lloyd-Jones
2. *Evidence that Demands a Verdict,* by Josh McDowell

There are many more I could recommend, but believe me, these are plenty to begin with (both are thick!) I pray that they will help you on your journey toward getting the real questions of life answered. After all, it is the most important thing you can do. Everything else comes second.

The Cumulative Effect of Incremental Change

It is fascinating to use historical examples to illustrate leadership principles. In our book, *Launching a Leadership Revolution*, co-author Orrin Woodward and I use several. What I do not think we have ever told anyone, however, is that we stumbled upon the idea by discussing Tom Brady, quarterback of the New England Patriots. His story was such a clear illustration of the Third Level of Influence; Performance, that it inspired us to find other individuals whose stories could serve to equally illustrate the book's concepts.

Tom Brady's story is extremely interesting. It caught our attention because of the deliberateness he used to climb from scrawny obscurity to international stardom. His success story is an excellent example of what can happen when a person commits to making steadfast, incremental, consistent improvements in one's self over a long period of time. Since we wrote the book in 2005, Tom Brady has driven himself even deeper into the record books, recently leading the Patriots to an undefeated regular season, and being named the league's MVP.

Author Robert Kiyosaki writes about what he calls the three keys to wealth:

1. Long term vision
2. Delayed gratification
3. The power of compounding

In the story of Tom Brady, all three of these principles can be seen at large. His story is covered from a slightly different angle in our book, so I will not rehash it all here. My purpose in this article is to focus upon #3: the power of compounding.

Most people, when they are new to the self-improvement journey, don't realize the power of proper steps applied over a long period of time. There is a saying, which I believe to be true, stating that "people overestimate what they can achieve in a year, and underestimate what they can achieve in ten." The challenge for most people is staying the course when they do not see any evidence of results for their efforts. Frustrated, they give up and quit, leaving behind the new ground they had gained. Later, perhaps, they get re-inspired and begin again. Only now, they are forced to re-plow ground they already covered before. This cycle then repeats itself.

Others, however, and a quite small number it appears to be, break out of this cycle. They make a decision based upon a long term view to improve or accomplish something in their life. Then they get to work doing what is necessary to head in that direction, delaying gratification, saying "no" to a thousand "good" distractions that come up along the way, focusing instead on the one great, over-riding goal they have set on the long term horizon. As the days go by, these people take the little steps of improvement, ever heading toward their goal, one tiny inch at a time.

At first, of course, no one notices any results. This phase can often last a long time. Then, their efforts are noticeable enough that critics are attracted to throw their bile upon the proceedings. Many times, this is enough to break the cycle and get the person to quit on their journey. At this point, though, champions persist. Eventually, results start to show up. Next, results become entirely obvious. At this point in the journey, people start to say that the achiever is "talented" or "gifted" or "lucky" and "was always going to make it big in something." These comments may be true to a small extent, but they are due more so to the weeks, months and years of work when no one was paying attention. No one, that is, but the achiever.

Whenever we see people who have achieved enormous success, stature, character, mental fortitude, or spiritual maturity, we can know for certain that it was the result of a long process of incremental change. Nothing truly good in the realm of human accomplishment comes easily or quickly. But incredible things can result from proper steps taken over a long enough period of time.

Benjamin Franklin, through his "Thirteen Virtues," forced himself to improve in his relations with people, transforming himself from an argumentative, dogmatic know-it-all into an ambassador capable of wooing the King of France in the middle of Europe's most complicated court environment. Theodore Roosevelt, a small, weak, and sickly child, transformed himself into a hearty and adventurous leader, even taking a bullet in the chest at point blank range and being able to give a ninety minute speech before receiving medical treatment! And skinny Tommy Brady, growing up in California dreaming of being the next Joe Montana, transformed himself into one of the best quarterbacks in the history of the game.

The inspiring part about this principle is that it applies to everyone reading this page. Anyone can grow and accomplish beyond their wildest dreams if they will take to heart what this principle teaches. Never forget the power in the cumulative effect of incremental change over time!

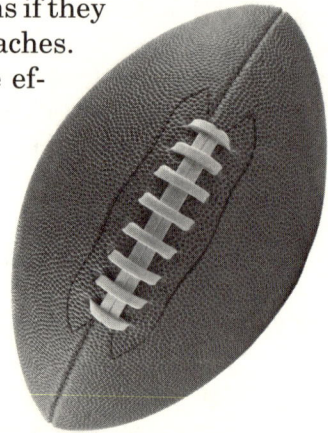

Four Common Myths About Leadership

The study of leadership is full of paradoxes. Author George Barna highlights an interesting list of misperceptions about leadership in his book *A Fish Out of Water*. His four myths are as follows (paraphrased where not quoted):

1. Influence is not synonymous with leadership. "You can have influence with someone without leading him somewhere. A true leader has a much deeper impact."
2. "Leadership is not the same as management." Managers are charged with doing things right. "Leaders do the right thing, for the right reason, at the right time."
3. Leadership is not about control and power. "Great leaders empower and release rather than dictate and confine."
4. "Leadership is not a popularity contest." Many times leaders are in fact unpopular, because they encourage people to change. Popularity may come and go, but leadership principles remain.

The chart on page 80 illustrates that true leaders can have a dramatic impact. In fact at the time this book is being written 30 of the 32 current head coaches in the NFL can trace their coaching line back to these three coaches. There are also several former head coaches in all three trees. (see chart) The underlined are all current coaches in the NFL.

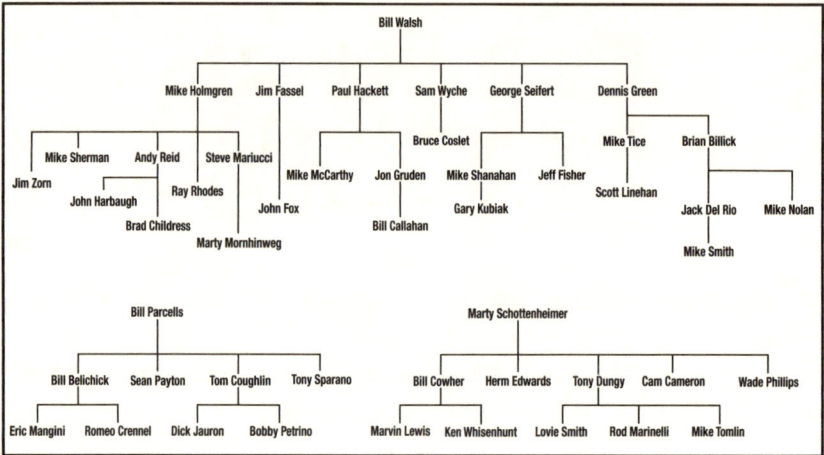

Circle of Concern vs. Circle of Influence

The leadership principle, "Focus only upon what you can control", is critical to success. Often, people get bogged down worrying or concerning themselves with things they cannot change. As the saying goes, if you are not part of the problem or solution, then it should not be your concern. Worry, fear, and anxiety often come from being concerned about things over which we have no control.

What is the weather going to do? What was that person thinking of me? Why did the President make that comment? Why did that zit come back? What is Bin Laden going to do next? Why are the Lions still losing? Our minds get filled with questions that are outside of our "Circle of Concern."

Ideally, we should aim to have our Circle of Concern the exact same size as our Circle of Influence, that is, the realm of things that we CAN control or have an impact upon. We would have very little anxiety, and would be very effective, if the two circles overlapped and were matched in size. Also, we would not waste time talking about or working on things that we really can't change. Let's face it; there are plenty of things we CAN change and OUGHT to change that we SHOULD be working on instead. Let us leave all that other stuff to the side.

> *If you can't sleep, then get up and do something instead of lying there worrying. It's the worry that gets you, not the lack of sleep.*
> *– Dale Carnegie*

"But if I am concerned about it, doesn't that mean that I am assigned to get involved and do something about it?" Maybe, as long as it is within the realm of possibility for you to actually do something about it. But putting valuable thought energy into something in which you can make no difference is a waste of time, energy, and talent...at least for now.

The best leaders know this cold. They find something that needs changing, and they go after it with all they have got. They do not waste time and energy on topics and causes beyond their influence. Then, as they grow in influence by focusing only upon what they CAN control, they eventually get a bigger and bigger Circle of Influence. Ultimately, then, they can have a bigger and bigger Circle of Concern to match. It must be influence first.

Work and focus primarily within your Circle of Influence, and it will grow as your leadership ability grows. Then, your Circle of Concern can grow to match. But worry about a Circle of Concern beyond the scope of your immediate Circle of Influence, and you have got a recipe for frustration, ineffectiveness, and failure.

Lead where you are, right now, with what you have got. Sufficient for the day is the evil thereof.

Mortimer Adler:
Reading Great Books - Past and Present

I would like to cover a subject today that has changed my life. I believe everyone's life will be enriched greatly by the discipline of daily reading. Ronald Reagan once said, "I am not a great man, but I deal in great ideas." President Reagan was a reader and he thought deeply on the ideas he read. One of my lifetime assignments is to help create a hunger for men and women to read again. With television, radio, music, movies, video games, etc., many are failing to develop a reading habit. I was 26 before I began reading to learn and think. Before this time, reading was a task to do for school or to learn a specific function for work. I had no interest in the classic ideas and people from history, religion, or philosophy. Our society has created a nation of specialists and frowns upon the generalist. I was one of the specialists with a deep understanding of a very specific area. The fact that I was clueless of the world around me did not seem to faze me at all, since I did not know what I did not know.

I now realize our society is in dire need for leaders who are generalists. What is a generalist? A generalist is someone who can tie the disparate information from different fields into a unifying vision and plan. For example, a specialist that knows the genetic code for a living cell does not necessarily qualify for leadership of the country, if that is all they know. So many specialists are great in their specific area, but the lack of reading in a range of subjects has made them hopelessly narrow. A generalist, on the other hand, has learned a little about many things and

has specialized in one specific area. I like the quote, "Jack of all trades and master of one." I personally have chosen to master the field of leadership. Why leadership? Leadership teaches you about human nature and the battles within someone to grow and change into the person they were called to be. Leaders create a hunger in their students to read and grow in all areas, with a focus on their specialty. Yes, I know you have specialized in your chosen field, but do not stop there. Shut off the TV when you get home and dig into the classic books; civilization is discussing the great ideas of the ages and you are missing it! Become part of the "Great Discourse" going on daily between the hungry minds of today and the wise men and women of history. Mortimer Adler spent his life teaching and encouraging others to read the classics. Here is an answer from Dr. Adler on why to read the great books.

Q: Dear Dr. Adler, Why should we read great books that deal with the problems and concerns of bygone eras? Our social and political problems are so urgent that they demand practically all the time and energy we can devote to serious contemporary reading. Is there any value, besides mere historical interest, in reading books written in the simple obsolete cultures of former times?

A: People who question or even scorn the study of the past and its works usually assume that the past is entirely different from the present, and that hence we can learn nothing worthwhile from the past. But it is not true that the past is entirely different from the present. We can learn much of value from its similarity and its difference.

What are the top books in different areas you have read: Economics, History, Biographies, Leadership, Personal Development, Philosophy, Christianity, Politics, etc? Are you aware of others' top lists? Expand yours and start reading more classics. The world is counting on you!

A library is a hospital for the mind.
- Anonymous

Show me the books he loves and I shall know the man far better than through mortal friends.
- Dawn Adams

Books are the legacies that a great genius leaves to mankind, which are delivered down from generation to generation as presents to the posterity of those who are yet unborn
- Joseph Addison

Reading is to the mind what exercise is to the body.
- Joseph Addison

You don't have to burn books to destroy a culture. Just get people to stop reading them.
- Ray Bradbury

The best effect of any book is that it excites the reader to self activity.
- Thomas Carlyle

Character

There are people of character who believe a good name is more important than any amount of wealth. They have been blessed with both a good name and wealth because they understood success is from the inside out. You must take care of the inside person before you will see the outside results. True leaders are models of character and integrity and do the right thing, even if other options may have been easier personally. Leaders understand that it takes years to build character, but only minutes to lose it.

I want to share a story from a book I read recently. It is so powerful and exemplifies the battles people must wage to keep their character. As you read this story, think through the times in your life where selling out would have been the easy thing. There are many opportunities for compromise in a person's life, whether it be for money, fame, power, fear, lust, etc. Men and women of character will not compromise their principles. Here is the story:

A man aboard a plane propositioned a woman sitting next to him for one million dollars. She glared at him but pursued the conversation and began to entertain the possibility of so easily becoming a millionaire. The pair set the time, terms, and conditions. Just before he left the plane, he sputtered, "I—I have to admit, ma'am, I have sort of ah, led you into a white lie. I, um, really don't have a million dollars. Would you consider the proposition for maybe—ah, say—ah, one hundred thousand dollars?" The lady was incensed at the lie, but still imagining the use of $100,000 reluctantly agreed. As the man was getting up from his seat, he confessed, "Ma'am I really don't have one hundred thousand, but can we close the deal for one hundred dollars?" On the verge of smacking him across the face for such an insult, she snapped back, "What do you think I am?" The man looked into her eyes, "That has already been established," he replied. "Now, we're just haggling over the price."

When I read this I was floored! It is the best story I have read on the powerlessness of your convictions when you begin to compromise them. If I were to plead with you to do one thing in your life, it would be to develop character and principles that you will not compromise. Show me a man or woman of character and I will show you someone who knows the non-negotiable principles in their life. In this story, the lady's purity was not a non-negotiable, and once the compromises started, there was no end. Compromising on core convictions is like taking the first step onto a children's slide—you can control the first step, but not how far you slide before you stop.

Can you think of other examples of selling your character for money? Is your character for sale? Think about all the great men and women from history. One of the things we admire in our heroes is their convictions and willingness to stand for their core principles. This is character, and if you sell your character, you have sold something of permanent value for something of temporary value. If you have failed in this area, begin today to rebuild your most important earthly asset.

Assignment: Can you give examples in your life where you held to your core principles and maintained your character? Maintaining your convictions is not easy or else everyone would do it, but it is essential to leadership!

You Only Get What You Picture

We do not always get what we want (for instance, I never made it as an NFL quarterback), nor do we always get what we deserve (I have not been struck down by lightening yet), but we do generally get what we expect.

This thinking becomes critical to success. Our actions tend to line up with the picture we have of ourselves in our mind's eye. People who expect the worst tend to bring it on themselves. People who expect the best seem to make great things happen.

None of this is black and white, but I am sure all of us can think of times when we wanted something so badly we could picture what it would be like. We could feel it, see it, and sense it in every way. Then, one day it comes true, and we think back to when we had pictured it so clearly.

This is why envisioning a successful outcome is so important. Dennis Waitley calls it "Pre-Programming." We can envision an outcome so often and so clearly that our actions automatically line up to bring it to fruition. We will head in the direction of our most dominant thoughts.

Reality can be beaten with enough imagination.
– Anonymous

Most of us have seen Olympic slalom skiers preparing before a run, sitting with their eyes closed and moving their hands in the air to mimic the route of the course: rehearsing every turn and rise and picturing a perfect performance. Football coaches have learned not to say "don't fumble" because the picture of a fumble immediately pops into a player's head, and often, he complies by going out and fumbling!

Famously, when Disney Land was completed after Walt Disney's death, someone commented how they thought Disney would love to have lived to have seen it all. A relative of Disney's replied that he already had seen it in his mind's eye and that was how it came to be! When Seinfeld was asked if he expected to meet with the success he had in television comedy, he simply replied "yes." Napoleon would invest days in the planning of complex battle maneuvers for his army. When the conflict actually occurred, forces would advance here, problems would erupt there, and everything seemed to be confused and chaotic; nevertheless, more often than not, the final defeat of the enemy would occur exactly where he had predicted it!

So, what are you picturing in your mind's eye? Are you rehearsing success or failure? Do you parade a bunch of junk before your mind, or do you continually focus upon a victorious picture? Are you envisioning success or failure? Are you setting yourself up for a beautiful picture, or more of the same?

It's a tough lesson to learn, but very true: we only get what we picture! So envision it, picture it, imagine it, and rehearse it, whatever you want to call it, but employ your mind to create your future. Then work like crazy to make it come true, refreshing it regularly to keep it real. One day, it is likely you will wake up inside the picture you once imagined. It is not magic, and there is no Heaven on Earth, but you can lead yourself in the most positive direction by the force of your will and imagination.

Remember, success is not an accident. If it occurs accidentally it will not last and it is not a true victory. REAL victory comes through preparation and rehearsal. So succeed - on purpose!

Goals in Stone, Plans in Sand

The War of 1812 for many was more properly called the Second War for Independence. The new United States was struggling to make it in the tough world of foreign affairs, and its troubles with England had bubbled up into a war for which the new nation was not ready.

Much of North America was still unsettled, at the time, and the "frontier" was the Ohio valley and the dense forest regions around the Great Lakes. Control of these inland waterways was critical to control of the frontier territory, and both the United States and England were eager to dominate there.

Onto this scene sailed a twenty-seven year old American named Oliver Hazard Perry. In a small, fresh water sailing fleet, Perry engaged the bulk of England's Great Lakes squadron in what became the Battle of Lake Erie. Perry commanded the *Lawrence*, a ship named for a recently killed captain of the American navy who had foolishly lost one of the United States' six powerful frigates in direct disobedience to his orders. Lawrence's reckless conduct had pitched his awesome ship against one of the ablest captains and best trained crews in the British navy. Lawrence's ship the *Chesapeake*, was destroyed in less than fifteen minutes! Strangely, Lawrence's dying words, "Don't give up the ship", caught on as a sort of battle cry among the American sailors. Even though Lawrence had foolishly put himself and his crew into a position where giving up their ship was inevitable, the phrase became almost as powerful as "Remember the Alamo" would decades later. Because of this, as Oliver Hazard Perry sailed to confront the British Great Lakes fleet that day, his ship, the *Lawrence*, flew a flag that proudly stated, "Don't Give up the Ship!"

Although all the ships in the engagement were tiny by ocean-going standards, the Battle of Lake Erie would be the biggest, most violent naval engagement the Great Lakes would ever see. Perry sailed directly into the British ships and fought furiously. The *Lawrence* was one of the two biggest, most powerful American ships on the Great Lakes. The other one was called the *Niagara*. For some reason, though, the *Niagara* did not engage in the battle. It stood off in the distance, out of harm's way, and watched Perry get torn to shreds in the *Lawrence*. Although Perry was fighting a losing battle, he had inflicted heavy casualties on five British ships at once, firing furiously and refusing to quit.

Finally, the *Lawrence* was almost a complete wreck. Four-fifths of Perry's men had been killed or wounded. The gun deck was littered with bodies and refuse, the dead and dying sprawled everywhere. With so much death and destruction, hardly a gun was left firing aboard the *Lawrence*. Still, from the mast of the ship flew the flag that said, "Don't Give up the Ship!"

At this point in the battle, Perry did the unthinkable. He lowered one of his only remaining ship's boats into the water, and with a small contingent of men, he rowed away from the battle and toward the untouched *Niagara*, which was still watching the battle from a safe distance. Perry and his men in the little boat were fired upon by the same cannon that had torn his ship to pieces. However, many of the British ships were damaged badly enough that they neither destroyed his boat nor made much of an attempt to pursue. Perhaps they thought the battle was over and Perry was fleeing the scene. But as Perry reached the *Niagara*, he needed only moments to convince the crew to follow his orders instead of those of their timid captain. The *Niagara* made sail and headed directly for the fleet of damaged British ships.

It is interesting to imagine what the men aboard the British ships must have thought, seeing the heroics of this young captain and his bravery while rowing a boat through heavy enemy fire. How their attitudes must have changed as they realized he was bringing a new ship to engage them! And engage them he did. With the fresh fire-power of the *Niagara* brought to bear on the damaged British fleet, the outcome was not even a question. The bravery of Oliver Hazard Perry had won the day and secured the Great Lakes and the western frontier to the United States. Throughout the remainder of the War of 1812, the British would never regain what they had lost that day.

Perry's actions were impressive; given the bad advice he had flying from a flagstaff aboard his ship. Perry did not fall in love with the idea of winning the battle aboard his ship, committing to the chivalrous but silly notion that he should either win or sink on his ship. Instead, he had victory in mind, a clear goal on the horizon for which he would change his plans and disregard the popular naval passions of his time.

It is interesting to think about Perry's exploits that day in leadership terms. What he did was nearly unprecedented in naval history, but is even more powerful as a metaphor for how a leader should attack a goal. Many times, leaders set goals to accomplish something, and then proffer plans to achieve that goal. Somehow or somewhere along the way, however, the leader falls in love with the PLANS and gets overly committed to them at the expense of the goal. As the saying goes, and as Perry so deftly demonstrated that day, "Goals should be set in Stone, and Plans should be set in Sand". If the plans are not working, scrap them and come up with more plans. But never give up the goal! If one ship is not working, get another ship, but be sure and get to the victory!

Oh, and by the way, do not even ask me for the name of the original captain of the *Niagara*, who watched safely from a distance while his countrymen fought the battle; he does not deserve to have history remember it.

Purpose Transcends Pleasure

Victor Frankl, survivor of a Nazi concentration camp, who saw everything and nearly everyone in his life taken from him and destroyed, lived to teach the world from his experience. One of my favorite Victor Frankl quotes comes from his book *Man's Search for Meaning*:

> "Man's main concern is not to gain pleasure or to avoid pain, but rather to see a meaning in his life. That is why man is even ready to suffer, on the condition, to be sure, that his suffering has meaning."

The reason this is so powerful to me is that most people I meet never seem to be "happy" because "happy" is exactly what they are chasing. And as I have said before, happiness can never be captured by direct approach. Happiness, rather, is the result of living the life God called us to live, fully utilizing His gifts for the purpose in which they were intended. This always involves serving others, by the way, and may only minimally involve pleasure, although it always involves joy.

People in our society experience two points of confusion here. One can put a little too much emphasis on the phrase "the pursuit of happiness" which Thomas Jefferson penned in our country's wonderful Declaration of Independence. (This phrase is certainly better than others which were considered to go into the document in its place, namely: "The ownership of property.") Pursuing happiness is an empty endeavor. That is the first point of confusion. The more one tries to pursue happiness, the more it escapes and eludes them. Why? Because of the second point of confusion, which involves people thinking that pleasure brings happiness. Pleasure does not bring happiness; it only brings an increasing hunger for more pleasure. It is an endless spiral of self-serving consumption.

Do not get me wrong. I am not against having some fun and seeking some pleasure. My life has been full of such moments. However, neither I, nor any of the other top leaders with whom I am blessed to be affiliated, spend nearly as much time "playing" or "seeking pleasure" as people seem to think. I have boats I use occasionally, a plane I fly when I get the chance, dune buggies and other such toys, which are dusty much of the time. Most of these are slightly used until such a time presents itself for the entertainment and dream-building of other people. For the most part, however, the great leaders in my life invest their time in something a lot higher than the pursuit of pleasure.

> *Above all be of single aim; have a legitimate and useful purpose, and devote yourself unreservedly to it.*
> – James Allen

And that brings us back to Frankl's quote. Paraphrasing: "the main concern is not the pursuit of pleasure or avoidance of pain, but the yearning to see meaning in life, even to the point where suffering is found to be an acceptable cost in the name of purpose." Another Frankl quote goes like this, "In some ways, suffering ceases to be suffering at the moment it finds a meaning."

Why is all of this important? Because this principle of making one's life about purpose rather than pleasure, in the hunt for happiness, is the key to the beginning of leadership. I firmly believe that leadership is an inside job and relies upon the inner spark of an individual. It is not something that can be imposed from without, it is something that must be nurtured from within. Where do you suppose this comes from? Purpose!

Having trouble "gutting up" and leading? Keep getting distracted with the shiny objects on the side of life's road? Finding it hard to motivate yourself? Having trouble getting yourself to do what you know you should do? Making excuses for your lack of performance? Blaming others because they are not meeting your needs?

These are all signs that you are not in touch with your purpose. To quote author Dan Castro, "Happiness, therefore, does not come from the elimination of pain, but from the realization of purpose."

Want to be happy? Want real pleasure? Get in touch with God's purpose for your life. Remember: you do not determine your purpose, you discover it. Arriving at your purpose in life is a bit of an archeology project; it is something that is carefully unearthed one stone at a time. But it is there, deep inside, waiting to be found. Dig carefully and find it. And you will not only make a difference in this world with the gifts God has given you, but you just might find some real happiness along the way!

And stop waiting. You do not have forever.

Fruit on the Tree

"Whenever you purpose to consult with anyone about your affairs, first observe how he has managed his own; for he who has shown poor judgment in conducting his own business will never give wise counsel about the business of others." - Isocrates, letter to Demonicus

It is curious to me how quickly people are to proffer advice, even when they have no fruit on the tree. Many would-be "counselors" would do well to demonstrate success before feigning to be able to advise others.

Conversely, it amazes me at times to see people neglect, disregard, or even flat-out refuse to ask for advice or help from those who have obviously succeeded in a category far in excess of themselves. The best way to make it through a minefield is to follow in the footsteps of one who has successfully gone through ahead of you. Sure, we are all free to venture out on our own, but we can only be blown up so many times. The short cut is to follow success. In this, I do not mean blind loyalty. Rather, heeding the advice, attempting to learn the mindset, world-view, and perspective of those that have succeeded in an area in which we would also like to succeed.

Because of this, the greatest leaders are those that are also able to follow and ask for help. Orrin Woodward says, "If you are too big to follow you are too small to lead." I see so many people that will take advice for a time, that will listen for a season, but then venture off course and start heading right back into the bushes again. Why is this? I wish I knew. But what I DO know is that there is a tremendous difference in results between those who continually seek perspective and counsel, and those who drift off by simply "taking their own counsel."

Be smart enough to counsel with those seasoned by experience. Be humble enough to ask. Be a big enough leader to find someone you can follow, even while others are following you. The Bible says, there is wisdom in a multitude of counselors. At the same time, however, never let go of your own senses. Never follow blindly. Never disengage your own brain and thinking. Proper mentorship should encourage the protégé to think more and better than they did before. One does not seek advice and counsel to learn what to think, but rather how to think. When we learn how to think and learn the process of exercising our gray matter, we are able to think our own thoughts at a much higher level. We will then be utilizing the experience and thoughts of others to elevate our own.

Perhaps you, dear reader, ought to think on this.

Dwight Eisenhower:
Power of Perseverance

The story of Dwight Eisenhower is one of persevering through a long series of assignments with no glory and waiting patiently for his opportunity. At fifty years of age he was a Lt. Colonel and nearing the end of his career. Had it not been for World War II no one would remember his name, except for a few military historians. Stephen Ambrose in his biography of Eisenhower states:

> He was fifty-one years old; only the coming of the war had saved him from a forced retirement and a life with no savings and but a small pension to live on. Although he had impressed every superior for whom he had worked, he had no accomplishments to his credit that he could point to with pride for his grandchildren. Had he died in 1941, at an age when most great men have their monumental achievements behind them, he would be completely unknown today.

A couple of key points emerge from Mr. Ambrose's commentary. First, regardless of fame or fortune Eisenhower did all he could with each assignment. He persevered with whatever he was asked to do. He focused on getting the job done, not self promotion. Second, he was prepared when his moment of destiny came. Many people feel life has dealt them a bad hand and decide to go through the motions. Great leaders will play every hand life deals them. Instead of getting worked up over injustice and playing the victim roll, great leaders make lemonade out of lemons. Like the saying goes, "It is not what happens to you, but how you handle it that counts."

I believe some of the greatest leaders developing on the team are toiling away in obscurity. No one knows their name, but they will. Leadership cannot be hidden and by preparing and responding properly, your moment will come. Do the best where you are at! Do not cry over what you do not have, but focus on what you do have to get the job done. This is all part of the process to develop the leadership necessary to handle bigger assignments. Are you doing all you can where God has you in life? Are you crying over what you do not have or focusing on the gifts and resources you do have? If you want more you must prove to be faithful in the little you have.

Laurie and I decided a long time ago to go the extra mile in whatever we do. When you join the second mile club you are separated from the crowd. Your team knows you are special and responsibility naturally gravitates to the second mile club. Go the extra mile; accept responsibility even though it is not your assignment. Everyone likes to follow people who get the job done with a cheerful attitude. Eisenhower never cried about his fate, but worked diligently to be the best he could and look what happened. He was a fifty year old Lt. Colonel ready to retire, who rose to the Supreme Allied War Commander and then became President of the United States for two terms. Are you the next Eisenhower? Are you going to be prepared when your moment comes?

I think of all the people who look back on their life with regret and believe they never had an opportunity. I believe most were given their opportunity, but were not prepared mentally for the challenge. When opportunity knocked at the door, they were too busy entertaining themselves or complaining about their situation to hear it. Opportunity is knocking on your door. Are you preparing to greet her? Remember; "When opportunity and preparedness meet, success must happen." We have a responsibility to prepare and with confidence know that opportunity will come knocking.

Leadership Perspectives

By seeing a situation from another person's point of view or an experience from another perspective, the ability to lead and influence is increased. Every leader who wishes to build a large community must gain multiple perspectives on every key situation before deciding on a course of action. Before you judge any situation, be sure to hear from all the parties involved. You may discover that your one sided view was not the whole truth. I believe that most people want to do the right thing, and listening before acting is imperative to good leadership.

There are absolute truths in life, but human beings experience life through their own personal paradigms or world views. The same situation can be experienced by various individuals and each draws their own version of what happened. In most cases, the stories are different due to each person's unique perspective. Each one is telling the truth as they know it, but it takes a wise leader to discern how to proceed. I love the elephant story because it teaches us humility in our own interpretation of the facts and also a, seek first to understand attitude. This story also teaches us that Together Everyone Achieves More because working together helps us to identify the particular animal we are dealing with at the time. We are all blind in some areas and we each can see in others. By working together, we can quickly ascertain the facts and proceed to the solution without needless arguing or turf protection. Seeking first to understand builds trust and trust generates strong teams with fast responses to changing conditions.

Six blind men were discussing exactly what they believed an elephant to be, since each had heard how strange the creature was, yet none had ever seen one before. So the blind men agreed to find an elephant and discover what the animal was really like.

It did not take the blind men long to find an elephant at a nearby market. The first blind man approached the beast and felt the animal's firm flat side. "It seems to me that the elephant is just like a wall," he said to his friends.

The second blind man reached out and touched one of the elephant's tusks. "No, this is round and smooth and sharp - the elephant is like a spear."

Intrigued, the third blind man stepped up to the elephant and touched its trunk. "Well, I cannot agree with either of you; I feel a squirming writhing thing, surely the elephant is just like a snake."

The fourth blind man was of course by now quite puzzled. So he reached out, and felt the elephant's leg. "You are all talking complete nonsense," he said, "because clearly the elephant is just like a tree."

Utterly confused, the fifth blind man stepped forward and grabbed one of the elephant's ears. "You must all be mad, an elephant is exactly like a fan."

Duly, the sixth man approached, and, holding the beast's tail, disagreed again. "It is nothing like any of your descriptions, the elephant is just like a rope."

And all six blind men continued to argue, based on their own particular experiences, as to what they thought an elephant was like. It was an argument that they were never able to resolve. Each of them was concerned only with their own idea. None of them had the full picture, and none could see any of the other's points of view. Each man saw the elephant as something quite different, and while in part each blind man was right, none was wholly correct.

There is never just one way to look at something, there are always different perspectives, meanings, and perceptions, depending on who is looking.

Can you give an example where you experienced a disagreement of perspectives that created conflict? How does this story speak to you?

Levels of Influence

One of the key points in the book, *Launching a Leadership Revolution*, is that there are different levels of influence on a leader's journey. The five levels are:

1. Learning
2. Performing
3. Leading
4. Developing Other Leaders
5. Developing Leaders that Develop Other Leaders

Every leader must start at the first level of becoming a student. Since leadership is driven by a leader's hunger to change the status quo, that hunger naturally results in a leader's desire to learn all they can about the endeavor. Learning becomes a hunger in itself and one of a leader's greatest joys. A leader learns, this knowledge is not simply to be had for the sake of intelligence, or for the sake of theory or mighty thoughts, although these are fine in and of themselves, but this knowledge is supposed to lead to action. There are those who never leave the first level, and therefore their influence in the lives of others is limited to the relatively small reach that knowledge for the sake of knowledge alone brings.

Most people move on to the second level; their learning leads to performance. It should be noted that the first level of learning never ends, but continues on while the leader is performing at level two. Performing means that the leader actually demonstrates the habits of initiative and activation. At this level the leader becomes the player on the field, scoring and winning. This performance, over time, becomes attractive to others. This is what leads to the third level of influence. Some people, however, never get beyond this level. They do not develop the skills to deal with other people, or they have character issues that keep others away. Even though their performance is attractive and impressive, people do not volunteer to be influenced by them. Many, however, do move on to begin influencing others through the credibility of their own performance.

At the level of leading, others are attracted to the obvious competence of the leader's performance at level two. The leader's results speak for themselves, so people readily want to know what the leader knows and how to do what the leader does. In effect, people are now allowing the leader to have influence in their lives because of their results as a performer. The impact of the leader is really growing now. Whereas the first level of influence impacted predominantly the individual doing the learning, and the second level of performing demonstrated the competence as a result of that learning, now others are enabled, encouraged, and led to have an impact themselves. There is a process of addition going on where the leader is not the only one making a difference, but others are added to the equation and the overall impact is beyond what any one person could accomplish. Many leaders never grow beyond this level. They continue to learn, they continue to perform, and they lead people effectively, but they never realize that they should take the next step, or they never develop the abilities to do so.

The next step is developing other leaders that can do everything the leader does; this is the fourth level of influence. At this point, multiplication is going on because a leader reproduces their abilities in others. This level is where mentoring and leadership development come into play. My friend, business partner, and co-author Orrin Woodward and I like to call mentorship the "Lost Art of Leadership". Purposeful mentoring is not done in very many organizations. It is as if leaders do not realize that their job is to fill the "leadership pipeline" with people who can replace them. But systematic mentoring and developing of other leaders is the difference between good and great organizations. It is the art that separates the greatest leaders from the decent leaders. Perhaps one reason mentoring is not more heavily utilized is that it

takes an exceptional person to develop leaders that are potentially better than one's self. It requires humility! Leaders
who are trying to build a kingdom for themselves will never
make it to this level. But those who truly hunger for significance and maximum impact will strive with full effort to
learn how to operate at this level.

The fifth and final level is almost beyond scope for most of
us. It is the pinnacle of leadership influence, when a leader
can develop leaders that develop other leaders. The impact
of this level is exponential in scope. The work of the leader in
developing other leaders of leaders usually goes down through
the generations. In fact, the cause for which the leader stood
usually becomes associated with their name. The fifth level
of influence is only open to the most humble, serving, cause-
driven leaders. And it takes a significant amount of time and
consistency to reach this level.

Why is it important to understand the five levels of influence? First, it is a road map for self-assessment. A leader
can look at the levels and quickly deduce where he or she
stands, and therefore know exactly where to begin growing
and developing. Second, it is extremely useful for determin-
ing where the leaders in one's organization are in their leadership journey, and it pinpoints what steps they need to take
to advance. Third, it lets one know where each part of their
organization is in its leadership. Are the leaders in that area
performing at level two...three...four?

The five levels of influence are an exciting map for each of
our leadership journeys. Find out where you are in yours,
seek out the materials and mentorship you need to move on,
and enjoy the ascent as you make a greater and greater impact in the world! God bless you on your journey!

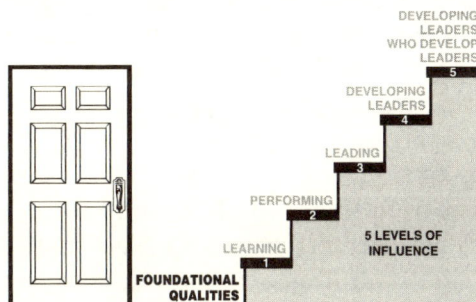

Life is Too Short to Be Little

"It is not what happens, it is how you respond." These are easy words to hear, but hard ones to live out. For most of us, it is easy to let people "hi-jack" us emotionally, to "blow our lid," or "get ticked off," or "blow our stack," or "lose our temper, " or "come un-glued," or "let them have it," or "lose control," or "boil over," or "erupt," or "fly off the handle," or "throw a tantrum," or "pitch a fit," or "get our knickers in a knot," or "get our tail feathers in a bunch" or "get jacked sideways," or "spout off," or any number of expressions. Perhaps there are so many expressions for this because there are so many instances of this in our lives. It would make sense that we would need a lot of names for something that happens so often!

But what a shame, really. How many phrases are there for the opposite? "Keep one's cool," or "stay calm," or "keep control," or "maintain composure," or "turn the other cheek," or "blow it off," or "let it lie," or "leave it alone," or "take it with a grain of salt," or "keep things in perspective," or "let sleeping dogs lie," or "don't rock the apple cart," or "leave well enough alone," or "keep the peace," or "take it all in stride."

In both cases, when we lose our temper or when we maintain control, our language is full of expressions to describe the event. It must be that this is a big deal. In the art of human relations, I can assure you that how we respond to the things that happen to us in life IS A BIG DEAL.

Many times the things that happen to us are with, through, about, or because of other people. The interesting thing about life is that we, as humans, are free to choose our response. We are different from the animals which have no choice but simply to react by instinct. Sure, we have instincts, but we also have overriding intelligence that offers us a choice of our response in any situation. It is how we choose our responses that matters.

Do we choose our responses because they make us feel better in the moment, riding the emotional wave that wells up in us and forgetting to engage our intelligence? Or do we stop and think for a moment, making a conscious choice about what our response will be? HOW we choose our response is important.

Additionally, WHAT response we choose matters as well. We should gain enough control over ourselves to choose the appropriate response. And which response is the appropriate one? Would it be the response of expediency, meaning the choice that serves our personal needs the best? Or would it be better to choose a response that serves the other person? Should our response be in line with the highest purpose we have for our life? Should our response have anything to do with God and His glory?

You see, asking these kinds of questions of ourselves (and what is thinking, if not the attempt at answering questions we ask ourselves?) produces the environment for us to CHOOSE our response, and to CHOOSE appropriately. Remember, we are the happiest when our actions are in line with the highest picture we have of ourselves. In other words, the closest in line with how God would have us live.

People who are given to emotional flights of fancy, getting angry and battling with the people in their lives for whom they are supposed to love, are the least likely to produce lasting relationships. They may have great "people skills" on the front end, but over time, their lack of emotional self-control will deliver misery and regret by the truckload. Many of the wounds resulting from a lack of emotional control are very painful and heal slowly. Trust is destroyed and is rebuilt painfully and slowly, if at all.

Work hard to grow emotionally. Experts agree that your "emotional quotient" is more important than your "intelligence quotient." Get control of yourself by getting clear on who you are and what your purpose is. Do not lose perspective on the big picture in your life. Get in touch with the fact that your life is finite. Keep in mind that the most important aspects of your life are how you touch and influence the lives of God's children around you. You will be remembered more for your contributions or subtractions from people's lives than anything else you will accomplish. And finally, it may be helpful to keep in mind two of my favorite quotes:

"Life is too short to be little"
"A man is only as big as the smallest thing that makes him lose his temper."

So grow big.

Benjamin Franklin's Leadership Example

The name Benjamin Franklin is so familiar it is almost a cliché. School children are introduced to him as the gray haired man flying a kite in a thunderstorm, or as the contemplative elder statesman sitting in the Pennsylvania State House and advising upon the drafting of the Declaration of Independence or the United States Constitution. Franklin is one of the most famous founding fathers, and after more than two centuries, there are still those who have trouble understanding why. Author Gordon S. Wood wrote of Franklin's return to North America after the signing of the peace treaty ending the Revolutionary War,

> "When he arrived in 1785, his fellow Americans did not know what to make of him. They knew he was an international hero, along with Washington the most celebrated American in the world, but they were not quite sure why. He had not led the revolutionary movement like John Adams. He had not written a great revolutionary document like Jefferson. He had not led armies like Washington."

When writing about or discussing leadership, it is relatively easy for military and political figures to be examined as examples. The reason for this is that their lives are lived very much in conflict and battle, and the principles of leadership that apply to "every day" life are seen in broader relief in the context of extreme and dangerous circumstances. This is why so many leadership books, including our own, are filled with generals and statesman. Examining Benjamin Franklin as an example of leadership principles is not so straight forward, however. Seeing his genius in the leadership category requires a little deeper inspection. But the reward for this extra effort is one of the richest and most motivating examples of leadership one can find.

The life of Benjamin Franklin can best be summarized by breaking it into three distinct phases. In the first phase, Franklin was a businessman. As most everybody knows, he rose from obscure and humble beginnings (a much larger barrier to advancement in those days than it is in ours) to become what we would today call a multi-millionaire. He worked hard, had a great mentor and patron, and learned his trade (printing) well. He became not just a wealthy printer but a sophisticated entrepreneur. He was involved in the establishment of over eighteen paper mills, owned an extensive portfolio of rental properties, was a creditor to other business owners, and was involved in setting up other print shops on the model of his first one in Philadelphia. He also became a famous writer during this time. He used his abilities and efforts to establish businesses that he could safely leave to the conduct of others, and by the age of forty-seven he was free to pursue other things. In the second phase of his life, Franklin was a philosopher and scientist. Although he had been sent to England as the colony of Pennsylvania's ambassador to the English throne, his passion was scientific thought and discovery. He became an esteemed member of the Philosophical Society in London and was world famous for his real contribution to the understanding of electricity. He also invented the Franklin stove, bifocals, an instrument for which Mozart created a musical score, and an almost endless list of contraptions. During this time, of course, he continued to write. It was in this second phase of Franklin's life that he was the most happy. He was famous, well-respected among his peers, dined with Kings and Lords all over Europe, and was friends with most of Europe's esteemed minds of the day. He fully expected to live out the rest of his life in England, and could not even be

> *The Constitution only gives people the right to pursue happiness. You have to catch it yourself.*
> – Ben Franklin

compelled to sail home for the marriage of his only son, the birth of his grandchild, or the waning health of his wife. But circumstances and his own convictions thrust him into the third phase of his life; that of a patriot and American "founding father." He would sail home in 1775 and become one of the most passionate patriots in the Revolution.

It is in the dramatic circumstances of Franklin's transition from the second phase of his life into this third phase that most demonstrates his leadership ability. What transpired would change his life, and the course of American history, forever.

Franklin was slow to comprehend the forces of change that were swirling in the North American colonies. The violent reaction in North America to the 1765 Stamp Act caught him by surprise. He had trouble understanding the feelings of repression brewing back home. An event took place that brought him into the revolutionary spirit with fervor.

By this time he was not only the representative of Pennsylvania to the English government, but of several others as well, including Massachusetts. Somehow a pack of private letters from the Massachusetts lieutenant governor Thomas Hutchinson got into Franklin's hands. In the letters, Hutchinson was imploring the British government to take more control of the colonies so that

> *Anyone who trades liberty for security deserves neither liberty nor security.*
> – Ben Franklin

they would remain dependent on England. Franklin sent these letters to officials in Massachusetts with the intent of demonstrating that the problems with the mother country were not official English policy, but the machinations of a few bad apples such as Hutchinson. In the words of Wood, "This was a gross miscalculation, for the letters he sent to Massachusetts only further inflamed the imperial crisis. Contrary to much conventional wisdom, Franklin was not at all a shrewd politician or a discerning judge of popular passions, certainly not of the pre-revolutionary passions of these years." The letters were printed in Boston newspapers. Word soon got back to England about the Hutchinson letters and Franklin's involvement in the affair finally became public once Franklin stepped forward and admitted to his involvement in order to stop a duel between others involved in accusations. Franklin firmly defended himself by saying that the letters were not private, but from public officials about public matters. As author H.W. Brands wrote:

"If any in England expected repentance [from Franklin] they certainly did not get it. Franklin's assertiveness condemned him the more in the eyes of those who considered Boston a nest of sedition and judged all who spoke for Boston abettors of rebellion. Until now Franklin – the famous Franklin, scientist and philosopher feted throughout the civilized world – had been above effective reproach. His admission of responsibility for transmitting the purloined letters afforded his foes the opening they had long sought."

Meanwhile, the Massachusetts House had petitioned the government in England to remove Hutchinson from his position. Franklin was called to the Privy Council hearing on the matter. The opposing counsel was not just a lawyer, but a man named Alexander Wedderburn, the solicitor general. Wedderburn was feared for his acidic and combative style and his lack of scruples when it came to his own political ambition. Brands wrote,

"Franklin had hoped to argue for Hutchinson's dismissal on political grounds; the appearance of Wedderburn indicated that the government intended to mount a legal – and personal – counteroffensive. Moreover, the target of the counteroffensive would not be Massachusetts but Franklin."

Seeing this, Franklin asked for legal representation and was granted three weeks before the Privy Council would reconvene. It is here where Franklin, normally the master of timing, became its victim. Between the first and second Privy Council meetings, the Boston Tea Party took place.

This event shocked London and confirmed for most that the inhabitants of Boston were rebels, making Hutchinson look like a heroic defender of the British interests in a hostile environment. Furthermore, and bad news for Franklin, the Boston Tea Party had outraged officials in London, and Franklin was on hand to feel the brunt of their wrath.

The second Privy Council meeting was a public spectacle, and very unlike normal, was overwhelmingly well attended. The large hall, called the "Cock Pit," was filled with dukes and viscounts and sirs and members of Parliament, including the Prime Minister. Forgetting any pretense of the purpose of the original meeting, solicitor general Wedderburn launched into a tirade against Franklin that was so severe, so slanderous, that most of it was deemed unfit for print. He attacked Franklin's character, his intelligence, his loyalty, his reputation, and made statements such as, "I hope, my Lords, you will mark and brand the man . . . He has forfeited all the respect of societies and of men." As the diatribe continued, the audience laughed and jeered at Franklin's expense. Franklin sat motionless and silent, refusing to change even his facial expression. Wedderburn continued by blaming the rebellious colonies on Franklin by saying, "these innocent, well-meaning farmers, which compose the bulk of the [Massachusetts] Assembly," were not responsible for the rebellion. Instead Franklin was the "first mover and prime conductor, the actor and secret spring, the inventor and first planner." This was quite a charge in itself, since Franklin had not even been there in years!

> *By failing to prepare, you are preparing to fail.*
> – Ben Franklin

Franklin maintained his composure. Wedderburn continued, feeding off the growing approval of the crowd, getting louder and more belligerent. Although his expression betrayed his feelings, Franklin grew hotter and hotter. He sat rigid and frozen, however. Eye witness Edward Bancroft wrote, "The Doctor was dressed in a full dress suit of spotted Manchester velvet and stood conspicuously erect without the smallest movement of any part of his body." Wedderburn continued for over an hour, and when he had finally finished,

Franklin refused to speak.

Two weeks later Franklin was still fuming. He was angrier for the public principles violated than for his own sake. He wrote to a friend,

> "When I see that all petitions and complaints of grievances are so odious to government that even the mere pipe which conveys them becomes obnoxious, I am at a loss to know how peace and union is to be maintained or restored between the parts of the empire. Grievances cannot be redressed unless they are known; and they cannot be known but through complaints and petitions. If these are deemed affronts, and the messengers punished as offenders, who will henceforth send petitions? And who will deliver them? Where complaining is a crime, hope becomes despair."

Following the events in the Cock Pit, the government moved to remove Franklin from his long-held and prestigious position of deputy post master. According to Brands, "Such action was discreditable in itself; it was even more pernicious in its prospect. Appointments to the post office . . . were being held hostage to adherence to the policies of whatever ministry happened to hold power." In other words, disagree with those in power, and they would use their power to break you. It was a classic case of "shoot the messenger." But the English government did not stop there. It immediately passed the Boston Port Act, effectively closing Boston down to commercial trade. This outrage was followed soon thereafter by the Massachusetts Government Act, the Administration of Justice Act, the Quartering Act, and the Quebec Act. These acts would come to be called the "Intolerable Acts," and would represent a point of no return in the conflict. In the following weeks the colonies began sending delegates to an emergency continental convention.

Any fool can criticize, condemn and complain and most fools do.
– Ben Franklin

To Franklin's credit, he hung around London for some time afterwards, and used all his skills and connections to get motions into Parliament attempting to reverse the path toward war with the colonies. Two of these motions became official, and both were defeated. Regarding the bullheaded charge of the officials in the English government down the path toward war, Edmund Burke said, "A great empire and little minds go ill together."

Finally, having lost all hope of finding cooler heads to prevail, Franklin sailed for North America. Wood wrote, "Franklin had had his deepest aspirations thwarted by the officials of the British government, and he had been personally humiliated by them as none of the other revolutionaries had been." The Franklin that stepped ashore in North America was a vastly different man that the one that had departed so many years before. This Franklin was a man on a mission, with a clear view of how things really stood with mother England. He had been there. He had seen it for himself. He had exhausted every bit of self control and diplomacy he could muster in the cause of maintaining harmony and justice between the two sides. And he had suffered personally for his attempts.

In the decade to follow, Franklin would be as instrumental in the success of the War for Independence as anyone. He would spend eight years in France as ambassador to King Louis XVI. He would leverage his international fame to garner good will and connections. He would hone his "folksy American" image to further his objectives. He would befriend the high-born, the nobles, and the many courtiers of Louis' court.

> *Even peace may be purchased at too high a price.*
> – Ben Franklin

He would patiently and persistently build a bridge of trust between himself and the French government. And finally, after years and years of painstaking effort, managing the squabbling ambassadors the colonies sent to help him, Franklin would accomplish his coup de grace. He would forge an alliance with the mighty French government on behalf of the fledgling colonies. The day he signed the former papers of alliance with England's only worthy rival, Franklin showed up wearing the same exact suit he had worn that day years before in the Cock Pit. He had not forgotten. He had gotten the final laugh. According to Wood, "[Franklin] was the greatest diplomat America ever had. Not only did he bring the monarchy of Louis XVI into the war on behalf of the new Republic, but during the course of that long war he extracted loan after loan from an increasingly impoverished French government. No other American could have done that." The money and munitions given by the French, followed by troops and finally ships, were irreplaceable in the colonial victory in the Revolutionary War. Without such support, Washington and his battered troops and Congress and its empty coffers would never have made it.

In the broad swoop of this story the leadership lessons to be learned from Benjamin Franklin are numerous. First of all, he reversed his position on the rebellion growing in America when new information presented itself. Next, he risked his reputation and world renown, and even a secure financial government post, by getting involved in the politics of the colonies' unrest. He handled himself with dignity under outrageous circumstances, and did not allow his personal pain to prevent him from making further overtures of peace. But once he saw the truth for what it was, he became a fervent champion of its cause. As a true leader, he could not stand to leave the status quo the status quo. Injustice was wrong, and no amount of personal prestige or comfort would be enough to make him "play it safe." Franklin was also patient, and never lost sight of the big picture, working steadily and methodically for years to accomplish his master stroke. To use military terminology, Franklin kept his view at the high "campaign" level, rather than get distracted at the detailed "battle" level. If leadership is influence, Franklin had droves of it: he found his way through a complicated French society and influenced a monarchy to support a rebellion attempting to overthrow another monarchy. That's influence. If leadership is having vision, Franklin was a giant. Arriving

back in the colonies in 1775, most historians agree he was among the first to realize that it was independence or nothing. While others clamored for middle ground and appeasement Franklin counseled whole-hearted resistance.

In the end, Benjamin Franklin is noteworthy for so many things he is almost an intimidating figure peering through history at the rest of us as though we could and should do more. But towering above his wide range of accomplishments is the legacy of freedom and independence he helped usher into existence. His greatest achievement did not come from his scientific mind, his inventive tendencies, or his philosophical wisdom. Franklin's greatest contribution came from his role as a leader. Anyone studying leadership and aspiring to utilize God's gifts to the fullest extent would be wise to study his example.

Ben Franklins Firsts:

- First scientist to study and map the Gulf Stream
- Invented the Glass Armonica musical instrument
- He invented a simple odometer to help measure postal routes
- First to promote a daylight savings time.
- Creator of the "Franklin Stove"
- Invented Bifocals
- Invented the Lightning Rod

On Becoming a Leader

Leadership is a lot like happiness: it cannot be captured by a direct run - the only way to BE happy is to GIVE happy. In the timeless leadership classic, On Becoming a Leader, author Warren Bennis makes an outstanding paradoxical point about leadership:

> ". . . the point is not to become a leader. The point is to become yourself, to use yourself completely - all your skills, gifts and energies - in order to make your vision manifest. You must withhold nothing. You must, in sum, become the person you started out to be, and to enjoy the process of becoming."

When a person fully invests themselves in a cause, in pursuit of some worthwhile and God-given vision, his or her efforts will have an impact on others. Others volunteer to follow, buying first into the leader and then into his or her vision. Never forget: it is the pursuit of the vision that makes a leader attractive to others. It is the pursuit of the vision that produces the influence in the lives of others.

With that said, what is the vision you have of what you can accomplish with the gifts you have been given? Is there a dream of something nestled way back behind the curtains of doubt and disappointment? Do you take it out every now and then and wonder what would happen if you actually pursued it? I hope you find the courage to chase after it. After all, you were built for that chase!

If You're Dumb, You'd Better Be Tough

"If you're dumb, you'd better be tough!" This is one of my favorite movie lines, partly because it is funny and partly because it is true!

Raising three sons keeps me in constant mindfulness of the need to be tough. As boys grow to men, there are a myriad of lessons to learn about life and how to handle it. Keep in mind that I am the same guy who chickened out of jumping off the high-dive in elementary school in front of all the girls, so I certainly have no corner on the market on toughness or bravado. I have, however, learned a lesson or two that I desperately hope to successfully pass along to my offspring. One of these is the lesson on toughness. Orrin Woodward likes to quote the phrase, "When the going gets tough, the tough get going." It is a simple, but ever-so important reminder. But notice that it only works on the assumption that "the tough" are "tough." What if they are not?

Life is not fair. Perhaps that is the starting point for my boys. There will not always be a referee or life-guard on duty. There won't always be someone (in the human sense) watching out for you. Things do not always go your way, and no, there are no free lunches. One thing I can still remember my own father telling me many years ago is; "No matter how good you get at something, or how much you accomplish, there will always be someone better than you. Be ready for it." Valuable advice. Competition out there is stiff. Evil is real. Health is fleeting. People will hurt your feelings. The list goes on. That is life. Get used to it.

Is that enough tough talk? Perhaps. And certainly we have spent a lot of time discussing the nicer, "softer," more sensitive aspects of life. However, success and greatness and

achievement and significance do not come without toughness. Without that understanding, sensitivity to the lighter
side and the softer stuff is not as valuable. We need both.
Rest assured, there will be a time, or many times, when you
will have to be tough. That is just the way it is. Prepare for
it, resist the temptation to baby yourself, and stiffen your
spine. Besides, it is worth it. The world loves heroes.

Please do not get me wrong. By being tough, I do NOT
mean being a bully, being mean, or being cold hearted or
mean-spirited. These are not tough; they are the imposters of
true toughness. Being tough does not take away from showing love, understanding or compassion. As Rocky said in the
latest sequel Rocky Balboa, "In life, it's not how hard you can
hit, that counts. It's how hard you can get hit and still be
able get back up and move forward (slightly paraphrased)."
Toughness is not about the hitting; it is about taking shots
and staying the course anyway. It is about responding to
life's turmoil's properly. It's about enduring. It is about attitude. It's about perseverance and resolution.

Oh yeah, I almost forgot.....You will still have to be tough,
even if you are not dumb!

A List of Principles

Some time ago I was speaking at an engagement in central Florida. During one of the conversations I had with the many fine people who were there, I was asked to make available a list of principles I had presented. The following leadership (and life) principles, along with several others have played a significant role in my journey toward success. My hope and prayer is that they prove as helpful in your life's journey as they have in mine!

1. Focus only upon what you can control.
2. The main thing is to keep the main thing the main thing.
3. It is not what happens it is how you respond that counts.
4. Everything happens for a reason.
5. God is sovereign and in control.
6. Most things you worry about never come to fruition.
7. One person CAN make a difference.
8. Anything worthwhile is usually difficult to accomplish and takes time to do so.
9. Who you are is much more important than what you accumulate.
10. There is such a thing as RIGHT and WRONG.
11. Action builds strength, inaction builds weakness.
12. People resist a challenge, but are the happiest when they are engaged in a challenge.
13. Leaders are just normal people who adhere to great principles and ideas.
14. We are all here for a purpose.
15. People matter (more specifically, INDIVIDUALS matter).

We Have Been Taught How to Do, But Have We Learned How to Be?

My sons and I were leaving a used book store this morning (one of my favorite south Florida haunts) and one of them, arms loaded with a stack of books, said, "I wish I did not have math to do today (he is home schooled) so I could read all these." The cashier laughed, I then replied, "I know how you feel! I felt that way all the way through college!"

I have two engineering degrees from excellent universities, and I learned a lot during those years: systematic thinking and analysis, mathematics, mechanics, dynamics, circuitry, more mathematics, computer architecture, mathematics, physics, chemistry, mathematics, mathematics, mathematics, etc. etc. By the time I graduated from those six grueling years I could reduce any equation that got within ten feet of me! Complex matrices' - no problem. Quadratics, integrals, friction cones - child's play. But I had never heard of Homer and did not know how to pronounce Herodotus or Beowulf. I had never heard of Machiavelli, did not know anything about the classics, learned only rudimentary history, and had been assigned to read a total of FOUR works of literature throughout the entire time! I remember going to the campus book store and seeing all the cool history, literature, philosophy, sociology, and theology books and wishing I had time to read them. But there was never time. It took every ounce of my energy to keep up with my course load and stay on track for the Dean's List and scholarships in math and science.

Would I trade it? Would I change it if I could go back and do it all over again? These are interesting questions. I have no regrets about it. I was supposed to learn what I learned and to have those experiences. Those years have become a part of who I am and what I know. Besides, I personally believe that there are not enough kids in North America focusing on math and science and keeping up with the global technology race. As Thomas Freidman warned in The World is Flat, the West is losing its hold on the technical expertise of the world. More and more American and Canadian kids are losing ground to those overseas who excel in technical educations. Besides that, my education was hard for me, it toughened me up and taught me to work.

However, and the point of this rambling, is I wonder how I might have gained a bit more of a "Classical Education" in the process. How could I have been better exposed to the thoughts and ruminations of the top thinkers of history? How could I have been given broader understanding of the human issues man has always faced?

I have been blessed with great friends and mentors who have shared their love of learning, reading, and study with me over the past fifteen years or so. Through this process, what I might call a self-induced continuing education, I have filled in some of the blanks that I missed during the "math years." This has been one of life's greatest pleasures for me!

There is nothing so stupid as the educated man if you get him off the thing he was educated in.
– Will Rogers

What about you? In the kaleidoscope of your life, whether you had formal education or not, what were the gaps in your learning and understanding? What were you taught about the classics, history, mankind and the great questions of life? Were you ever allowed or given time to THINK? Was your education vocational or fundamental?

I hope more and more people realize that there just is not the time in a few short years of high school and/or college to learn everything necessary or desirable for life. Continuing education must go on. We alone are responsible for self-improvement, and it should be a life-long process. Identify some areas where you feel you are not sufficiently informed, and get busy filling those holes!

On this same theme, I would like to quote an excerpt from one of the world's foremost leadership authors, Warren Bennis. His view is perhaps a little more critical than mine, but a great thought starter at any rate:

> "Universities, unfortunately, are not always the best place to learn. Too many of them are less places of higher learning than they are high-class vocational schools. Too many produce narrow-minded specialists who may be wizards at making money, but who are unfinished as people. These specialists have been taught how to do, but they have not learned how to be. Instead of studying philosophy, history, and literature - which are the experiences of all humankind - they study specific technologies. What problems can technology solve, unless the users of that technology have first grapples with the primary questions?"

With that, I will leave you to ponder!

Captain Pellew and the Indefatigable

The French Revolution of 1789 had begun on the high ideals of Liberty, Equality, and Fraternity, but had descended into the Reign of Terror and the guillotine. Eventually, the more moderate Directory took over the affairs of the country, and set its sights on dominance and dominion.

In its war with Great Britain, France had seen momentum swing its way. By 1795 it had recaptured islands once lost to the English in the Caribbean, and had secured three of its borders in mainland Europe. Spain then decided to sign on as an ally of France. With this development, the Royal Navy's presence in the Mediterranean was threatened, and it was forced to withdraw from those waters for the first time in ages. This withdrawal forced Britain's one remaining ally, Austria, to give up hope and sue for peace with France. Now Great Britain stood alone.

According to Herman, "The Directory sensed final victory. One more blow directed at Britain might do it. But how to bring its invincible army to bear against an enemy protected by the English Channel – and the fleet at Spithead? This was the problem that would perplex and baffle France's best military minds, including Bonaparte, for more than a decade. It equally baffled Hitler and his generals in 1940. Philip II and Louis XIV had each failed to find the solution, even when they enjoyed naval superiority. There was England with its puny army, its exposed beaches, its capital vulnerable to attack: the last barrier to complete French domination of Europe. Yet it would not give way." The French struck upon an idea to attack the Irish coast, hoping to take advantage of rebel sentiment there and gather an army of Irishmen to assist them in their conquest of England.

Out of the port of Brest a French squadron of seventeen ships of the line loaded with 15,000 soldiers was dispatched for the attack. The British had been maintaining a blockade of the harbor, keeping watch on the French fleet and trying to keep it bottled up in port. The weather, though, had grown harsh, and the ships of the Royal Navy had been blown far off station and out into the Atlantic; except for one.

The Indefatigable was only a frigate, not a full size line of battle ship, and was of the class of faster, lighter ships meant for speed and reconnaissance. Through the foulest weather he could ever remember, Captain Edward Pellew had hero-ically managed to remain on his station. He alone was there to spot the large fleet making its way out to sea.

Realizing that there was not enough time to sail out in the Atlantic and alert the British squadron, Pellew seized the initiative. In the darkness of the night and in a torrential downpour, Pellew immediately sailed his tiny frigate directly into the middle of the French fleet. As the enormous French battle ships labored to maneuver their way around the rocks and shoals at the mouth of the harbor, Pellew and the In-defatigable deftly sailed amongst them, firing off guns and flares, attempting to imitate the French signals and cause confusion. Pellew and his tiny ship were everywhere. The result was chaos. One of the large battleships, the Sedu-isant, ran onto the rocks. Several others were scattered out into the Atlantic, including the one carrying the French ad-miral and general.

Pellew had acted courageously and decisively and had demonstrated ingenuity all at the same time. Pellew's ef-forts had caused just enough of a delay. The French fleet took time to reassemble, and once it did the weather had turned into an ice storm. The winds were contrary to a land-ing on the shores of Ireland, and the invasion had to be called off. The initiative of one leader and his crew had made the difference.

Captain Pellew did not deliberate in the face of a chal-lenge. He did not need to get orders before acting. He saw what needed to be done, exhibited great courage and ingenuity, and took responsibility to get results. One leader's initiative made an enormous difference.

Famous Mis-quotes

Everything that can be invented has been invented.
 – Charles H. Duell, Commissioner,
   U.S. Office of Patents, 1899.

640K ought to be enough for anybody.
 – Bill Gates, 1981

Louis Pasteur's theory of germs is ridiculous fiction.
 – Pierre Pachet, Professor of Physiology at Toulouse, 1872

Airplanes are interesting toys but of no military value.
 – Marechal Ferdinand Foch, Professor of Strategy,
   Ecole Superieure de Guerre.

Drill for oil? You mean drill into the ground to try and find oil? You're crazy.
 – Drillers who Edwin L. Drake tried to enlist to his
   project to drill for oil in 1859.

The concept is interesting and well-formed, but in order to earn better than a 'C,' the idea must be feasible.
 – A Yale University management professor in response
   to Fred Smith's paper proposing reliable overnight
   delivery service. (Smith went on to found
   Federal Express Corp.)

There is no reason anyone would want a computer in their home.
 – Ken Olson, president, chairman and founder of
   Digital Equipment Corp., 1977

Doesn't Matter, Doesn't Matter, Doesn't Matter

Sometimes, things are going to hit you. Details will try to overwhelm you. Obstacles will pop up in your path. That is just the way life is. If you are a leader in hot pursuit of a vision, its best to learn to expect it. After all, resistance is what builds strong muscles. Ships are safe in the harbor, but they are not made for the harbor. Strong sailors are not made in calm seas. And leaders are just going to have to develop thick skin.

One little phrase I started thinking to myself a long time ago was,

"Doesn't Matter, Doesn't Matter, Doesn't Matter."

What I meant by this was that the goal remained the same; the obstacles were just there to add color to the story. And maybe I am just weird (okay, maybe it is more than a maybe) but it worked for me. It helped me remember that the big picture was still the big picture. The goal was set in stone and the path in sand.

As long as you have got the vision clear in your mind, and you have got the goal set in stone, perhaps keeping this little philosophy in your head will help you advance. It Doesn't matter what happens, it is how you respond. Respond appropriately with a little self-encouragement and press on. As Gandhi said,

"Your playing small does not serve the world."

So play big. Expect obstacles. And realize that those obstacles do not matter.

.....Speaking of OBSTACLES who do not matter.......(pay special attention to the next article!).....

Obstacles

My name is OBSTACLES, and for you English speakers it is Greek, so it is pronounced "Ob-stock-a-leez."

I am your worst enemy. It is my pleasure and privilege to haunt your every move toward self-improvement and success.

I have many weapons I can use against you. And I am so confident that they are superior to your pathetic little assaults on success that I can even tell you about them and it will make no difference. So here they are. (Maybe by knowing them, you can at least make it a contest between us. I am getting rather bored.)

- *Criticism:* This is one of my favorites! I am always surprised how much you ambitious ones are slowed down by the negative inputs of bystanders! It cracks me up, actually. If you spent half as much time worrying about your own future as you do about what others think you would be stinking millionaires!
- *Self Doubt:* This one is fun, too. I can convince you that despite all those other great things you have done in your life you are not worthy of your latest endeavor. This is the one you should see right through immediately, but, alas, many of you do not. Discouragement and Frustration: these are a joy to use. They stem from the most common of human indulgences: self-pity. If I can get you thinking you have paid a high price for very little gain, you will slow down and start thinking about yourself instead of the task at hand.
- *Contentment:* This is one of my most sneaky. It basically involves convincing you that you are already doing

"pretty good". After a few doses of this, you will be lucky if you can even get yourself off the couch.

- **Distraction:** Oooooh boy do I love this one. You get running toward success with all kinds of enthusiasm and then wham! Off to the side you go, chasing some little this or that which will add up to nothing in the long run. I can throw this one at you in the form of family changes, a promotion at work, a sports team that does well, a fight with your spouse; it is pretty easy, actually. And then years pass and it's too late! I love it.

- **Arrogance:** Yep, this is another reverse-screen-play. Sometimes you guys actually resist many of the above devices and make it this far into my defenses. That is when I hit you with cockiness. It is pretty easy, actually. Because if you make it through all of the above then you probably have a pretty secure self-image. It is a lot like martial arts, where one opponent uses the weight and momentum of the other opponent against him. Here you come charging ahead, all gung-ho for success, full of confidence and focus, and then I release it. You puff up like a peacock all sure that you are the end-all know-it-all. And you know what they say, pride cometh before the fall. Boy, how I love to watch them fall!

- **Suspicions:** If I cannot get you to doubt yourself, and then I fail to get you cocky and overconfident, then almost certainly I can throw a little 'blame' temptation at you. Just how much do your mentors *really* care about you? Can you not see, after all, that they are not *perfect?* Yep sir-reee! This one is a real hoot. It is great!

Well, that is probably enough for now. Do not want to give away all of my trade secrets in one blow. No matter, though, I am confident I can still decimate the masses that think they are heading towards their goals and dreams. In no time at all I can send them back to their previous 95% lives, watching television and heading nowhere.

I am the unstoppable!

I am OBSTACLES!!!!!

Come on, you guys. JUST WIMPIFY!!!! (You know you want to!!)

Obstacles cannot crush me; every obstacle yields to stern resolve.
- Leonardo da Vinci

One who gains strength by overcoming obstacles possesses the only strength which can overcome adversity.
- Albert Schweitzer

I have learned that success is to be measured not so much by the position that one has reached in life as by the obstacles which he has overcome while trying to succeed.
- Booker T. Washington

Obstacles are those frightful things you see when you take your eyes off the goal.
- Hannah More

The obstacle is the path.
- Zen Proverb

Ride on! Rough-shod if need be, smooth-shod if that will do, but ride on! Ride on over all obstacles, and win the race!
- Charles Dickens

We Grow When We Serve

The concept that leadership is service to others has received a lot of coverage in leadership literature lately, but it is still a concept that seems foreign to many people. When I discuss leadership with people, they automatically think of the perks of leadership: power, prestige, and status. These are not the true features of leadership. Real leadership involves service, sacrifice, dying to self, taking responsibility, calculated risk taking, empowering others, and struggle.

The decision to lead is a decision to take responsibility. Automatically, the leader is asked to take responsibility beyond what others are assuming. That is why I say that often times a leader is asked to carry an "unfair" load. He or she is the one out front hitting the resistance first, clearing the path for the followers to come.

Jesus was, of course, the perfect example of leadership. He came to serve, to show true humility, and to sacrifice for his beloved people. His example towers above the pretenders who try to teach that leadership is stepping on others to get ahead, or power or position. Jesus demonstrated just the opposite. As leaders, we must be willing to serve others before self. This is easier said than done, certainly, but is a source of great joy. In fact, leaders are the happiest when they are serving others. I believe this happens gradually within the leader

What do I mean? At first, a new leader might find it difficult to sacrifice their own self interest in the moment for the service of another person. When they make the sacrifice of time or resources on behalf of another they discover that it brings them happiness. This makes it a little easier the next time. Then, as the leader meets challenges, overcomes their own selfishness and learns to serve others more and

133

more, the opportunities for service grow bigger. The leader grows bigger at the same time. Eventually, what would have seemed impossibly difficult or imposing, is handled by the leader without a pause. The leader's contribution and impact grows larger and more significant. As this process continues, usually the leader's impact and following expands beyond what he or she ever could have imagined at the beginning. For this reason, the best way to begin growing as a leader is simply to begin serving. Do not worry about how far the journey will take you or what will be coming against you down the road. Serve right where you are, giving of yourself to the people God brings into your life. Make time for them. Find out what they need. Determine how you can help. Care. Share. Give. Grow. I think you will discover along the way, that the more you serve others, the more you receive in return. It is one of life's most beautiful paradoxes, and I hope you enjoy it to its limits (if there are any)!

Patrick Henry:
PART I
Courageous
Revolutionary Leader

"Give me liberty or give me death!" proclaimed Patrick Henry in his most memorable phrase. Patrick Henry was recognized as the best public speaker of all the revolutionary war leaders. After reading George Willison's excellent biography on Patrick Henry, I realized this was not his most influential act as a leader. There is a story from history that needs to be remembered as an example of a man and his principles. On May 29, 1765 a young twenty-nine year old Patrick Henry walked into the Hall of the House of Burgesses. Only 39 of the 116 members were in the hall as many had left assuming nothing great would be accomplished in the last few days of the session. In hindsight, nothing could have been further from reality.

The explosion of truth and courage displayed by Patrick Henry on this day would reverberate throughout the known world. More evidence that individual moral acts matter in God's eyes. England had recently passed the infamous Stamp Act and Virginia leaders were upset at the obvious power play by the English leaders. Virginia had always appropriated that taxes and "tyranny" was frowned upon by these freedom loving people. As Thomas Jefferson was later to say, "The power to tax is the power to destroy." A direct tax on the people was a new policy employed by the British. Virginians believed it violated the rights and privileges they had enjoyed since the founding of the colony. Although many members of the House were speaking behind the scenes, no one seemed to have the courage to go public with the complaints that the Virginians had with the English taxes. In walked Patrick Henry to fill that leadership gap and expose the hypocrisy of the English position.

The more conservative members of the house agreed the Stamp Act was wrong in policy and in implementation, but stressed an obeisance tone to the English leaders. Patrick Henry believed if Virginia had constitutional and inalienable rights then it was time to assert those rights; not grovel for them on bended knee at the whim of King George. Let me quote directly from Mr. Willison's book:

> In pioneer communities where people lived by hard toil and most men were their own masters, a new equalitarian society was evolving—one in which there were no marked distinctions in wealth and social status. Depending on his energy and abilities, one man was as good as the other, and none was disposed to bow to the pretensions and obiter dicta of their self styled "betters."

I translate this to mean, "When you are right you better stand, because to not stand for truth does not make you a peacemaker, but a coward." The Henry family had not raised a coward and Patrick believed strongly in his God given rights.

I will continue this historical essay in Part II. Here are some questions to ponder before the next leadership lesson. If you were part of the House and saw the English trouncing on the liberties of the colonies what would you do? Would you gripe behind the scenes and complain about those silly Englishmen and yet do nothing when you have a chance to speak in public? Too many would-be leaders know what is right, but they lack the character to stand for truth when they believe it may hurt. What kind of leader ducks and runs the moment things get tough? What do you think Patrick Henry will do when he has his moment to speak to the House of Burgess? History is so fascinating to me because you can learn from the moral stands that were made or not made. Where would our land be today had we not had a group willing to stand for truth regardless of the

If this be treason, make the most of it!

personal cost? You must use your own moral imagination to place yourself as a member of the House of Burgess and determine where you would be in the early conflict that set off the Revolutionary War. History remembers the names of the courageous few who stand for truth, yet relegates to the dustbin of history the cowardice majority who fawn obedience to policies they know to be wrong.

The Loyalty Effect

Frederick F. Reichheld, contributor to the Harvard Business Review and author of several books, defines The Loyalty Effect as, "The full range of economic and human benefits that accrue to leaders who treat their customers, operators, and employees in a manner worthy of their loyalty."

Reichheld's premise about loyalty might seem obvious at first. Loyalty is of course, important for business success. But studies have shown that loyalty, in fact, is a concept many companies might be able to talk about, but can rarely develop in their customers and employees.

Truett Cathy, legendary founder of the wildly successful Chick-fil-A restaurant chain, has taken the development of loyalty to an art form. In fact, Chick-fil-A fosters so much loyalty among its customers and operators, that Reichheld wrote, "I cannot imagine a serious discussion of loyalty in business that does not reference the Cathy family and their accomplishments. Why? Because Chick-fil-A has succeeded by designing its entire business system around customer loyalty; because Truett Cathy recognizes that a company earns customers' loyalty by consistently delivering superior value; because Chick-fil-A has created a degree of loyalty among its customers, employees, and restaurant franchise Operators that I had never imagined possible . . ."

Cathy himself writes, "The more we can foster the feeling that we are a group of people working together, depending on each other, and not just bound by a franchise agreement, the more likely we are to be loyal to each other. In our case . . . the extra measure of trust has brought us the success we enjoy today."

Imagine that! A company whose "secret sauce", "crown jewels", or "proprietary advantage" is the way it treats peo-

138

ple! Ideas like that almost sound, well, out-of-date. Can it really be that simple?

One of the most important things to understand in the world of leadership is that principles never change. There is no such thing as an "out-of-date" principle. Absolutes are never trendy. The longer I live, the more I am convinced of the truth of the saying, "Methods are many, principles are few, methods always change, but principles never do."

Loyalty as a business strategy sounds both obvious and out-of-date at the same time. I find that interesting, but what I have witnessed in my own life shows the wisdom of Cathy and Reichheld. Wherever loyalty has been earned and developed, great things happen. Wherever it is demanded or compelled, bad things happen.

Personally, I appreciate the people who have taken the time to earn my trust, make deposits in my life, and add value to me as an individual. They have earned my loyalty. I am also thankful for all the people in my life who have shown me loyalty. It is encouraging, but also comes with massive responsibility. I would never want to let them down!

As leaders, I think we would do well to duplicate the example of Truett Cathy and the culture he has built at Chick-fil-A. Whether our leadership is in the home, at work, in a business of our own, at church, or in our community, we should build loyalty in all that we do.

This brings up an interesting question for discussion: In what ways can we as leaders "build loyalty?" How, exactly, does that get accomplished?

The Leadership of Proverbs: Part Two

This is a foundational verse for the Christian faith and the beginning of all true wisdom and knowledge.

Proverbs 1:7 - The fear of the Lord is the beginning of knowledge: but fools despise wisdom and instruction.

When you go to any large shopping mall and have never been there before, look for the sign that displays all the stores. These signs are typically at the entrances and in the middle of the mall. Although the signs contain all the information you will ever want, they would be practically useless without a "You Are Here" sticker. If you do not know where you are, how can any directions help you? You could be holding exact directions on how to get to a store, but unless the directions know where you are starting from it will only get you further off track. Whether in life or in the store you must have a reference point or foundation point. God is the proper foundation to live your life upon and from there one creates a unity among all the disparate points. In our natural state, we do not want to serve God anymore than we want to serve others. Part of the fall is the belief that we shall become as gods. If we feel we are a god, why would we fear another God or choose to serve Him?

We do not fear the Lord in our natural state because we are at war with Him. An analogy would be two gunslingers in a small western town. They are walking at each other saying, "This town isn't big enough for both of us." We cannot worship the one true God and yourself at the same time. What Solomon brings up here is that the beginning of knowledge is realizing you are not to worship yourself, but the one who created you. Without this admission you will fight against God and reject the foundation on which to build true knowledge. Fear of the Lord is reverence and obedience to the One who gave you life and all of your gifts. How many people do you know that attempt to impress you with their talents? If we are to boast, we ought to boast in the One who has given us all of our gifts.

Why would someone despise wisdom? It reminds me of the common joke about men never asking for directions. I know I am as guilty as anyone. Laurie will suggest we stop and ask for directions. "No" I say, "I know how to get there." Thirty minutes later I have to admit I went the wrong way. The difference in life from the analogy is; decades, and many times a whole life, go by without men and women admitting they are lost. Are you lost but making good time? Why do people resist stopping to ask for directions in life? One answer is that it offends their sense of being god over their life. God's are all knowing and do not need any help because they have all the answers. The problem is when they have the accidents and roadblocks in life; they are not prepared to handle them. Many, instead of admitting they are lost, will only harden their heart more and blame or curse God for the tough times in their life. Why? Because fools despise wisdom and instruction since they feel like Gods.

The real problem occurs when people who are lost are the one's teaching others how to live their lives—the proverbial blind leading the blind. Sir Francis Crick was still a graduate student when he along with James Watson discovered the double helical structure of DNA. Doctor Crick received the Nobel Prize for his work on DNA and the genetic code. I respect greatly the work Dr. Crick has performed for the scien-

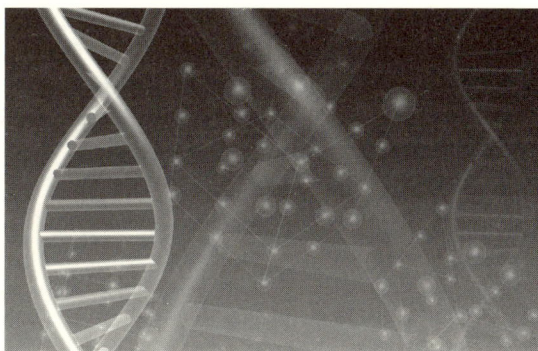

tific community. Dr. Crick also thinks life on earth may have begun when aliens from outer space sent a rocket ship containing spores to seed the earth. In a 1973 article entitled, "Directed Panspermia" in a science journal called *Icarus* he expounded his theory of alien spores seeding life on earth. Why did he pursue such an elaborate hypothesis to describe life on earth? Let's hear Dr. Michael Behe's explanation from his book Darwin's Black Box:

"The primary reason Crick subscribes to this unorthodox view is that he judges the undirected origin of life to be a virtually insurmountable obstacle, but he wants a naturalistic explanation."

Did you catch that? He wants a naturalistic explanation and cannot accept the idea that God created life, a very intelligent man is willing to jump to space aliens depositing life on earth. Dr. Crick understood the level of complexity in the genetic code made it impossible for him to conclude chance. Rejecting chance and previously rejecting God; the only alternative was to accept alien bacterial invasions.

As human beings God has created us as moral agents. We are free to reject God, but we are not free to choose the consequences of this rejection. By rejecting God we become fools willing to buy anything but the truth. I was a fool for twenty-six years of my life. By God's grace, I was introduced to a personal relationship with God's son Jesus Christ. It has made all the difference in my life. When I am lost I can go to my map (The Holy Bible) and find out where I am. How can you possibly be a leader when you are lost yourself? Leading people requires you to know where you are going so people can follow. What do you believe and where are you going? Do you fear God or man? Until you know God aright, you will never know yourself aright. On this day contemplate God and His creation. Everything created is created for a purpose.

Why did God create you? What is your purpose?

Blessings in Disguise: God's Providence

Human beings cannot know the future like our omniscient God does. When apparent bad things happen to us, we can question why God allowed it to happen. I believe a critical choice for all leaders is to learn to walk by faith. Many seemingly negative situations are actually blessings in disguise. The key is to know events cannot be evaluated in the short term. Who knows whether an event was positive or negative until enough time has elapsed to determine how we have responded and grown? Why do some people thrive on challenges, while others shrivel in the face of adversity? Faith must be a key component in all leadership. I believe a strong faith will see you through the tough times even when you cannot see clearly. Here is an excellent story about a King and his Friend:

An African King had a close friend who had the habit of remarking, "...this is good!" about every occurrence in life no matter what it was. One day the King and his friend were out hunting. The King's friend loaded a gun and handed it to the king, but alas he loaded it wrong and when the king fired it, his thumb was blown off.

"This is good!" exclaimed his friend.

The horrified and bleeding King was furious. "How can you say this is good? This is obviously horrible!" he shouted.

The King put his friend in jail.

About a year later the King went hunting by himself. Cannibals captured him and took him to their village. They tied his hands, stacked some wood, set up a stake and bound him to it. As they came near to set fire to the wood, they noticed that the King was missing a thumb. Being superstitious, they never ate anyone who was less than whole. They untied the King and sent him on his way. Full of remorse the King rushed to the prison to release his friend.

"You were right, it WAS good!" The King said.

The king told his friend how the missing thumb saved his life and added, "I feel so sad that I locked you in jail. That was such a bad thing to do."

"NO! This is good!" responded his delighted friend.

"Oh, how could that be good my friend, I did a terrible thing to you while I owe you my life".

"It is good" said his friend, "because if I was not in jail I would have been hunting with you and they would have killed ME."

Can you see the faith and attitude of the King's friend? Both the King and his friend experienced apparent adversities, but they responded differently. How do you respond to the appearance of setbacks in your life? Think of an example of what seemed to be a setback, that you now know was a blessing in disguise. Always remember; coincidence is just God's way of remaining anonymous!

Courage of Your Convictions

"Courage is the most important attribute of a leader, because without this one—none of the others matter." - Winston Churchill

The longer I lead people; the more I realize the importance of courage. Courage is following through on the principles you hold dear even when it hurts. Anyone can espouse great principles, but influence begins when you model the principles. Remember, people buy into the leader before they buy into the leader's vision. An important question to ask yourself, "Are you the type of leader people should follow when principles are put to the test?" In other words, are your principles just words or your core convictions? If they are your core convictions—then in surrendering them—you surrender your leadership! I read a couple of quotes that teach the principles of courage. One memorized quote can keep your resolve firm in times of duress. I have made it a habit to sum up discussions into one-liners that captures the essence of the subject. Joseph Joubert said, "There are single thoughts that contain the essence of a whole volume, single sentences that have the beauties of a large work." With this thought in mind, let us discuss the single thoughts that capture the essence of the whole concept of courage. Notice how each of these quotes captures different aspects of courage.

Nothing splendid has ever been achieved except by those who dared believe that something inside of them was superior to circumstances
- Bruce Barton

He that would be superior to external influences must first become superior to his own passions
- Samuel Johnson

Obstacles will look large or small to you according to whether you are large or small
- Orison Swett Marden

Courage is convictions in action
- Orrin Woodward

What the superior man seeks is in himself: what the small man seeks is in others
- Francois La Rochefoucauld

All the significant battles are waged within the self
- Sheldon Kopp

True courage is a result of reasoning. A brave mind is always impregnable
- Jeremy Collier

Courage is resistance to fear, mastery of fear—not absence of fear
- Mark Twain

Courage is a special kind of knowledge: the knowledge of how to fear what ought to be feared and how not to fear what ought not to be feared
- David Ben-Gurion

The beauty of the soul shines out when a man bears with composure one heavy mischance after another, not because he does not fell them, but because he is a man of high and heroic temper
- Aristotle

What you have outside you counts less than what you have inside you.
- B.C. Forbes

If I were asked to give what I consider the single most useful bit of advice for all humanity it would be this: Expect trouble as an inevitable part of life and when it comes, hold your head high, look it squarely in the eye and say, "I will be bigger than you. You cannot defeat me."
- Ann Landers

To have character is to be big enough to take life on
- Mary Caroline Richards

Little minds attain and are subdued by misfortunes; but great minds rise above them
- Washington Irving

These are phenomenal quotes on the attributes of courage! Have you displayed courage in your life? Have you experienced courageous leadership examples that helped you have courage before? Can you give me your definition of courage and a time you experienced courage in action? How about an example where lack of courage hurt an organization, community or country? A courageous example strengthens the resolve of others around them.

The Ripple Effect

Leadership matters. It makes a difference. In fact, its results cannot really be measured. A leader's influence spreads through society and time and often has a much bigger effect than most can imagine. This is called the Ripple Effect. Remember, a forest fire starts with just a tiny spark. The tallest oak grows from a small acorn. So it is with the efforts and influence of a leader. One person can and does make a difference.

Never underestimate the impact of your decisions in the lives of others. Never doubt that you, as a lone individual, can make big things happen. Follow the vision you have got to make something better, to attack the status quo, to assault the present in the pursuit of a better future, and allow the compounding effect of incremental efforts to do its wonders. And just know this: you are probably thinking small!

Booker T. Washington: Bitter or Better

The life story of Booker T. Washington may be the most inspirational I have read yet. Very few people in life have overcome as much as this former slave did to accomplish so many things. If success is measured by how far you have come, from where you started, then Booker may be the most successful American in history. Booker was born a slave in Virginia shortly before the Civil War. He was born on the Burroughs farm and life was the drudgery of labor for no gain or purpose. Young Booker was fascinated by the one room school house that he walked the young Burroughs girls to everyday. He was amazed when people could take the letters and make them into words. Booker was hungry to learn the magic of reading, but had no books or teachers.

After the Civil War, life did not get any easier for young Booker. He worked in the salt mines as a pre-teen to put food on the table for the newly free family. In an effort to escape the Malden salt mines—Booker took a job working for Viola Ruffner. Mrs. Ruffner was the wife of the owner of the mines and was the embodiment of the Protestant work ethic. Booker was exposed to the exacting attention to detail which he would adopt as his own. Booker also was taught to read by this saintly lady and allowed to peruse her extensive library. Young Booker's mind devoured the information as a thirsty man would drink water on arriving at an oasis. Mrs. Ruffner would be the difference maker in Booker Washington's life and develop the habits that changed a man's destiny.

There are so many incredible moments in Booker's life. He

> *Character, not circumstances, makes the man.*
> – Booker T. Washington

was truly a driven man that understood it is not what happens to you, but how you handle it that counts. Booker had to deal with prejudice and criticism his whole life. Instead of getting bitter and allowing other to control his thoughts— Booker chose to get better and maintain responsibility for his attitude and life. He had learned a powerful truth from his experiences: hatred does more damage to the hater than to the hated. Washington insisted, "No race can cherish ill-will and hatred toward another race without its losing all those elements that tend to create and perpetuate a strong and healthy manhood." Most of us will never experience the amount or type of rejection and prejudice that Booker experienced. But we all have had moments of conflict and unfair attacks. How did we respond? Did we respond like Booker and know that, "It is better to be wronged than to commit a wrong" or did we respond with hatred and bitterness in our own heart. I love the quote, "Bitterness and resentment is like drinking poison and expecting someone else to die." Life is too short to be filled with bitterness and resentment.

Booker built a college in Tuskegee, Alabama and affected many young men and women with his message of work and hope. I believe Booker Washington is the best example in America regarding someone who chose to get better instead of bitter about his circumstance. If Booker can overcome and contribute, then certainly you and I can do the same. I just picked up Booker's life story, *Up From Slavery* and plan to read it. I am always inspired by dream, struggle, victory stories because I find that they model real life. No great dream is accomplished without great struggles. Instead of fighting God's plan, we must ask what we are to learn from each struggle that comes our way. Booker went on to become one

> *Associate yourself with people of good quality, for it is better to be alone than in bad company.*
> – Booker T. Washington

of the most influential Americans of his time and a hero to many people. I encourage you to read his story of overcoming and reflect on our own small challenges in comparison to his. This will give you a perspective to charge ahead in faith to accomplish your life's purpose. Let me close with another quote from Booker T. Washington: "You may fill your heads with knowledge or skillfully train your hands, but unless it is based upon high, upright character, upon a true heart, it will amount to nothing. You will be no better than the most ignorant." Yes character is destiny and character is an inside job!

I have learned that success is to be measured not so much by the position that one has reached in life as by the obstacles which he has overcome while trying to succeed.
– Booker T. Washington

Slavery can only be abolished by raising the character of the people who compose the nation; and that can be done only by showing them a higher one.
– Maria W. Chapman

Is life so dear or peace so sweet as to be purchased at the price of chains and slavery? Forbid it, Almighty God! I know not what course others may take, but as for me, give me liberty, or give me death!
– Patrick Henry

Whenever I hear anyone arguing for slavery, I feel a strong impulse to see it tried on him personally.
– Abraham Lincoln

Today's the Day

One of my favorite quotes comes from treasure hunter Mel Fisher, who would show up at the dock every day for seventeen years encouraging his employees by saying,

"Today's the day!"

Fisher and his gang were on a mission to find the Atocha, a Spanish treasure galleon bound for Europe with a load of gold, copper, and precious gems. It was rumored to be the richest lost treasure ship ever, and had remained hidden off the dangerous coast of Florida for centuries. Finally, after an incredible story of perseverance, unfair governmental interference, greedy competitors, and family heartbreaks, Fisher and his crew hit the mother load and found the Atocha! His daily doses of positive prediction that "Today's the Day!" had finally paid off.

I like the quote as a daily encouragement, to be sure. We all need to say something like this to ourselves when the going gets tough, when we start to feel discouraged, or when the vision starts to fade a little. It is important to develop positive "self-talk" that keeps us focused and propped up. However, I also like Fisher's quote, because it has a second meaning that I am not even sure he intended. "Today's the Day!" also means that we should cherish this day, and forget the past, while not living too much in the future. Yesterday is gone. Tomorrow can only be hoped for, but is not promised, and today is all we really have! As the Bible says, "Sufficient unto the day is the evil thereof" (Matthew 6:34 KJV). I like this quote because as we repeat it to ourselves and others, it helps us to be encouraged about the great things that we can discover this day, the treasures we can experience and share this day, and the fact that we can't really become too enamored or concerned about future days, or hung up on failures of past days, because, in fact, Today is the Day!"

We should certainly learn from our past. And we would be fools not to prepare for tomorrow and dream about possibilities, but these things should never be done at the expense of today. Let us each make today count for all it is worth, remembering that indeed: Today is the Day!

The estimated $450 million cache recovered, known as "The Atocha Motherlode," included 40 tons of gold and silver and some 100,000 Spanish silver coins known as "Pieces of Eight", gold coins, Colombian emeralds, golden and silver artifacts and 1000 silver bars. Large as it was, this was only roughly half of the treasure that went down with the Atocha.

It is How You Think That Counts

People will often say that they are in search of an opportunity, assuming that they have the correct thinking to carry an opportunity through to success. What is most surprising, however, is that the challenge is usually just the opposite.

I know in my own case, I was convinced I knew how to think systematically. I was confident I could perform. I thought I had a good attitude. I had a great formal education, and it seemed all I needed was an opportunity.

Reality, however, was just the opposite. I did not so much need an opportunity as I did correct thinking. As it turns out, I had a lot to learn (and still do). I needed to develop emotional maturity, long term vision, attitude control, proper perspective, perseverance, and a long list of other things with which I was not equipped. I was correct in my confidence that I could succeed, but not without a lot of personal change.

People who are unwilling to confront this brutal reality are the ones that go from "opportunity to opportunity" and never quite seem to make it. They are always on the brink of something big, but just never seem to get there. The reason is that they take the root of their problem with them into each new endeavor. That root, of course, is their old self! Without learning the thinking that leads to success, by studying the great achievers, finding a mentor, and making learning and personal change a constant in their life, they basically just experience the same failure over and over. Such a person that claims ten years experience actually just has the same experience over and over again for ten years because they have not grown personally.

If you are reading this, however, I think it very unlikely that you are in this category of people. You, instead, are reading and seeking information to help you develop your own thinking. If you place yourself on a program of personal growth, learning with hunger everything you can to improve, and if you strive to learn systematic thinking and grow in your leadership ability, you will suddenly begin seeing opportunity everywhere! The truth of the matter is, opportunity abounds, but people qualified to take advantage of it are in short supply!

I sincerely wish you enjoyment, success, and significance as you take the self-disciplined road of personal growth. You probably have no idea how big the opportunities are out there that await you!

Urgency - The Press of Time

One thing that strikes me as I read biographies of the great contributors to our history is a certain trait they all seemed to have in common: an urgent awareness of the press of time. It seems that most people who wind up doing great things are a little impatient about getting them done.

When Abraham Lincoln lost his last election (prior to finally winning the Presidency), his law partner told the story of Lincoln's dejection. Lincoln supposedly had always felt he was called to accomplish great things, and suddenly felt that his time was up. Theodore Roosevelt was famously impatient toward accomplishing greatness, perhaps to a fault. I could list many more individuals that felt similar. Other leaders, it seems, awoke to their calling once in the throes of some great challenge. It was only at that point that they grew impatient, understanding the fleeting nature of time.

In all cases, though, leaders come to understand how important time is in their quests. There is simply not enough time to do everything. When hit with a great challenge, when in pursuit of a vision, leaders suddenly switch things into a higher gear. What used to be entertaining is not so entertaining anymore. What used to be relaxing only stresses them out more. Priorities suddenly become apparent, and leaders begin focusing on the "great" things and realize they can not do every "good" thing that comes along. It's called a sense of urgency, and it is the mark of a genuine leader.

Understand that you will not live forever. As the Roman ruler Marcus Aurelius said, "Do not live as though you have a thousand years." Make your time count. Once it is gone, it is gone. There is no getting it back.

The Surprising Leadership Example of Mark Twain

There is a preponderance of leadership examples to be taken from the annals of military conflict. These are both interesting and instructional. Perhaps the reason so many demonstrations of the principles of leadership are available from battles and wars is true leadership becomes most visible at times of extreme circumstances. War is as extreme as it gets. But most of us are not engaged in wars and battles, at least not of the military variety. We can benefit from the examples of everyday people living everyday lives that utilize and implement the same leadership principles demonstrated by war heroes.

One such example is Samuel Clemens, whose famous pen name became Mark Twain. Few would be quick to consider Twain as a leader. In fact, a case could be made for calling him a coward: twice he fled the scene when faced with dangerous circumstances. After causing a conflict with another man, Twain skipped town when threatened with a duel. Also, many have speculated that when Twain went to Nevada with his brother it was largely to escape the American Civil War. But Mark Twain's example is enriching precisely because he resists the stereotypical hero cast. He was not brave or courageous in the physical sense, or influential in assembling teams of people aligned in some great common purpose. But leadership and leadership principles are more profound and at the same time more subtle than the expected heroic examples. Leadership is also about results, change, assaulting the status quo, having the determination and the individuality to express oneself sincerely in the face of opposition, and about persisting through trying circumstances. And largely, leadership is about taking a group of people to a place where they have never been before. These are precisely the things

Mark Twain did.

Born in 1835, Mark Twain has been accused of living a life of profound "accidental" timing. He came of age coincident with the great (but short-lived) steamboat era, and became one of its romantic captains. Twain was on hand as a speculator in Carson City just after silver was discovered there at the world famous Comstock Mines. He experienced the Wild West when it was still wild; seeing gun fights, buffalo hunts, stage coach travel, and the Pony Express first-hand. He had also seen slavery up close and personal. His father-in-law was active in the Underground Railroad and helped Frederick Douglass escape. Twain saw first-hand the birth of the American Red Cross, the Great Fire of Chicago in 1871, the beginning of the United States Income Tax, experienced some of the first oceanic steamship travel, was a participant on the first organized luxury tour in U. S. history, was on hand in the gallery to see the vote for the impeachment of president Andrew Johnson, and had the first private telephone in his city installed in his house.

Examining the life of Mark Twain is like taking a tour around the globe and meeting all the people of caliber alive at that time. He was personally acquainted with President U.S. Grant, and was instrumental in encouraging Grant to write his now famous memoirs. Twain was friends with Artemous Ward, Henry Ward Beecher, Harriet Beecher Stowe, William James, Oscar Wilde, Rudyard Kipling, Henry James, Charles Dickens, Ralph Waldo Emerson, Oliver Wendell Holmes, Henry Wadsworth Longfellow, and Daniel Beard, the founder of the Boy Scouts. He worked for Senator Stewart while the statesman drafted the fifteenth amendment to the U.S. Constitution. Twain was on hand with Anson Burlingame and the first treaty of the United States with China. Twain was instrumental in encouraging rich benefactors to give scholarship money to Helen Keller. He met the original "Siamese Twins" Chang and Eng. He introduced Winston Churchill at the Waldorf Astoria. He dined with Teddy

Roosevelt (who hated him), and played putt-putt golf with Woodrow Wilson. Twain was friendly with Franz Joseph, the Emperor of Austria, and the Prince of Wales ("Edward the Conqueror", later King Edward VII). Andrew Carnegie made his famous admonition to Mark Twain about "putting all your eggs in one basket and then watch that basket," commenting on Twain's terrible history of speculative investing and diversification. Twain knew Brigham Young, Jefferson Davis, Napoleon III, and stayed with Czar Aleksandr II, Emperor of Russia. He was photographed by Matthew Brady, was friends with Frederick Douglass, and knew Horace Greeley the abolitionist and founder of the New York Tribune. Twain knew P.T. Barnum of circus fame, and the famous British statesman Benjamin Disraeli, he dined with Kaiser Wilhelm II of Germany, who would lead that country and the world into the First World War.

Arguably, there has never been an American who was so intermingled with the trends and trend makers of his day as was Mark Twain. As a writer, Twain could not have hoped for more exposure to material upon which to comment and be inspired. Twain was on hand with a front row seat for most of the changes taking place in the new United States and around the world. His personal contact with dying trends and his direct involvement in new ones gave him a unique

> *Whenever you find yourself on the side of the majority, it's time to pause and reflect.*
> – Mark Twain

perspective that found its way to his pen. When Twain got involved in journalism the profession was just entering its own budding era. Twain began writing just as America, an infant country struggling for eminence on the world's stage, was finding its own voice. Again, Twain was right in the middle of change. He was one of the first writers to begin using recorded dictations, he turned in the first type-written manuscript to a publisher, and he conducted some of the world's first newspaper interviews.

Twain's involvement with trends new and old, his familiarity with the great names of his day, and his extensive experiences are not really the sum and substance of his leadership example. The reason Mark Twain is noteworthy as a leader is because of the changes he himself brought about in the American literary voice. He was a daring pioneer and a "first of firsts." He was one of the first to write dialogue phonetically as it is actually spoken. He was one of the first to give slaves, children, southerners, and a wide range of dialects their true voice. His writing was not seen as proper and did not follow the unwritten rules that were expected at the time. He enraged literary critics with his style because it was seen as lowly and disgusting. Mark Twain, whose works seem so harmless to our standards today, was nearly scandalous in his own. Twain's new territory was the staking out of honesty in writing. He wrote it the way it actually was, without bowing to pretense or aristocratic rules, and he wrote to a country about a country at a time when that country was itself coming of age. According to biographer Ron Powers, ". . . the American Vandal was more than the sum of these parts. In his hard-headed, bull-in-a-china-shop way, he was the ambassador of a newly industrialized, populous, and therefore consequential America – no longer the familiar apologist for a backwoods culture sneered at by the French and English and Italian aristocracy, but the envy of all these, and damned proud of it." Twain's leadership was evident in the way he showed America to itself.

> *The man who does not read good books has no advantage over the man who cannot read them.*
> – Mark Twain

Toward the end of his life, Twain got even more outspoken, especially against the tendencies in America toward imperialism. Also, according to Powers, "Mark Twain was virtually alone among journalists in his reportage of Jewish Europeans as caught in the pincers of rising nationalist antagonisms." When warned of how his new tirades might erode the goodwill he had accumulated through years of being America's top entertainer, Twain responded:

"I can't understand it! You are a public guide & teacher, Joe, & are under a heavy responsibility to men, young &

old; if you teach your people – as you teach me – to hide their opinions when they believe their flag is being abused & dishonored, lest the utterance do them & a publisher a damage, how do you answer for it to your conscience? You are sorry for me; in the fair way of give & take, I am willing to be a little sorry for you."

Powers wrote, "The publishing industry could not handle his [Twain's] strongest ideas." Twain himself wrote, "Sometimes my feelings are so hot that I have to take to the pen and pour them out on paper to keep them from setting me afire inside. Then all that ink and labor are wasted, because I can not print the result." Leaders assault the status quo. They can not stand to leave things the way they found them. Leaders also deal in reality, no matter what other people think. They are driven by what they believe and have to do what they feel called to do. And leaders must be true to their conscience. They do not compromise their principles; they stand for what they believe in, even if it is costly. Leadership is also about getting results. Here again, Twain's example shines through. Mark Twain changed the face of American literature, entertainment, and the public image of the new country itself.

Each of us must understand that we are all called upon to lead at some point, and probably many points, in our lives. We will be called upon in big ways and small. We need not be military leaders involved in colossal struggles. We need not have positions of power or authority. We simply need to follow our convictions, respond to the inner call to greatness, take a hold of whatever it is God has seen fit to assign us to do, and do it with all honesty and might. Confronting brutal reality, assaulting the status quo, and doing that which is in us to do, are the hallmarks of leadership available to everyone. May the Mark Twains of our history inspire us to lead in whatever capacity in which we find ourselves.

Economics, Politics and Madmen: John Maynard Keynes

Here is a John Maynard Keynes quote that describes why we must discuss economics in life. I could take the easy way out and not discuss any controversial issue. However, if we do not discuss any controversial subjects, how do we learn the truths to live life by? I understand that thinking through issues can be tough, but I promise to not attack anyone personally; I will only attack error and focus on leading people to truth. If someone does not agree, then develop a reasoned argument of why you think differently and help me grow. I believe that when people go into labeling and name calling, then it signals a lack of rational points to discuss and have resorted to attacking personalities not principles. I encourage all of us to not take the low road and focus on principles instead of personalities. Let us fear ignorance more than disagreement and focus on iron sharpening iron as we all grow on our way to serving and leading. As Tim Marks states, "Know why you believe what you believe." I am proud of everyone for thinking. Whether they agree or disagree is not as important to me as logically thinking through why you think what you think. If you do not know why you believe what you believe, you may be a victim of some defunct economist or political philosopher. John Maynard Keynes was an economist who lived in England during the Great Depression. I personally disagree with much of his thinking, but I respect the fact that he thought deeply about economic issues. Keynes' ideas still hold sway in many economic circles and his thinking made an impact in our world. Keynes' quote below is an appropriate quote for our discussion on the presidential elections and will help us to hold all of our beliefs to critical reasoning.

"The ideas of economists and political philosophers, both when they are right and when they are wrong, are more powerful than is commonly understood. Indeed, the world is ruled by little else. Practical men, who believe themselves to be quite exempt from any intellectual influence, are usually the slaves of some defunct economist. Madmen in authority, who hear voices in the air, are distilling their frenzy from some academic scribbler of a few years back. I am sure that the power of vested interests is vastly exaggerated compared with the gradual encroachment of ideas."

What intellectual influences have helped you develop the way you think about the economy and government? Have you studied and read for yourself or have you developed your ideas through parents, teachers, and the media?

Wolf at the Door

Ever stop to consider what the word "Freedom" really means? Ever wonder what is truly meant by liberty, and those "Unalienable rights of life, liberty, and the pursuit of happiness" that were spoken of by the United States' founding documents? I certainly have. Consider this:

> "Single acts of tyranny may be ascribed to the accidental opinion of a day; but a series of oppressions, begun at a distinguished period, and pursued unalterably through every change of ministers, too plainly prove a deliberate and systematical plan of reducing us to slavery." -Thomas Jefferson

When I read history, I see one long, painful struggle of men trying to exert their control over others. In many instances, this resulted in tyranny.
Tyranny is defined as:

1. Oppressive power, or
2. A rigorous condition imposed by some outside agency or force.

Jefferson said, these acts, over time, constitute a deliberate plan of enslavement. It was this continuing oppressive behavior by the English government that led the thirteen colonies to revolt, and resulted in the loss of Great Britain's most valuable territory. Great Britain could have held the territory if it had won the hearts of the people. Instead, she bullied the people, threatened the people, encroached upon their freedoms, and pushed them to the point of open rebellion.

Sadly, in our society today, we are losing many of our personal, economic, and spiritual freedoms. We must meet the oppressors at the point of encroachment, and fight to preserve what we have, even pushing back the tide, if we can. As Lawrence Patton McDonald wrote:

> "Early Americans adhered rather closely to the free market ideal that people should remain free to find their own solutions for economic problems, whether caused by industry or by nature. The force of government would be used, if deemed necessary, only at the local level, under local control, to meet local needs. And as a result, America became a new promised land"

> "We later Americans have all but forfeited the great charter of liberty that made possible the miracle of America. It still exists for us to examine. If we still like it, we can reestablish it. Doing that will require as much persistence and dedication and plain hard work on our part as was required of the eighteenth-century gentlemen who created it. It will require as much labor to regain it as it did to create it, but thankfully not more."(Lawrence Patton McDonald, We Hold These Truths, p. 14-15, '76 Press, 1976)

Otherwise, I feel, the oppression of the common man, the infringements on his freedom by bigger, more powerful bodies, and the loss of something special will come to pass. As Ronald Reagan said,

> "Freedom is never more than one generation away from extinction. We didn't pass it to our children in the bloodstream. It must be fought for, protected, and handed onto them to do the same, or one day we will spend our sunset years telling our children and our children's children what it was once like in the United States where men were free."

Never take for granted the freedoms we still enjoy. On the other hand, never forget that those freedoms will always be under attack by some force somewhere who either wants to see it taken from you, or simply wants it for itself. Greed, jealousy, power lust, hatred, pride, and covetousness are behind nearly every example of tyranny in history. This has not changed.

Stand at the ready. For, there is always a wolf at the door.

The Leadership of Proverbs: Part Three

Proverbs 1:10 *...my son, if sinners entice thee, consent thou not.*

This proverb contains a very important principle for success and Godliness. As Christians we are called to be in the world, but not of the world. Because we are in the world, we will be enticed to do wrong. The first line of defense is to not willingly go into bad situations. I have read that Billy Graham will not go into a house or hotel room alone with a woman, except his wife. I think this is a good policy. Billy is avoiding even the appearance of sin and ensuring that no enticement to sin can occur. Pastor Dickie states that sin is to miss the mark. Sin is like a fire; it may start small, but it cannot be controlled once it is started. The best defense is to not light the match of sin when it is offered to you. The rule should be to never go near a fire that you know can burn you. If we can avoid the enticement, then we have a responsibility to do so.

The second line of defense is to just say no. This can be easier said than done with peer pressure and the desire to conform, but it must be done in order to follow biblical principles. When someone is doing something off track, they usually have a desire to get others involved to ease their conscience. If you have children, you have probably heard, "but everyone is doing it!" Following biblical principles is not a popularity contest, but it is a discipline contest. Say no and then extricate yourself from the environment that is causing the temptation. Proper association with other Godly people will reduce the enticement of sin in your life. An old southern saying states, "If you hang out with dogs, you will get fleas." One of my first mentors used to say, "If you put two geniuses and one idiot in a room for a day—when you come back, there will be three idiots." I always laugh at this saying, but I realize the truth in it. It takes a lot of positive associations to make up for one bad association. I have learned to control my association as much as humanly possible.

The Bible states clearly that all have sinned and fallen short of the glory of God. This is not an excuse to sin, but a fact of our fallen nature. We must choose to feed our spirit and starve our fallen human nature. Look at your life. What areas do you know of that need to change? What better time than today to ask Christ to forgive you and repent of your sins. All of us must turn from our sins and follow Christ example. Will we reach perfection? No, we will not, but that does not mean we should not be striving to hit the mark set before us. When I fail, I look to Christ and ask God to forgive me. What a wonderful gift it is to know we are forgiven in Christ. The great preacher D.L. Moody once said, "The Bible will keep you from sin or sin will keep you from the Bible!" Are you reading God's instruction manual for life or are you following the world's path? Your choices will make all the difference in your life and leadership. Remember, when tempted by sin, consent thou not!

How have good or bad associations made an impact in your life?

How does association influence the messages going into your thought life?

The American Creed

On many stages recently, I have spoken about the need for a leader to respect the individual. It is not enough to talk about "people" like many politicians do so dangerously at this time in the electoral process, but rather it is of supreme importance for leaders to focus upon and respect the rights and "evidence of the Creator" apparent at the level of the individual. What this means is that each individual is special and has equal rights under law.

Whenever we get off track and sacrifice individual rights on the altar of "people" as a broader category, we begin treading down a path where eventually no one will have individual rights or liberty. For proof of this, witness the murderous and bloody results of the French Revolution, which was founded on principles at first similar, but upon closer inspection, radically different than those of the American Revolution. The difference between the two is the American Revolution focused upon the rights of the individual, versus the French focused upon "Fraternity" or "the group."

Interestingly, the foundation for this belief system in the United States of America originated in a document that was intended to be revolutionary. The Declaration of Independence was drafted as a document to justify to a watching world why thirteen disparate colonies were choosing to do the impossible and unthinkable and overthrow their sovereign monarch. Only as a bi-product was the Declaration of Independence supposed to enumerate the fundamental creed that America would base its system of law and Bill of Rights upon.

Thomas Jefferson is given credit for the authorship of the Declaration, even though he was part of a five man committee responsible for its creation, and even though the document went through revision by the entire Second Continental Congress. Still, history shows that the opening salvo of words that establish the foundation of the American Creed of which we are speaking, were indeed Jefferson's creation. Interestingly, these opening fifty-five words were hardly debated or modified at all by the committee or the Congress. They read as follows:

> "We hold these truths to be self-evident, that all men are created equal, that they are endowed by their Creator with certain unalienable rights, that among these are Life, Liberty, and the pursuit of Happiness. That to secure these rights, Governments are instituted among Men, deriving their just powers from the consent of the governed."

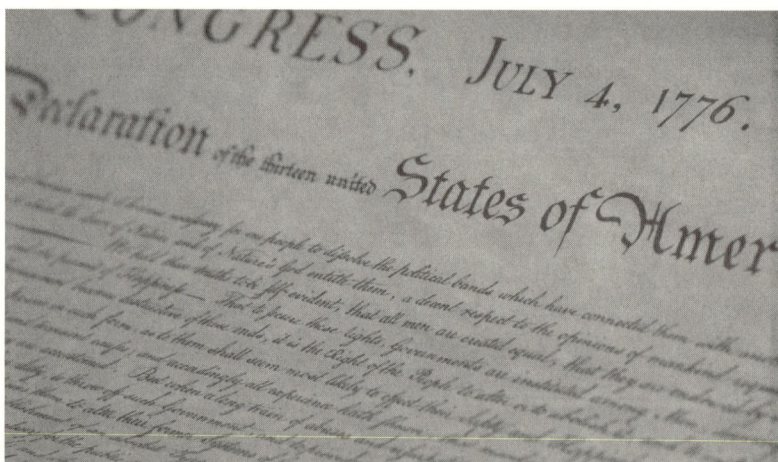

Apparently the truths of these opening words really were "self-evident" to the founders. According to my favorite historian, Joseph Ellis, these opening words would "grow in meaning to become the seminal statement of the American creed. With these words, Jefferson had . . . casually and almost inadvertently planted the seeds that would grow into the expanding mandate for individual rights that eventually ended slavery, made women's suffrage inevitable, and sanctioned the civil rights of all minorities."

Abraham Lincoln also, understood the significance of these words on the direction of America, writing, "All honor to Jefferson - to the man who, in the concrete pressure of a struggle for national independence by a single people, had the coolness, forecast, and capacity to introduce into a merely revolutionary document, an abstract truth, applicable to all men and all times, and so to embalm it there, that today, and in all coming days, it shall be a rebuke and a stumbling block to the very harbingers of the re-appearing tyranny and oppression."

Whenever our candidates or representatives or elected officials veer off track, whenever our leaders begin steps towards tyranny (read Communism, Socialism, etc.), whenever the rights of an individual are sacrificed for the "common good," the words in the opening paragraph of the Declaration of Independence are there as a timeless protection. May we never forget them.

It is Not Enough to be Busy...

Henry David Thoreau said, "It is not enough to be busy, so too are the ants. The question is, 'What are we busy about?'" We live in busy times. Our technology makes everything much easier, but it also tends to make things more hectic, too. Sometimes it seems that everybody is "busy, busy, busy" and that the world is all about hustle-bustle. As a matter of fact, in segments of our society, people have taken to the belief that being busy is in-and-of-itself a sign of success. The busier one is, the more important he or she must be!

Is this bad? Certainly idleness is not desirable, either. The law of inertia states that, "A body at rest tends to stay at rest, and a body in motion tends to stay in motion." I have written articles about initiative, and I would suggest getting busy doing something! Nobody likes a couch potato, and they especially do not like the tater tots that couch potatoes raise!

The best way to look at this is perhaps to view "busyness" and "idleness" as extremes. In the middle is effectiveness. The most effective people in life are certainly not idle, but they really are not busy, either.

Busyness really comes from a lack of ability to prioritize. Each of us has only twenty-four hours in a day. And life quickly becomes a struggle for what is and is not allowed to consume that time. When we prioritize our time properly, (and this goes beyond the mere concept of time management), we can work on the most important things first and allow the others to wait their turn. One of the best pieces of advice I have ever heard in this regard is, "Only do what only you can do." Only I can be a father to my children; only I can be a husband to my wife; only I can do what God has purposely built me to do, and I should be extremely careful not to allow anything else into my schedule. This can be taken to extremes, of course, and I do not mean it in that sense. We should always allow time for the unexpected but important matters: a friend in an emergency, a spontaneous hug, etc. But understanding our purpose very clearly, and being realistic about what our main strengths and duties are in life, will free us to "keep the main things the main things." Remember, the enemy of GREAT is GOOD. There will always be a myriad of GOOD things we could spend our time doing, but they will always be done at the expense of the one or two GREAT things we could be doing! Everything is a trade off.

Conversely, idleness is a form of wastefulness. It is when we take the precious gift of time and return it unused. Usually, it comes from a lack of purpose or understanding of what God would have us to do. Sometimes it can be caused by doubts, fears, or even hurts. But idleness is a thief that steals our life from us one minute at a time. This thief is very subtle, So beware.

Why is effectiveness the balance between busyness on one side and idleness on the other? Because idleness and busyness are actually different forms of the same thing: waste. Busyness wastes our time just as severely as idleness does. People with active personalities are more prone to waste their life with busyness, while those with more easy going personalities are more prone to do so with idleness. Either way, effectiveness was held at bay.

> *Diligence is the mother of good fortune, and idleness, its opposite, never brought a man to the goal of any of his best wishes.*
> – Miguel de Cervantes

Coach Lou Holtz once said, "Decisions are easy to make if you know what your purpose is," and I believe he is right. If we are not clear on what our purpose is, we will not make decisions that serve that purpose! Instead, we will make decisions that serve other ends, such as pleasure, comfort, happiness, personal peace or affluence. Notice that these things are all temporal and temporary. But if we understand our purpose, we will make decisions that are in line with that purpose and will be more effective in our lives. Usually, these things are of a higher and more lasting caliber.

So how do we fight off the evils of busyness on one side and idleness on the other? We get clear about our purpose in life, prioritize accordingly on a regular basis, and "only do what only we can do". Of course, life is not that simple, but these steps will get us a long way down the road to effectiveness.

A good example of this effectiveness is found in the daily battle cry of Mel Fisher, "Today's the day!" While in Fisher's case he would use it when showing up on the dock each day before setting out to discover lost treasure, I would use it in the understanding that today is really all we have. Yesterday is a memory and tomorrow is up to God to provide. Today is all we have. If we are to live for God's purpose and make something effective out of our lives, then truly, "Today's the Day."

I will close how I opened: It is not enough to be busy, the question is, what are we busy about?

Do not Survive: Thrive in Adversity

Here is a wonderful parable on learning to thrive through adversity. All of us will go through moments of boiling in our own life. How we respond to these challenging times will determine our destinies. Enjoy the parable and ask yourself which of the three items: Carrot, Egg, or Coffee Bean, best describe how you handle the boiling waters of life.

You may never look at a CUP OF COFFEE the same way again. A young woman went to her mother and told her about her life and how things were so hard for her. She did not know how she was going to make it and wanted to give up. She was tired of fighting and struggling. It seemed as one problem was solved a new one arose. Her mother took her to the kitchen. She filled three pots with water and placed each on a high fire. Soon the pots came to a boil. In the first, she placed carrots, in the second she placed eggs and the last she placed ground coffee beans. She let them sit and boil, without saying a word. In about twenty minutes she turned off the burners. She fished the carrots out and placed them in a bowl. She pulled the eggs out and placed them in a bowl. Then she ladled the coffee out and placed it in a bowl. Turning to her daughter, she asked, "Tell me, what do you see?" "Carrots, eggs, and coffee," she replied. She brought her closer and asked her to feel the carrots. She did and noted that they were soft. She then asked her to take an egg and break it. After pulling off the shell, she observed the hard-boiled egg. Finally, she asked her to sip the coffee. The daughter smiled as she tasted its rich aroma. The daughter then asked, "What does it mean, mother?" Her mother explained that each of these objects had faced the same adversity, boiling water, but each reacted differently. The carrot went in strong, hard and unrelenting. However after being subjected to the boiling water, it softened and became weak. The egg had been fragile. Its thin outer shell had protected its liquid interior. But, after sitting through the boiling water, its inside became hardened. The ground coffee beans were unique, however. After they were in the boiling water they had changed the water. "Which are you?" she asked her daughter. When adversity knocks on your door, how do you respond? Are you a carrot, an egg, or a coffee bean?" Think of this: Which am I? Am I the carrot that seems strong, but with pain and adversity, wilt and become soft and lose strength? Am I the egg that starts with a malleable heart, but changes with the heat? Did I have a fluid spirit, but after death, a breakup, a financial hardship or some other trial, have I become hardened and stiff? Does my shell look the same, but on the inside am I bitter and tough with a stiff spirit and a hardened heart? Am I like the coffee bean? The bean actually changes the hot water, the very circumstance that brings the pain. When the water gets hot, it releases the fragrance and flavor. If you are like the bean, when things are at their worst, you can get better and change the situation around you with God's help.

How do you handle adversity? When adversity strikes, ask yourself...ARE YOU A CARROT, AN EGG, OR A COFFEE BEAN?

Patrick Henry: PART II - The Seven Resolutions

This is the second part of young Patrick Henry's courageous stand for truth against the tyranny of British King George the Third. What will Patrick Henry do? Will he stand for what he knows to be right or bow to the older members? The older House members fear the King and are not representing the people they are under oath to represent. The House of Burgess began its session and by all indications it would be a few days of closing up previously discussed items. The monotonous proceedings clipped along until someone made a proposal to review all the actions the House had done in protest against the notorious Stamp Acts and consider any further steps that could be taken to convey their displeasure with the tyrannical actions of King George. Patrick Henry stood up in the opening debates with seven resolutions he had written out on a blank page of an old law book. He drew the page from his pocket and began to read the resolutions. (I will paraphrase and abridge the resolutions.)

1. *Resolved:* That subjects of his Majesty's colony have all privileges, franchises, and immunities (rights) enjoyed by the people in Great Britain.
2. *Resolved:* These rights have been confirmed by two royal charters.
3. *Resolved:* The taxation of the people by themselves or by a person representing them is the distinguishing mark of British freedoms.
4. *Resolved:* The Virginians have always been thus governed by their own Assemblies in the areas of taxes and internal policy.

By this point the conservative Tory members of the House

were getting nervous. No one could argue with Patrick Henry's logic or the correctness of his points. But they did not like the tone or the direction that Patrick was heading with his reasoning. In 1765, subjects did not talk like this against the King's proclamations. Patrick Henry knew there were principles stronger than the King's commands. Conservatives attempted to close the debate by saying they should wait until they heard from the British Ministry and Lord George Grenville on their earlier protest letter. (In fact, they never heard from Lord Grenville, author of the Stamp Act as he scarcely glanced at the protest before dumping letter into wastebasket.) After much discussion, Patrick's first four resolutions were adopted by the slimmest of margins. Patrick Henry did not sit down and what happened next was a major force that changed the thinking of the colonies and forged the unity which led to the United States of America. The conservatives' worst fears were being realized.

5. *Resolved:* That the General Assembly have the exclusive right and power to lay taxes on the subjects of the colony.
6. *Resolved:* That the subjects of this colony are not bound to obey any law designed to impose taxes upon them—other than the laws and ordinances from the General Assembly.
7. *Resolved:* Anyone maintaining a contrary opinion to this either in writing or speaking shall be considered an enemy to the Virginian Colony.

This was a new and bold innovation in the colonies. Although the Virginian colony enjoyed incredible freedom from British Parliament, it was more from neglect than by design. The British had left the Colonist alone and their freedoms had thrived. Now with the British desire for money and power they began to tax and regulate the colonist freedoms away. Patrick Henry would not take this sitting down. The fifth resolution passed by one vote, but the 6th and 7th caused an uproar amongst the members. Members attempted to shout down the twenty-nine year old Patrick Henry. Patrick stood his ground and spoke with the eloquence of a backwoods Demosthenes.

"Tarquin and Caesar had each his Brutus, Charles the First, his Cromwell; and George the third....."
"Treason!" cried by Speaker of the House. Numerous members of the House followed the Speaker in castigating the young leader. Patrick patiently waited for the fury to subside and continued.
"......and George the Third may profit from their example. If that be treason, make the most of it."

The House appeared to accept all seven resolutions, but the next day the inflammatory 6th and 7th were rejected by the more conservative majority in the House of Burgess. On the following day the 5th resolution was rejected also. Even with this setback the die was cast. The political foundations of the Virginian conservative order was cracked and soon to be broken. Copies of all seven resolutions were sent to the other colonies and the ideas that would lead to the Revolutionary War were disseminated into the leading minds of the colonies. Here was the spark that lit the flame inside of the Revolutionary leaders burning for independence. Let me quote from George Willison's excellent biography again:
"If Virginia—the oldest, largest, richest, and traditionally the most loyal and royalist of the colonies—was prepared to take the lead in resisting British "tyranny", why should her sister colonies hesitate to follow? The answer was: They shouldn't. And they began organizing associations to boycott British goods and take other measure to force repeal of the Stamp Tax."
Years later, when assessing the relative influence of American leaders on the eve of Independence, it was Jefferson, always in the vanguard himself, who said of Henry: "He left all of us far behind . . . He gave the first impulse to the ball of Revolution . . . He was the idol of the country beyond anyone that ever lived."
Can one man with courage and convictions make a difference? In my reading of the Revolutionary War, I believe

this single event was the catalyst that united Massachusetts and Virginia together. This unity created leadership teams across all colonies that formed together to resist the tyranny of the British. I can only imagine the amount of courage it took for a twenty-nine year old country lawyer to stand up in front of the wealthy Virginia aristocracy and speak the truth.

Where would you have stood in the Virginia House of Burgess? Would you have rationalized the wrongs for your own personal peace and affluence? Or would you have stood with the truth and young Patrick Henry? Perhaps you will have an opportunity in your life to test your courage. When you need courage, reflect back to the young lawyer from Virginia who stood up to the English empire and sparked a revolution.

Leaders Carry an Unfair Load

Often, it seems, leaders are asked to carry an unfair load. In fact, this is one of the hallmarks of leadership. Leaders are the ones taking responsibility when everyone else waivers. Leaders are the ones accepting the blame for a situation when it was actually the accumulative affect of others' involvement that caused it. Leaders are the ones paying the price of going somewhere first, where many times they have not even been there themselves. Leaders take the flak, the responsibility, and the bulk of the wind resistance from being out front. For sure, leaders are put in a position of higher responsibility. They are held under higher scrutiny and loftier standards than the rest, and they are expected to have a great attitude when everyone else has failed. Leaders are expected to be the toughest, the most consistent, the strongest, the fairest, the hungriest, and the most courageous. No wonder we admire them so! And no wonder the apostle Paul had to encourage his protégés with the phrase, "never grow weary in well-doing."

If this list of requirements sounds daunting; it is. Leading is dangerous, exhausting, exposing work. So why, again, would anyone volunteer for the position?

Because!...At least that's the way my four year old would answer.

For the real answer (with apologies to my son), we must go back to the definition of a leader. As defined in the *Launching a Leadership Revolution* book, Orrin Woodward and I defined leadership as:

"... the influence of others in a productive, vision-driven direction and is done through the example, conviction, and character of the leader."

Notice that leadership involves someone who is "vision-driven." And what causes the drive toward the vision? Conviction in the cause they pursue, and their strength of character. What does this mean?

It means that a leader does not set out to become a leader, as such. A leader becomes a leader the moment he or she decides to act on their conviction. A leader's character is such that he or she simply can not leave well enough alone, and must do something about whatever situation confronts them. Someone in danger, a cause not making enough progress, a project that stimulates the imagination, a group of people without direction, etc. all make up the type of situations that spark a leader into action.

All men have an instinct for conflict: at least, all healthy men.
–Hilaire Belloc

Once the leader realizes the situation, sees the problem to be solved, or the challenge to be embraced, he or she takes immediate initiative towards the vision. It can not be helped. It is the natural outpouring of the leader's character and vision.

So a leader is driven into a position where he or she accepts more responsibility, accepts a higher percentage of the "shots" from the "peanut gallery," and volunteers to carry an "unfair" load. Interestingly, true leaders do it willingly and with enthusiasm! Why? I think it is because leaders come alive when they are infused with a challenge. Real leaders are overcome with joy at being called to apply their gifts to a worthwhile cause....And what about everyone else?

Usually, "everyone else" looks at the leader with a bit of admiration, but also with a bit of curiosity. It is like looking at a dog chasing a rabbit, and then removing the rabbit from view. Without the rabbit to explain the dog's behavior, he looks mad. And for many leaders, people can not quite make out the vision the leader is chasing as clearly as the leader can. As a result, leaders look a little mad to the uninformed.

Just what is it that makes that leader behave like that? Why would anyone want to put themselves in harm's way as a leader does? What makes them tick? Is it not it better to be comfortable, play it safe, mind one's own business, and take it easy? It may appear that way to some people, but never for a leader. A leader carries an unfair load, and believe it or not, loves it! Why? Because what a leader does makes a difference, it matters, it changes things, and that's what a leader lives for!

People Skills

One of the biggest challenges leaders of all types will face is the difficulty in dealing with people. Some people are easy to deal with, while others can be tough. But it is even more complicated than that. Sometimes the easiest people to get along with harbor quiet resentments, while the difficult ones will at least "tell it to you like it is." Additionally, each person is a fallen, sinful creature (as is the leader!), with foibles, quirks, oddities, fears, blind spots, and weaknesses. Then there are gender differences, culture differences, age differences, religious differences, differing world-views, hormonal influences, sicknesses, and mood swings! Wow! What a list! (I am sure that we could expand the list even further!)

Like it or not, a leader must learn to deal with all these issues in a continually effective way. Leaders without people skills will not be leaders for long, if at all. It is amazing for me to see this displayed time and again: people who think they are leading that can not get along with others! Remember, leadership is with, for, and about others. If you can not succeed in starting and maintaining valuable relationships over time, you will not be able to lead effectively, period.

Further, let me mention that I believe there are two groups of "people skills" to be considered. The first deals with initial impressions. These include the ability to "come across well" to others, the ability to build quick rapport, and the capability of connecting with strangers by finding common ground or identifying areas of respect. The second area is maintaining relationships with people over the long haul.

There are five main books we recommend people read on a recurring basis to grow and continue to improve in their ability to work with people:

1. *The Magic of Thinking Big* by David Schwartz
2. *How to Win Friends and Influence People* by Dale Carnegie
3. *How I Raised Myself from Failure to Success in Selling* by Frank Bettger
4. *How to Have Confidence and Power in Dealing with People* by Les Giblin
5. *Personality Plus* by Florence Littauer

These five books cover a broad range of approaches and principles that have been proven extremely effective in elevating one's ability to deal with other people. Of course there are other books I could recommend, but reading these five over and over will hurt no one.

Now, let us delve a little deeper. I believe the best way to develop "people skills" is to forget about the "skills" part of this for a moment. First, it is important for one to get one's heart right toward people. This, I believe, like everything else, can only come through faith in Christ and the resulting Biblical world-view. Without a true and proper understanding of WHO you are, and WHOSE you are, you will not have a real heart for people. Without an understanding that others are created by God in His image, with their own special and unique design, while simultaneously understanding one's own fallen condition and need of grace, relations with people will be strained and continually incoherent. This is because we will not be interested in serving others, but instead in having others serve us. Also, we will be more interested in winning "battles" with people and squabbling with them when we feel affronted, offended, and wounded. We will feel that we are righteously indignant when wrongs are done to us and will not be forgiving of others.

With the proper Biblical view, however, a heart for others is readily at hand. The Bible teaches that we are to love our neighbor, and we are to be as forgiving of others as the Savior is of us. For those of us that are believers, we are commanded to be as salt and light in a fallen world. This means that our Godly example is meant to be a witness for the God in heaven that is the power behind our ability to love others.

Do you now see why I said that this rises above mere "skills" and gets into "heart" issues? Truly, the best way to have "people skills" is to begin with getting our hearts right toward others. If we do not, the "skills" may open some doors, fool some people, and get us some results for a while. But eventually, our hearts being focused on self, rather than on others, will be found out, and as a result people will lose trust in us and over time will flee from our influence.

Once a person has his heart in the right place, focused on others (although it is not that easy!). We can then move on to the "skills" part. Building upon a firm foundation of a heart that is right toward others, willing to serve and to love and to forgive, people skills can become very important. Learning to smile, to listen, to be interested in the other person, to get the other person to open up about themselves, to affirm, approve, and appreciate others are incredible lessons we should all learn. Remembering names, refraining from interrupting, and making good eye contact are all "skills" that will get results with others. The five books I mentioned are full of interesting stories and applications of these concepts. Read them again and again. Practice these skills until they become habits. But don not get so caught up in the "skills" part that you become a cheesy fake. Instead, apply well-meant people skills to a servant's heart toward people, and watch them adhere to you and offer you a chance to influence them.

When in doubt, lead with the heart!

Counter-Productive Compassion

According to Ronald Reagan, some of the most dangerous words anyone could ever hear are, "I'm from the government, and I'm here to help." With his characteristic home-spun style, Reagan in that one little quip summed up what plagues much of the United State's current condition.

Author W. Cleon Skousen coined the term "Counter-Productive Compassion" to describe what I see displayed across nearly the entire current landscape of national candidates for President. Somewhere, somehow, the American populace got it into their head that "the government" is responsible for solving the people's problems. Even most of those on the "conservative" side barely represent a conservative platform. It seems as though the citizenry has realized that they can vote "benefit providers" into office to serve their individual needs.

Do not get me wrong. It is not that we should not care for the poor. It is not that we should not provide cushion to displaced workers caught in industry shifts. It's not that we should not get involved in addressing a whole host of human needs across our country. Of course we should. To do less would be cold, uncaring, and the farthest thing from compassionate. What I am suggesting is that we merely consider who the "we" is in these sentences. Exactly who should care for the poor? Exactly who should help the displaced worker?

187

Our compassion is correct, our implementation is flawed. Why? Because, just as Reagan indicated, governments are notoriously bad at executing (unless we are speaking of despotic governments, of course, in which case executions are some of their most efficient work). Have you ever had to work with or inside of a bureaucracy? If you have (and who among you has not invested hours inside a DMV or Secretary of State's Office?), you know exactly what I am talking about. The U.S. government, although founded upon some of the most sound political theory and documents the world has ever produced, is the world's largest bureaucracy. Worse, it has a nagging tendency to continue to grow. Each new "program," no matter how well intentioned, the pig just gets fatter, bigger, slower, and less effective. What began in compassion ends in a pile of paperwork and waste, with very little, if any, of the intended benefit actually finding its way to the proper recipient. Consequently if that benefit does reach the right place, often times the compassion then breeds entitlement instead of its original purpose. This is because most government programs, being so bureaucratic, are cold and impersonal, and therefore are not very caring, specific, or good at holding people accountable. Instead of a hand up, which is what most well-intentioned compassionate people hope to enable the government to provide, it turns into a hand-out. Let us look at the principles involved, which I borrow from Benjamin Franklin:

1. Compassion which gives a drunk the means to increase his drunkenness is counter-productive.
2. Compassion which breeds debilitating dependency and weakness is counter-productive.
3. Compassion which blunts the desire or necessity to work for a living is counter-productive.
4. Compassion which smothers the instinct to strive and excel is counter-productive.

We see that compassion improperly applied leads to bad results. We see that the government is especially gifted at "improperly applying" its compassionate funds.

So if compassion is a dangerous weapon that must be yielded properly so it does not backfire, and if government has continually demonstrated its inability to properly implement compassion, how then should it be handled?

The founding fathers had an answer for this, and it comes from a principle called "fixed responsibility." The principle works much the same as the structure of government they instituted at the birth of the United States, in which local governments controlled everything except what belonged to the states and national government, and in turn the states handled everything the local governments could not, and finally, the federal government handled only what was beyond the local and state governments. "Fixed Responsibility," according to Skousen, works like this:

"The first and foremost level of responsibility is with the individual himself; the second level is the family; then the church; next the community; finally the country, and, in disaster or emergency, the state. Under no circumstances is the federal government to become involved in public welfare. The Founders felt it would corrupt the government and also the poor. No Constitutional authority exists for the federal government to participate in charity or welfare. By excluding the national government from intervening in the local affairs of the people, the Founders felt they were protecting the unalienable rights of the people from abuse by an over-aggressive government."

In relation to this, where do you think we are today? And how did we get there? Was it because politicians learned that they could get elected by promising benefits to special interest supporters, thereby "selling votes," or was it because the government must handle these things because individuals, families, churches, and communities will not? Is our counterproductive governmental compassion a result of power hungry politicians (the kind that can not really solve the problem they crusade for because then they would be without their base of power), or is it due the selfishness and indifference of individuals, families, and churches in our society?

Leadership is an Inside Job

"I need someone to make me do what I know I need to do," said one, "I need someone to motivate me," said another, "I could do more if you would just hold me accountable like a boss," said still another. These and other comments by the hundreds of this nature I have heard in my years of working with and trying to develop other leaders. These statements, although all well-intended and hopeful, are way off the mark.

Leadership is an inside job. If someone from the outside is required to push you, or to motivate you, or to manage you like a boss does an employee, in order for you to perform as a leader, then you probably need to get out the *Launching a Leadership Revolution* book and read it again. Leaders are not pushed from without, they are driven from within.

One of the precepts of the book is that leadership begins and ends with Hunger. If a person is not hungry deep inside for achievement, for changing something about her world, for making something better, for winning or advancing, then she is not a leader at all. Do not get me wrong. People can still be productive, honorable, and valuable outside of the realm of hunger, but they should never be called leaders, no matter what their official title or position.

What happens inside of people that makes them decide to take personal responsibility for leading? What is it that makes up the substance of leadership? This is not an easy question to answer. Thousands of books, including ours, make the attempt. But no matter how much it is studied, or how much it is written about, leadership will always have an elusive quality to it. That is because it is partially art, not all science. It is wrapped up in the very identity of the leader. But it is spark has everything to do with hunger. How it is manifested is largely art, but how it begins is through the courage of conviction that becomes a hunger.

I have nothing but the highest respect for the people who choose to push, strive, grow, and advance when times get tough or confusing. It is when people are left more to their own in the turmoil of the storm that you find out the level of their leadership abilities. Tough times reveal tough leaders, and conversely, they expose imposters.

Do not ask your mentor to motivate you. Do not ask to have your hand held. Do not ask to be coddled. Such is not the territory of a leader. Ask for a challenge. Ask for danger. Ask for something that causes your heart to beat faster and your palms to sweat. Ask for a test of your courage, your character, and your staying power. Ask for that, and I will know you have the infant spark of hunger that starts all leaders. Finish the journey through thick and thin and I will know you ARE a leader. Help others to do the same, and I will know that you are among the rarest of leaders.

You can make excuses and blame your spouse. You can say the challenge was too hard, or that conditions were not right. You can say timing was not good, or blame someone else for your circumstances. You can say you were busy, or tired. You can blame confusion and lack of information. You can blame your mentor, or even the President. Bosses make good scapegoats, too. You can blame your health or your age or your birth. Hide behind your color or your gender or your past. You could also blame your parents. You could claim offense and say someone hurt your feelings. You could blame your finances, too.

Leaders never fix blame, they just fix problems. Leaders never make excuses, they make progress. Leaders never hide behind circumstances, they throw themselves in the way of danger. Leaders do not cower at the dock when the sea kicks up; they head out on the open ocean with all sails a-flyin'! Oh yes, it is a rare person that musters the courage to lead. It is a tough individual that answers the call of courage. There is nothing that says that it cannot be YOU.

Lead on! And be prepared to do most of it yourself.

William "Billy" Mitchell's Courageous Leadership

Leaders assault the status quo, and somehow just cannot stand to leave things the way they find them. For true leaders, this comes from a deep sense of hunger that burns inside. Often this yearning is extremely costly to the individual pushing for the change. What might have been a comfortable existence is traded for the pursuit of a vision the leader sees more clearly than anyone else. This, in short, is what makes him or her a leader; he or she sees further than others see, sooner than others see, and with more conviction. Ultimately, the personal cost is worth it to the leader because of his or her strong belief in the outcome desired. Whether ending in triumph, or flaming out in defeat, the leader is vindicated by the chase of the vision and the principles upon which he or she stands. The conviction of the leader, backed by his or her courage to act on that conviction regardless of cost to self, is the stuff that makes the world go around. It is also what all of us admire when we are fortunate enough to get a glimpse of it.

For just such a glimpse, let us examine the life of aviation pioneer and advocate William "Billy" Mitchell. It was the year 1898 when Mitchell saw his first military action as an infantryman in the Spanish-American war in Cuba. He later gave up prestige and promotion hopes to get involved in the United States' infantile aviation efforts, and was at the center of many of aviation's "firsts." During World War I Mitchell became the first U.S. officer to fly behind enemy lines. He next became involved in a joint bombing effort between the French and the Americans which assembled the largest force of aircraft ever to amass up to that point. Repeatedly, Mitchell was given organizational control and command of large scale joint-bombing efforts by his French allies: something pretty unusual and indicative of his leadership abilities.

After the end of the Great War, Mitchell began campaigning for the creation of an independent branch of the U.S. military that would be focused strictly upon air power. His ideas were radical and threatening and were fiercely resisted. The army had thought air power should be subservient to its needs, because airplanes could provide cover to troops on the ground and tactical bombing ahead of troop movements. The navy had claim to air power as well, needing planes to attack enemy shipping and provide visuals across the vast seas. William Mitchell saw further than the established bureaucrats in either branch of the military. He foresaw the advent of airpower as preeminent, and certainly worthy of a single, autonomous branch of the U. S. military that would transcend control by either the army or the navy.

Mitchell's campaign grew louder and more vehement, until he was called upon to prove his "wild" theories. In a demonstration utilizing a German dreadnought captured during the war, Mitchell's bombers sunk the great iron ship in about twenty minutes. This was astounding to the large assortment of navy brass on hand to witness the event, and out of this demonstration ultimately came the development of the aircraft carriers that would be so critical to winning the war in the Pacific during World War II.

These encouraging developments aside, Mitchell continued to push for his great vision of a stand-alone military branch that would control all forms of air power. The harder Mitchell pushed for something he felt was so obvious, the more resistance he met. Not only did he have to deal with skepticism and shortsightedness, but he also ran into commanders trying to protect their turf, pride, the "Not Invented Here Syndrome", cost cutters, peace nicks, small thinkers, and commanders who wanted to have air power fall under their own control. Mitchell did not play by the rules. He wanted change. He was upsetting the status quo. He was attacking long-held paradigms and beliefs about the way things were supposed to be done. He was preaching to the military establishment that had played a big part in winning the "war to end all wars" and was riding high on its success. Finally, as with many a bureaucracy, the innovator had to be silenced. Mitchell was demoted and transferred to a remote location in charge of a small corps. However, typical of a leader on a mission, Billy Mitchell was unable to stop there. When his crusade fell on deaf ears, he took his story to the press. This resulted in his court martial and conviction of insubordination. Mitchell was given a suspension of five years without pay. Mitchell resigned in protest instead, but continued his quest for an independent air force until his death.

According to author Alan Axelrod:

"Billy Mitchell was a leader ahead of his time, and he was a man willing to sacrifice his career for the sake of his country's defense. Virtually all of his doctrinal theories about the role of aviation in warfare would prove true – including his assessment (much ridiculed) that the navy's fleet at Pearl Harbor in the Hawaiian Islands was vulnerable to a carrier-launched air attack, which, Mitchell predicted, would be made by Japan. After his death, his major positions were vindicated, and he came to be considered the founding spirit of the U.S. Air Force."

Billy Mitchell's crusade to create a United States Air Force is a clear demonstration of the courage and conviction of a leader. At great personal cost and ending in much frustration in his own life, Billy Mitchell pushed to the end for the vision in which he believed. Mitchell was driven by what he could "see" long before it was seen by others. Rare indeed are those who will act at such great cost for a cause that transcends their own personal peace and affluence. Rare they may be, but history is rich with glimpses of individuals like Mitchell who have risked it all for what they believed was right. May they be an inspiration to us all!

The Great Awakening

Often we can identify a leader by examining the wake of change left in his or her path. Two such glaring examples are the fiery preacher Jonathan Edwards, and his inexhaustive contemporary, George Whitfield. Together, these men of God sparked a religious fervor that turned into a movement that spread throughout the North American colonies beginning in about the year 1734. The events that took place over the subsequent fifteen year period became known as the Great Awakening.

Edwards and Whitfield, of much differing temperament and style, were both at the apex of a massive shift in religious sentiment in the colonies. The Puritan era was drawing to a close, and much decline had been seen in the strength, breadth, and width of spiritual standing of many in the colonies. The light which had burned so brightly and inspired the Pilgrims and others to establish footholds in the new land for the purpose of the freedom to worship had dimmed. Edwards and Whitfield, each independently inspired, began to rail against what they saw as decaying religious belief. Edwards, Whitfield, and the others who all at roughly the same time began preaching against man's muddling of the gospel message and indifference to the work of the Savior, became known as the "New Lights." These men rode from town to town delivering their stirring sermons, calling sinners to repentance, and spreading the message of the gospel. Often, several sermons would be delivered in different cities in just a single day, sometimes from horse back. Benjamin Franklin himself was instrumental in procuring a large hall in Philadelphia for the use of George Whitfield, and Jonathan Edwards during this time would deliver what remains the most famous sermon in American history: "Sinners in the

Hands of an Angry God."

It is quite obvious that the work of the Holy Spirit was evident in the efforts of these men. However, from a leadership perspective, this story of one of the greatest religious movements in American history is evidence of the principles of leadership at work. Edwards, Whitfield and others, railed against the status quo. They used their health and resources to attack that which they could not stand to let alone: spiritual apathy and unrepentant sin in the colonies. They spent themselves in the pursuit of a vision which drove them to exhaustion. Others were inspired by the thousands and followed the example of Edwards and Whitfield.

The resulting leadership of these men was both enormous and timely. Their impact on the colonies was instrumental in returning people's thoughts to their blessings and their Creator. This established a foundation for the political turmoil to come. According to authors Alan Axelrod and Charles Phillips:

> "In a period . . . characterized by the increasing political tensions that foreshadowed the French and Indian War, and, ultimately, the War of Independence, people were looking desperately for faith and religious guidance . . . . The Great Awakening was founded on an especially American belief that the individual is the ultimate arbiter of truth and that any person can have an intimate, direct, unmediated relation to the Almighty. On principles akin to these, the Declaration of Independence was based, as well as the thought of those philosophers considered most typically American - Ralph Waldo Emerson, Henry David Thoreau, William James, and John Dewey - and the writing of the nation's greatest authors, including Nathaniel Hawthorne, Herman Melville, Walt Whitman, Emily Dickinson, Ernest Hemingway, William Carlos Williams, and Norman Mailer, to mention a few."

If leaders can be identified by their impact on events and those whom they have inspired, this commentary from Axelrod and Phillips is enough to settle the case. Edwards, Whitfield, and the other "New Lights" were an excellent example of character in motion. Their dedicated work, based on conviction laid the cornerstones of a nation.

Could these men, driven by their beliefs and convictions, have known the extent of the outcome of their efforts? Do any leaders ever grasp a true measure of the reach of their service? Perhaps not. But studying this example should be an inspiration to anyone moved to lead. Once again, we can see the far-reaching impact of a handful of leaders standing firm upon the truth.

Lead on!

The Leadership of Proverbs: PART FOUR

Proverbs 1:14-16 *Cast in thy lot among us; let us all have one purse: My son, walk not thou in the way with them; refrain thy foot from their path: For their feet run to evil, and make haste to shed blood.*

Today's verses teach against communism and spell out the punishment for anyone attempting such a man centered idea on earth. Communism has failed wherever it has been attempted and has produced more misery than any other economic system. Why have so many seemingly intelligent people supported this bankrupt system? I think the answer can be traced back to a rejection of God. The communist system is based upon the works of Karl Marx who drew his inspiration from Charles Darwin. Darwin's thoughts were so influential on Marx that Engels, speaking at Marx's funeral stated, "Just as Darwin had discovered the law of development of organic nature, so did Marx discover the law of human history." I love the saying, "Wrong doctrine leads to wrong living." Darwin was wrong when it came to evolution of species to other species; therefore, Marx was wrong in using Darwin to develop an inaccurate view of human history.

Communism is a system that abolishes private property and everything is owned by the state. Communism believes everyone will work their personal best and put all the wealth in a pot to draw on equally among the citizens. There are two major problems with this. First, whoever is in charge of the state always takes liberties to ensure they stay in power and to justify why they deserve more than their fair share. Lenin, the founder of Communist Soviet Union defined dictatorship as power that is limited by nothing, by no laws, that is restrained by absolutely no rules, that rest directly on coercion. Second, no one wished to give their best efforts so someone else could gain at their expense. Outside of threats, there was no way to motivate people to work. One worker cynically explained, "They pretend to pay us and we pretend to work." Communism was based on an inaccurate view of man. Communism believed man was perfectible and not fallen by nature. Because of this, communist dogma insisted man would willingly work to benefit all mankind with no thought of personal reward and others would willing accumulate the wealth of the state with no thought of a special deal. Both misguided thoughts were dead wrong!

The three P's explain what is wrong with Communism and what is right with Free Enterprise.

The first is *Private property*. No system will work that is not based on the right to own property. The ancient Greeks were the first group of people to develop the idea of property as a commodity. Because of this, they were the first to deal with the inequalities of wealth created by different levels of performance. Free enterprise believes inequalities are a given and slowing down the front of the train for the caboose only hinders the whole system. Communism took a different approach. They believe by taking all private property and giving it to the state that inequalities would be eliminated and a heaven on earth would result. History has proven the fallacy of this evil concept. The Bible, over 2000 years before Communist Russia, had clearly stated the result of these foolish ideas. Private property is the bedrock of free enterprise and anything that reduces property rights also reduces freedoms. If you thought you owned a field and worked hard for years to develop the best acreage in your county; imagine your shock if you learned it could be revoked at any time. If the farmers knew it could be revoked at the states discretion, who would apply their personal best to the field? Free enterprise gives the field and 100% ownership to the farmer; Communism takes the field and gives 100% ownership to the state with the farmer an employee of the state. Nazi Germany tolerated the farmer owning the field, but treated it as an irrevocable trust to be repealed at states discretion.

The second is *Power*. Every form of Communism ultimately falls into the hands of a power hungry statist who desire control and perks. Lord Acton's famous quotation, "Power corrupts and absolute power corrupts absolutely", applies here. Because man is fallen there must be checks and balances in a system. Communism's errant view of humanity causes a centralization of power and their ideology becomes a cover for blatant power plays. The state has no ability to motivate the citizens (employees) to work and implements threats, punishments or death sentences to coerce the people. The French thinker of the 18th century argued that proper instruction and legislation would enable and compel humans to attain complete virtue. This man centered theory is the common heritage of liberalism, socialism, and communism and has failed wherever it has been implemented. Why does it fail? Because human beings convinced against their will are of the same opinion still. This is why I do not believe electing all Christians will significantly change our country. Our country will only change by changing the mind, heart and will of the people by leadership, not dictatorship. Power is positional leadership; you will do this because I say so and I am in authority over you. True leadership is teaching and serving and leading people to truth. You cannot hit someone over the head with truth and expect to influence them.

How do you tell a communist? Well, it's someone who reads Marx and Lenin. And how do you tell an anti-Communist? It's someone who understands Marx and Lenin.
– Ronald Reagan

The third is *Press*. Because the Communist system did not work the press had to be controlled or else the truth would get out. I have learned that anyone attempting to control the free flow of ideas is fighting a losing battle. The communist had all the facts against them, but instead of admitting they were wrong, they attempted to control the press and keep the facts hidden. Andropov, the former head of the KGB and successor to Brezhnev, had warned that relaxing controls on speech could bring the whole Soviet system down:

"....Too many groups have suffered under the repression in our country....If we open up all the valves at once, and people start to express their grievances, there will be an avalanche and we will have no means of stopping it."

The only way to stop a genuine criticism is to address and fix the root cause. In order to do this with Communism, they would have to scrap the whole system and admit their error. This was too much to ask the fallen humans who had perks and power even though the people were suffering greatly from their errors. Boris Yeltsin, the first elected head of state of Russia took a trip to the US in 1989. The journey for him demolished many stereotypes and clichés fed to him by Soviet propaganda. After inspecting a Houston supermarket he exclaimed, "What have they done to our poor people?" Any economic model that cannot be examined under the light of day and discussed freely is broken. All communist countries control the press and determine the messages delivered to the people. A free press would call out the propaganda and the whole communist edifice would fall. My advice to all countries, business, and people is: everything you do, be sure it can be written in the cloud for all to see. If it cannot, then why are you doing it? The Communists knew they were not following the principles they espoused and the truth would get out. Communism fails not because it is a good idea poorly implemented. Communism fails because it is a bad idea and anti-biblical. A simple reading of the Proverbs would have saved a lot of pain and misery.

The last verse in this set of proverbs states, ". . . they make haste to shed blood." The Bible is again true to life. The estimated global number of humans sacrificed on the altar of Communism is between 85 and 100 million people. This is over twice the amount of deaths caused by the two world wars! Lenin said, "In order to make an omelet, you will have to break some eggs." The problem with this is: Human beings are infinitely more valuable than eggs and we are still waiting to see the illusory omelets.

Abraham Lincoln - Stephen Douglas Debates

Abraham Lincoln and Stephen Douglas had a series of debates during the senatorial elections of Illinois in 1858. These debates were extremely popular and catapulted Abraham Lincoln into a national level politician. He may have lost the battle for senator, but he won the war of ideas and was elected president in 1860. There were many subjects up for debate, but let me discuss the main issues of slavery and popular government. Author David Donald wrote an excellent book called Lincoln. Let us start with a quote from Donald's book:

"One way to formulate that difference was to see Douglas as the advocate of majority rule and Lincoln as the defender of minority rights. In Douglas' view there were virtually no limits on what the majority of the people of a state or a territory could do—including, if they so chose, holding black-skinned inhabitants in slavery. While Lincoln also valued self-government and would make no attempt to end diversity on, say, cranberry laws in Indiana and Illinois, he felt passionately that no majority should have the power to limit the most fundamental rights of a minority to life, liberty, and the pursuit of happiness.

This is a powerful paragraph and filled with meaning that has importance in the modern world. Stephen Douglas was arguing from the law of the land and holding as his highest principle the right of people to vote in a government of their choice. Abraham Lincoln believed in this principle, but held a higher principle. The higher principle was tied back to his Biblical beliefs that all men were created equal before an Almighty God. This is the essence of wisdom—to build a hierarchy of beliefs for which you stand. All beliefs cannot be equal. For example, I believe in representative government and the rights for people to vote for their representatives. However if the people voted by a 51% margin to perform euthanasia on anyone over eighty to reduce taxes should we go along with this? If we objected, by what principle would we object? Lincoln objected to the law of the land by a higher law, an absolute law derived from Biblical teaching. In our government, one person with the truth can back down a majority. Majorities can be wrong and we must follow the rule of law if it conflicts with the law of the land.

What makes the Civil War so tragic to me is that, good people on both sides neglected higher principles and attempted to settle the dispute on lower principles. I believe the person who throws the first punch has shifted from reason to emotion. As a country we must let reason and principles rule our choices. Both Lincoln and Douglas were holding on to different aspects of truth. Lincoln had a higher truth and if reasonable men would have discussed the issues, a Civil War could have been avoided. Instead passion ruled the day and honorable men and women on both sides were hurt. Both sides used force to settle the discussion and force is a terrible principle to use to settle a disagreement. Douglas used reason, but had a myopic vision of the world as it was. Lincoln used reason, but with a larger vision, he saw the world of absolutes and the hierarchy of principles. The mass of people used passion, and war resulted with terrible losses on both sides. Every truly great leader must be a person of principle. They must be willing to go against the majority, company, state or even country if the majority is violating an absolute principle. Lincoln was great leader. If both sides of conflict had come to the table and reasoned together the posterity of many men and women would be alive today.

Do you believe there are absolutes even above majority rule? If you do, where did you get those absolutes? Every country must have a rule of law that the people agree to or chaos will ensue. If the majority of people in your club, organization, state, or country are going against the absolute principles—will you make a stand? Lincoln made a stand and history remembers him.

Creative Destruction

One of my favorite things is to create something new. There is a satisfaction in conceiving something in one's mind and then working to bring it to reality. For me it could be a book, an article, a business activity, home designs, or a drawing. I think this is true for most people, as evidenced in the technical, business, medical, scientific, and certainly artistic worlds.

There is, however, an interesting downside to creating something; namely, pride of authorship. Many times the creator falls in love with the creation. When this happens, it becomes difficult to maintain a non-biased perspective and we begin to cling to our creations. As the saying goes, "Love is blind."

What separates great leaders from all the rest is their ability to wreck the present in pursuit of the future. This is the phenomenon that can make a leader feel as though he or she is "going against the grain" or "running up hill." To the leader on a mission, it can often seem as though it is "them against the world". This is because people fall in love with the status quo and do not want to see change. One speaker joked that the only person that likes change is a baby. But there is one other group of people, in addition to babies, that love change: leaders.

As author Maury Klein wrote, "The process of discovery, whether in art, science, business, or any other field, must always swim against the powerful tide of conventional wisdom. If discovery disrupts, its execution destroys. The new concept acts as a death ray seeking to destroy all obstacles in its path, indifferent to anything that is incompatible with it. In virtually every field of endeavor or production, innovation brought with it obsolescence of some kind." Joseph Schumpeter, who coined the term "creative destruction," said, "This process of Creative Destruction is the essential fact about capitalism."

People and organizations can become encamped on the hill of their last victory, resting on their laurels while proclaiming "this is what got us here." For leaders, it is important to learn, as a recent book was entitled, that "what got you here won't get you there." Greatness comes from having the courage and conviction and vision to attack the status quo, assault the comfortable and the "known," and to turn "best practices" upside down, pursuing a vision that transcends "conventional wisdom." It takes guts to do this, but real leaders thrive upon it.

And why is assaulting the status quo so difficult? Why does creative destruction nearly always coincide with pain and anguish? The answer: status quo is comfortable for someone. The status quo is a power source for someone. The status quo is a source of pride for those involved in its original creation or in sustaining it. Never forget: changing the status quo almost always threatens someone else's position. With few exceptions, leaders will need to learn how to overcome stodgy "experts" and managers in positions of authority "above them," or organizational structures and any other beneficiaries of "the way things are."

There is a choice, and sadly, many individuals and organizations take the path of "that's how we've always done it." As one of my favorite quotes so aptly describes it, "Nothing is so firmly entrenched as the opinions of the experts."

But in the case of creation, the experts are always wrong. The leader's choice is to assault the status quo, to tear down strongholds and ask the tough questions, slaying sacred cows and striving for the greater good at the expense of the ensconced and privileged few. It is uncomfortable and it requires courage, staying power, and conviction in the eye of the storm. But no matter how tough or resistant the status quo is to the change efforts of a leader, it is still better to be exhausted in the attempted pursuit of great things, than to rust while clinging to outmoded ideas and practices that guarantee, sooner or later, irrelevance.

Choose creative destruction in your greatest areas of endeavor, and steer clear of the "safe" path to irrelevance and slow-but-certain ruin through failure to keep up with changing times.

It is your future.

Create it.

Three Steps for Leaders in the Fog of Battle

Leaders must deal in reality, and often that reality is complicated and ever changing. Complexity, however, is no excuse for lack of results. Leaders, despite their circumstances, the pressures they face, the long odds they brave, and the machinations against them, are still, in the end, held accountable for results. If there were a Leadership Hall of Fame (as I think there should be), there would certainly be no section dedicated to the "Yeah, buts."

So what is a leader to do? How best to battle difficult circumstances and unfair pressures? The key is to keep things simple. Focus in upon priorities. The easiest way to do this is to go all the way to the "thirty thousand foot view", and remember your overall purpose. Just what got you into this position of responsibility in the first place? At one point, I would hope, you were convinced that what you were doing was worthwhile. What was the basis for that decision? Why did it matter so much to you? More succinctly, what was the vision you had of what could be? What part of the status quo did you absolutely deplore? You see, leaders are leaders because they find something they cannot stand to leave the way they found it. Some situation seemed wrong to them, or perhaps not as right as it could be. Somebody was hurting or suffering and needed a leader to step in. Someone was being wronged and needed defending. Some rule was unfair. Some government was unlawful. Some person was disrespectful. Some project was unfinished. These are the roots of leadership, because they speak directly to a leader's discontent. Automatically, when a person of character is confronted with such a situation, they become a leader because they cannot stand to leave the situation the way they found it. A vision forms in their mind of how things could be better, and they cannot let go of it, nor it of them. This vision of what things could be like causes a hunger inside the leader for change. The tension that a leader feels when considering his or her vision, is priceless, because it is the driving force behind leadership. A leader confronted with unfair circumstances and overwhelming pressures must first go back to the vision and his or her overriding purpose in life. From there, everything will look a little clearer.

The next thing to do is prioritize amid the fog. Find out the one or two BEST things to do, and get started on them right away. Remember, there are a lot of GOOD things to do, but usually only one or two BEST things to do. Focus upon those and temporarily disregard the rest. As the Bible says, "Sufficient for the day is the evil thereof."

After remembering his or her purpose and focusing on priorities, the leader must next find someone to serve. When things get tough, when times get hard, when the way seems unclear, finding someone to help, love, and serve is the biggest pressure reliever known to man.

A leader who implements these three basics during the "fog of battle" will be surprised at his or her results. After all, results are what a leader is held accountable for.

---

3 Steps:

1. Remember Your Purpose

2. Focus On Priorities

3. Find Someone To Serve

Quiet Strength

I recently read the excellent book by Super Bowl champion coach of the Indianapolis Colts, Tony Dungy entitled, *Quiet Strength*. One of the most pertinent sections of the book, which really summarized some great leadership truths, was one that relayed what Coach Dungy learned from studying the book of Nehemiah in the Bible. He and one of his spiritual mentors took a whole summer to focus just on that one book. His summary of the leadership lessons from that study are simple and important. I will include them in their entirety here:

"Tom pointed out that most of the failings of biblical leaders were spiritual rather than tactical. I learned three key truths from Nehemiah. First, Nehemiah's opportunity came in God's time, not his own. Second, Nehemiah diligently prepared his mind and his heart so he would be ready when God's time arrived. Third, Nehemiah needed to be prepared to take on the problems, doubts, and adversity that would come his way both from the outside and from within."

In summary of Dungy's summary
1. Opportunity is in God's timing
2. Prepare so you are ready when opportunity hits
3. Learn to handle struggle

I think Dungy's summary here is excellent. **As to God's timing:** Who among us has not gotten frustrated at least once about the timing of things? Who has not gotten impatient wondering why increase and success seem slow to find us? It is salve to a wound to realize it is all in God's perfect timing!

As to preparedness: I used to think that all I needed was an opportunity, but what I really needed was proper thinking and the maturity that could only come through proper preparation. For this reason I am thankful to the many authors, speakers, and great examples that have gone before me that have become so much a part of my preparation. I have really only just begun the journey of growing and learning and getting better, to which many of you are much relieved to hear, I am sure! As the saying goes, success occurs when opportunity and preparedness meet. It is interesting, though, how few people prepare properly for opportunity. They adopt a "wait and see" attitude, or an entitlement mentality. In a fast food culture they want everything instantly and refuse to put in the long, often hard hours of preparation. But those who prepare, who get their engines running before the gate drops, are those that prosper the most.

As to the struggle: Well, it is the struggle that builds strength and proves depth of character. We hate it while going through it but realize in retrospect that our struggles sometimes become our greatest allies.

So rely on God's timing and allow that understanding to give you patience. Meanwhile, prepare and prepare, knowing that your day will come. And when it does, do not expect a bed of roses; know that anything worthwhile will require effort and expense. Apply these three truths to your leadership arsenal and see if you do not notice the results.

Do you have stories or experiences related to these three truths?

Leadership is Character in Motion

It was another late night reading session and as my eyes scanned the pages searching for a nugget to improve as a person and leader I read, "Leadership is character in motion." I stopped reading grabbed my red marker and underlined this quote. I began to ponder the truth of this simple statement overflowing with meaning. I looked at my own life of leadership and the lives of other leaders I have studied, and realized the truth in this quote. There are many ways to describe leadership. Some authors have spent their whole lives studying the method of leading others, never to correctly summarize it, but this statement succinctly captures the essence of leadership. Leadership involves two parts that author Chris Brady and I describe as the art and science of leadership. The art is who you are and the science is what you do. Character is who you are (art) and motion is the action (science). It has been said that much of learning is reminding us of what we already know rather than learning something new. This quote reminded me of something already learned but deepened the meaning of the art and science to me. Let's take a few minutes to look at the character and motion side of leadership

Character is a look past the outside of the person into the core of what they represent. Character is what you do when no one is looking or will ever find out. Here are a few questions to contemplate as we discuss character:

1. Are you the type of person who will cut corners on the truth for your own personal gain or reputation?
2. Are you the type of person that can negotiate win-lose deals and have no pangs of conscience?

3. Are you the type that will sell out your friends if it benefits you at the moment?
4. Are you the same person with each group of people you are with or do you have a chameleon effect based on who you are with?
5. Would you sell your character out for money, recognition, or power?

The toughest thing when looking at your own character is the unbelievable ability for the human heart towards hypocrisy when it looks at itself. We have no problem reading this list and identifying people we know who violate it, but we tend to make excuses or reasons why the same rules

> *The moment there is suspicion about a person's motives, everything he does becomes tainted.*
> – Mahatma Gandhi

do not apply to us. The philosopher Socrates said, "A line that is crooked will not know this until it compares itself to a straight line." How many would-be leaders were destroyed because they never ensured their lines were straight. Character is the only non-negotiable in leadership. There are many characteristics that you can find in leaders, but the only non-negotiable for long term leadership is an unquestioned character ethic.

Think about this in your own life. How many people know someone they absolutely cannot trust? Now imagine giving this person leadership in your life. It is not going to happen is it? This would violate one of God's laws of life. You give no one influence in your life unless you trust them unequivocally, and trust is earned through consistent application of a person's character to the situations of life. That is why it is foolish to aspire to be a leader and yet not build a foundation of character. Who will truly follow you long term unless you have dug deep into your own heart to answer the question, "Am I who I say I am?" If this is not answered before a leader goes into motion there will be a construction accident on your building journey. You will destroy what you wish to build because you have not properly prepared the foundation to handle the growing edifice of influence. If I were to give one piece of non-negotiable advice to anyone desiring to grow in leadership it would be, "Do not take short cuts on character because the only person you cut short is yourself." Leadership, just like a high rise building requires a solid foundation and the foundation of leadership is character.

This does not mean I recommend hiding away for a couple of years waiting to get your character right before going into motion. The beautiful thing about leadership is that while you are learning how to lead there are few fatal mistakes. In other words working on the ground level, you can fall without being seriously hurt, but the same accident on the 50th floor is "game over". Motion means to begin doing the things you know leaders have to do. You can study other people riding bikes, watch videos, interview great bike riders, but to ride a bike you must get in motion. Albert Einstein once said, "We are born geniuses and taught to be idiots." A baby attempts to walk 999 times before it takes its first successful step. Babies inherently know that failure is a necessary step (pun intended) to success. When we get older we are less willing to take necessary steps to succeed. Our fear of failure has overcome our natural genius and we accomplish only a sliver of our total potential. Why do we let the opinion of others hold us back from our personal best? Imagine if a baby internalized failure like adults do. We would have a generation of adults who crawl from place to place explaining that walking just isn't for them. They tried it ten times and they are just not the type of person who can walk. Ridiculous you say? I agree, but how many times have you told yourself that you are 'just not a leader', or that "just is not the way you are"? Of course that is not the way you are and that is why you need to start learning the skills.

None of us are born leaders any more than we are born knowing how to walk. Both are learned skills and we must develop the hunger and drive to learn the skill if we wish to walk or lead. When I started my leadership journey I was a no-people-skills engineer. I went to the same school for eleven years from elementary to high school. The best thing that my classmates could think to say about me in my senior yearbook was, "Arguing, arguing early and late, if a line were crooked, he would argue it straight." You could not describe someone with less leadership influence than that! I wanted to be a leader bad enough to change and that raises a question for you. Do you want to be a leader bad enough to improve your character and begin the leadership journey? When a person wants something bad enough they will do the work to get it. Remember, "Leadership is character in motion." Character is an inside job and motion is the action behind the inside thinking. The art and science of leadership are available and you have the ability inside to lead already. Do you have the courage to pursue your God given destiny? You can answer today by placing your personal character in motion.

Famous Leadership Definitions:

My definition of a leader . . . is a man who can persuade people to do what they don't want to do, or do what they're too lazy to do, and like it.
– Harry S. Truman, 1884-1972, Thirty-third President of the United States

If your actions inspire others to dream more, learn more, do more and become more, you are a leader.
– John Quincy Adams 6th US President (1825-29)

Managers have subordinates—leaders have followers.
– Murray Johannsen

Leaders Get Results - The Battle for America

Everyone should be interested in leadership, because everyone will be called upon to lead sooner or later. What surprises most people, is just how often they are thrust into a situation of leadership. This may occur in small ways or big ways, or a thousand variations in between. But rest assured, everyone must lead.

Every time we take a young child's hand, we are called to lead. Every time we are asked for advice, we are called to lead. Every time we are looked to for our example, we are called to lead. Any crisis that arises in our life is a call to leadership. Any time we are asked to compromise our principles, it is a test of leadership. In fact, in many ways, each of us is leading others every day without even realizing it. The question becomes whether we will rise to the challenge or shrink from it.

Fortunately, the topic of leadership is also infinitely interesting. It is challenging enough to wake us up and hold our attention. As author Dan Allender wrote, "Leadership is a walk on the wild side. If we didn't have to deal with people or problems, leadership would be a piece of cake. Instead, leadership is all about . . . moving toward a goal while confronting significant obstacles with limited resources in the midst of uncertainly and with people who may or may not come through in a pinch. Leadership is about whether we will grow in maturity in the extremity of crisis."

Let us get one thing clear. Management is not leadership. Position or titles or fame is not leadership. Acting the part is not leadership. Seniority is not leadership. In the realm of true leadership, there is no "fake it 'till you make it." Leadership is about trust, truth, influence, and example, and it cannot be faked. People are incredibly adroit at spotting a phony. When it comes right down to it, leadership is about getting results. Those who talk a good game, or have the right position or title, or look the part, but do not produce results are simply imposters.

In the short period of peace between the end of the Seven Years War and the start of the American Revolution, an interesting development took place in Great Britain's Royal Navy. The English had been dominating the French navy for years. In battle after battle, more often than not, the British navy had been victorious. In large fleet engagements and small skirmishes, it was invariably the British royal navy that would capture the most ships and inflict the most casualties. However, in the peacetime of the mid-eighteenth century, the British became enamored with the "scientific" approach the French took toward naval affairs. The Enlightenment was in full flourish throughout Europe, and its center of orbit was Paris, France. Enlightenment thinking placed a heavy emphasis on man's ability to reason, the scientific method, and the formal ability of humans to steadily increase toward perfection. In this environment, the French navy pontificated endlessly about the "science of naval warfare." They wrote in-depth studies and treatises on the subject. They formed sophisticated academies of naval study. They developed complex signaling systems for commodores controlling fleets, and they preached their theories on hydrography, gunnery, ship construction, and maneuver. They developed theories of warfare at sea that supposedly could not fail. Somehow, caught up in the fervor of Enlightenment thinking, the British swallowed the French philosophy whole. But as author Michael Palmer wrote, "While there can be no argument that the navy of France was more militarily formal and "professional" than that of Great Britain, that "professionalism" did not necessarily translate into success." As another popular phrase puts it, "Big hat no cattle."

It was not long, however, until the British recovered from their stupor and got back to what had made them the "ruler of the seas" in the first place: effective leadership. But before they did, they were defeated and outmaneuvered by a

French fleet off the coast of Virginia in North America. This fleet was instrumental in entrapping British General Cornwallis and bringing to a close the American Revolution, and giving victory to the fledgling American colonies.

To blame the loss at Yorktown on a lapse in British naval leadership, I know, may be a bit oversimplified. War and geopolitics are complicated and subject to a myriad of factors. But most historians agree that the performance of the British navy during the action off the Chesapeake was less effective than it should have been, and certainly less effective than it had been in past engagements. The reasons for this have been debated and analyzed in depth, and culpable in most of these analyses is the leadership of the British fleet at that time.

Leadership makes a difference. And the results of leadership have lasting implications that can often be enormous. One can never underestimate the ripple effect that the decisions and examples of a leader set in motion. One should never be taken in, as the British were during the Enlightenment, with fancy theories and would-be leaders who look and act the part, have the resources, the prestige, or the "professionalism" that appears to be genuine. True leadership comes down to results. Proper results can only come from following true principles. That is why the study of leadership and its principles is so important. We will be called upon to lead, and more importantly, we will be held accountable for our results.

Robert E. Lee: Self Denial

Robert E. Lee the Virginian, American and Civil War general was a great leader because he had great character. General Lee taught that you are not worthy to lead until you take your focus off yourself and focus on serving your team. Here are some thoughts out of H. W. Crocker's phenomenal book called Robert E. Lee on Leadership:

> Lee recognized that most men—especially soldiers—have every reason to regard selfishness as a vice, and to regard an officer who thinks first of himself and then of his men, who is casual about their lives and well-being but selfishly protective of his own, as unworthy of his commission. Vice, however tempting to the individual, rarely invites respect in practice. Leaders who lack the respect of their subordinates must rely on force—something Lee regarded with acute distaste and a confession of failure, necessary only under the most extreme circumstances. For the modern business leader it might be appropriate to point out that leaders who rely on force are ultimately ineffective businessmen—especially in a competitive marketplace operating with a free exchange of labor and capital.

Did you catch that? First, if a leader is more concerned about protecting his income or his position and not the welfare of the people under his leadership, then they are not worthy of the title "leader". People followed General Lee because of who he was, not his title. General Lee's army followed him even when they had not been paid. They followed even when they knew their cause was lost. Why? People knew they were following a leader who had given his all to the cause.

Second, personal character faults such as lying, stealing and adultery will destroy your ability to lead. No one willingly follows a person they do not trust. The poorest form of leadership is that of positional leadership, which occurs when the so called leader is not capable of building a relationship based on trust. With no trust the relationship reverts to threats and uses of force. "You will do this because I am the boss!" "You will do this or I will take your Christmas bonus!" "You will do this or I will see you in court!" In my opinion there is a better way for leaders to solve issues. I am a firm believer that two reasonable parties can agree to disagree. By displaying mutual respect they can still treat each other with God-given dignity. General Lee disagreed with his subordinates at times, but he always treated them with dignity and respect. This allowed General Lee to find win-win solutions to every issue that developed.

Third, free enterprise allows the free flow of people, capital, and ideas. If someone has a better idea and cannot apply it at their current employment or business, our free enterprise system allows them to go elsewhere to test that idea. This is what makes America great. Economist Joseph Schumpeter used the term "Creative Destruction." Mr. Schumpeter explained the term to mean the constant flux of people, capital and ideas to recreate the marketplace.

What makes the free enterprise system so much better than a state controlled system? It is the reward for entrepreneurs to make changes and then receive the benefit if they are right. In the process of creating the new, they by definition, destroy the old. That is free enterprise! This is why leadership of

> *I cannot trust a man to control others who cannot control himself.*
> *–Robert E. Lee*

the quality that Robert E. Lee possessed is so important. People will follow leaders over money, perks, and position. Ironically, the person who leads out of desire to lead, not because of the money, will often see money flowing to them. If people, capital and ideas are free to come and go, then the only competitive advantage is the ability of leaders to lead and teams to learn. All over America today people are leaving jobs and businesses because the management team is not leading with vision and competence. The industrial age is over and the information age is upon us. Lead, follow, or get out of the way!

I love free enterprise and I love the chance to test new ideas in the marketplace. I encourage you to read up on free enterprise. Our country is what it is today because it allows entrepreneurs to enter the marketplace and compete with their ideas, capital, and leadership skills! Robert E. Lee won some battles and lost some battles, but he was always a man of character and won in the game of life. General Lee won and lost his battles with honor. Free enterprise demands that type of honor. True leadership is the strength of character to compete honorably and give everyone an equal opportunity.

What has free enterprise and personal growth meant in your life?

Get correct views of life, and learn to see the world in its true light. It will enable you to live pleasantly, to do good, and, when summoned away, to leave without regret.
– Robert E. Lee

The education of a man is never completed until he dies.
– Robert E. Lee

In all my perplexities and distresses, the Bible has never failed to give me light and strength.
–Robert E. Lee

Leaders under Managers

It is when the chips are down that true leaders rise to the surface. During times of struggle, confusion, and challenge, real leaders take stock of the situation and lead others through the chaos. For some reason, the others are happy to follow. The substance between the leader and those who voluntarily follow his or her direction is called influence. Influence is the mark of a leader. Without influence, one might have a title, a position, decorations, degrees, authority, and many other things that are designed to bestow power or title or status, but he will not have true leadership.

When analyzed in this manner, it becomes apparent that leaders pop up in inconvenient places within organizations, and that's the point. Leadership is not always found at the top of organizational charts or on the voting ballot, and sometimes it seems as though it is rarely found in such places. No, more often, leadership is displayed by ordinary people in ordinary positions.

I have become recently intrigued by the concept of "Leaders under managers." Quite often, leaders are trapped in a position "under" people of greater authority or power who possess much less leadership ability. As I survey the pages of history I find countless examples of this. I have often written of Horatio Nelson, England's (and the world's) most famous sea captain. When speaking of Nelson, it is easy to call him an Admiral, which is the position of command in which he died. At that point, even though he was in charge of an entire fleet, he was still subservient to the Chief Lord of the Admiralty back in London. We must remember that Nelson, throughout most of his career, was in a position under other captains, squadron commanders, commodores, and admirals. In fact, although he was never out rightly insubordinate, Nelson did have to struggle to overcome stodgy senior commanders and take liberties with his orders from time to time in order to post some of his most magnificent achievements.

If you are going to be a leader, it goes with the territory that you will be held back or potentially frustrated by those in "authority above" you. The first thing to do in such a situation is to realize that it is common. Secondly, you must realize that your day will come, that leaders always rise to the surface, and it will likely just be a matter of time and opportunity before you are able to spread your wings. Thirdly, understand that you can still lead, right where you are, with what you have and in what you have been given to do. This is done by accepting responsibility, taking command of the situations that are within your circle of influence, and striving for excellence in all you do. As you live this way, others will be persuaded to your cause and allow themselves to be influenced by you. As you continue to perform, inspire and enlist others, your opportunities will grow. Sometimes your opportunities will grow through normal means, other times they will grow through calamity, but opportunities for a leader always come. The key is to be in motion and be prepared.

> *Winning is the science of being totally prepared.*
> –George Allen

The wrong way to handle being a "leader under a manager" is to allow yourself to get frustrated. Do not get angry at the circumstances that hold you back. Resist jealousy, pettiness and bitterness; which are all cancers that will kill a leader's influence if allowed to fester. Understand that the obstacles in your way actually serve a purpose in and of themselves: they test your leadership abilities and make you stronger. Instead of resentfulness toward those who do not share your vision or ability, foster a spirit of servanthood and help them as much as you can while you are there. If they stand opposed to you as an enemy, pray for them and keep your eye on the ball. As I wrote in an earlier post, your goals should remain set in stone and your plans can be in sand. Adapt to situations and circumstances as necessary, holding the line on your integrity and refusing to sink to your enemies' level.

Keep your attention fixated on your vision and cause, all the while strengthening and building yourself so that when your opportunity comes, you are prepared. Those who waste their time in bitterness or political games with those who would hold them back, lose focus on the big picture and sometimes miss their chance.

Understand this: Success comes when opportunity and preparedness meet. Leaders cannot always control their opportunities, but they can be prepared. And this will only happen if leaders do not waste their time on the obstacles in their way, but instead focus on the bigger picture of fulfilling their destiny.

- Keep your eye on the ball.
- Focus on the bigger picture.
- Lead where you are, with what you have got, right now.

And never forget: If you are a real leader, your chance will come!

Creative Leadership: Walt Disney

Walt Disney was not a good student in school. He would just as soon doodle and draw cartoons in class as learn something. But, like most leaders, he was a big reader and a hard worker; holding down several odd jobs at once while still a young lad. His earliest dream was to become a cartoonist. He sent dozens of submissions to publishers only to receive rejection after rejection.

While still in his teens he formed a small company that produced cartoons. He hired some cartoonists to execute his many good ideas. The little firm prospered for a while and then floundered. He tried again and lost again. But along the way he was gaining experience and beginning to surround himself with the type of capable people who would share his vision and help bring his ideas into American folklore.

At one point in his early, lonely, broke years, Disney was offered a secure job at a jelly factory. To the disbelief of his family, Disney refused. He was not interested in a secure job. He had a vision for being involved in the entertainment industry and he knew his talents pointed him in that direction. With the drive and determination common to all great leaders, Disney refused to sell his dreams for the lure of security.

Walt Disney dreamed continually about making it in the entertainment industry. Over time he came to realize that the only way to reach his vision was through cartoons. In his relentless efforts to achieve this, Walt Disney learned a lesson every leader must; the lesson on how to be tough. In the words of biographer Bob Thomas, "It wasn't enough to be an original and creative artist, Disney learned; survival in the film business required a jungle toughness."

Disney was no great administrator, but he had a knack for surrounding himself with talent. His brother Roy proved to be an invaluable partner, financial wizard, and loyal supporter throughout Walt's career. Ub Iwerks was perhaps the nations' top cartoon talent, and Walt teamed up with Iwerks to create Disney's most timeless character, Mickey Mouse.

Most of all, Walt Disney had that key leadership ingredient of being able to get others caught up in his vision. He would enthuse about this idea or that until a whole room of artists were infected with his picture of what could be. Then, Disney would allow their individual creative efforts to flourish toward the completion of that vision. Bob Thomas said, "Walt was developing one of his most valuable traits: the ability to recognize a man's creative potential and force him to achieve it."

Walt Disney was also an extremely hard worker. He was often the first in the office and the last to leave. As a matter of fact, his late night tours of his artists' desks became legendary, and artists would often leave their most prized unfinished work out at the end of the day in hopes that Disney would see them and make comment. More often than not, he did. The secret of Disney's hard work was his passion. He would get onto an idea or vision for something and pour himself into it with everything he had. All too often throughout his storied career, Disney would pay no attention to finances or the monetary risks of a project. He was committed to making real the vision he carried in his mind's eye, and no price was too big or risky to bring it about. It was this boldness, this passion, this contagious enthusiasm that was the source of his ability to inspire so many talented people in his organization. Walt Disney once said, "I happen to be an inquisitive guy, and when I see things I don't like, I start thinking, why do they have to be like this and how can I improve them?"

In 1931 Walt Disney suffered a nervous breakdown. He had been repeatedly double-crossed in a cut-throat industry. He had lost many talented artists to competing studios. He had been continually wracked by financial problems. His ideas had been stolen by cheap imitators, and, just like any leader, he had his skeptics. Bob Thomas wrote, "Many worries and the stress of leading a crew of volatile, talented artists through uncharted territory began to wear on Walt." And in a statement that clearly demonstrates Disney's inability to rest on his achievements, Thomas wrote, "He had been pushing himself and his animators hard, seeking greater quality in the cartoons instead of coasting on his already substantial reputation." But Disney's eternal optimism soon revived him and he was as driven as ever to make his dreams come true. Those that were close to Walt Disney, said that he seemed to have a strong sense of his own mortality. This weighed on him heavily and drove him in a race against time to accomplish all the work he could.

In all, Disney's work spanned almost the entire spectrum of the entertainment industry. His name became synonymous with quality family entertainment. He was a pioneer in animated short films, then the first to add sound to a short animation. He was the first to produce animation in color, and again the first to produce a full-length animated film. He progressed to live-action movies, nature films, and pioneered children's programming on television. As a crescendo to an already staggering list of achievements, he pioneered the world of outdoor entertainment by creating Disneyland and launching Disney World before his death.

In the late 1960's Disney was invited to the White House by President Lyndon Johnson and awarded the nation's highest civilian honor, the Medal of Freedom. The citation contained the words, "Artist, impresario, in the course of entertaining an age, Walt Disney has created an American folklore." That citation could have just as easily stated that Walt Disney was a leader. Disney's leadership ability was the engine behind his success. He was a man driven by his dreams and a vision for how things should be. He could not accept the status quo and felt called to change things for the better. He worked very hard throughout his life, not even slowing down when his success and fame eclipsed him. Disney was optimistic and perseverant, and he knew how to spread his enthusiasm to others, even those with more talent in specific areas. Risk taking was natural to him, to the point where he did not even worry about the risk because he could "see" the vision so strongly he just knew he could get there. At several points during his life he said no to the temptations of complacency and security, always pushing forward for the next big dream. He would master one form of entertainment and then move onward to the next.

From a young man learning to lead a small group of intractable artists, to an elder scion of industry leading millions through a magical world of make-believe, Walt Disney was an excellent picture of leadership. Perhaps his brother Roy said it best, "My brother Walt and I first went into business together almost a half century ago. And he was really, in my opinion, truly a genius – creative, with great determination, singleness of purpose and drive; and through his entire life he was never pushed off his course or diverted to other things."

Today, the name Disney connotes many things. For most, it is a place where they dream of taking that special family vacation someday before the kids grow up. For many, it is cartoon characters and Mickey Mouse and family movies. But for everyone, the name is familiar. Disney's world of creations continues to grow and prosper to incredible proportions long after the death of the man who envisioned it all. The story of Walt Disney should be an inspiration to anyone who cherishes the hope that one person can make a difference. Because Disney and its parks, characters, cruise lines, television network, and brand images are an everyday part of our lexicon, most people do not stop to think that, not so long ago, the Disney empire was non-existent. What is common everyday reality for us was once a dream in one man's mind. Success on such a staggering scale should make each of us stop and think about what special gifts we have, what dreams we harbor, and what contributions we can make. Driven by those visions, we unlock our potential with the keys of leadership, first leading ourselves away from complacency and security and toward our dreams, then leading others by contagion in the same direction. Over time, the ripple effect of our leadership, like that of Walt Disney, can be immeasurable.

Ideas Have Consequences - Economic Thought and Karl Marx

No economic system has been proven more erroneous than Karl Marx and his communist revolution. With this being said, no system that has failed so miserably has so many of its ideas still in practice. It is like a person who realizes that drinking a whole cup of poison will kill him, but determines that half a cup a poison will help him. The communists spent years, along with millions of dollars on propaganda to inject their poison into the thinking of Americans. It is now a documented fact that the communists worked to control the media and change the American values to communist positions. I would like to take you back to the recognized father of modern communism, Karl Marx. I believe economic understanding is one of the keys for the future of America. With so much misinformation out there, I run the risk of being labeled by many sincere people who do not fully understand what is at stake.

> *The theory of Communism may be summed up in one sentence: Abolish all private property.*
> – Karl Marx

America was founded on strong free enterprise and rule of law principles. The fact that very few voters understand this and freely buy into communist positions ought to concern of all us. The whole goal of this article is to generate discussion and a better understanding of what the media war is about. I am not offended in the least if you disagree with our discussion. All I ask is we think together in an effort to learn truth. Here is an article on the Ten Planks of the Communist Manifesto. Do you recognize some of these originally radical ideas as now mainstream American thought? The ideologies of free enterprise and communism are polar opposites on their view of man, God, and government. Please read carefully and think about the 10 Planks. Does it concern anyone else that America would adopt so many principles from a communist system that is Godless, defunct, and such an abject failure, and from an atheist economist Karl Marx? Why have so many of us been taught these principles as the American way of life? Some will say I am paranoid, but are we paranoid if they really are after us? Here is the article:

Karl Marx describes in his communist manifesto, the ten steps necessary to destroy a free enterprise system and re-place it with a system of omnipotent government power, so as to effect a communist socialist state. Those ten steps are known as the Ten Planks of the Communist Manifesto... The following brief presents the original ten planks within the Communist Manifesto written by Karl Marx in 1848, along with the American adopted counterpart for each of the planks. From comparison it's clear MOST Americans have by myths, fraud and deception under the color of law by their own politicians in both the Republican and Democratic and parties, been transformed into Communists.

Another thing to remember, Karl Marx in creating the Communist Manifesto designed these planks AS A TEST to determine whether a society has become communist or not. If they are all in effect and in force, then the people ARE practicing communists.

Communism, by any other name is still communism, and is VERY VERY destructive to the individual and to the society!!

The 10 PLANKS stated in the Communist Manifesto and some of their American counterparts are...

1. *Abolition of private property and the application of all rents of land to public purposes.*

Americans do these with actions such as the 14th Amendment of the U.S. Constitution (1868), and vari-ous zoning, school & property taxes. Also the Bureau of Land Management (Zoning laws are the first step to government property ownership)

2. *A heavy progressive or graduated income tax.*

Americans know this as misapplication of the 16th Amendment of the U.S. Constitution, 1913; The Social Security Act of 1936; Joint House Resolution 192 of 1933; and various State "income" taxes. We call it "paying your fair share".

3. *Abolition of all rights of inheritance.*

Americans call it Federal & State estate Tax (1916); or reformed Probate Laws, and limited inheritance via arbitrary inheritance tax statutes.

4. *Confiscation of the property of all emigrants and rebels.*

Americans call it government seizures, tax liens, Public "law" 99-570 (1986); Executive order 11490, sections 1205, 2002 which gives private land to the Department of Urban Development; the imprisonment of "terrorists" and those who speak out or write against the "government" (1997 Crime/Terrorist Bill); or the IRS confiscation of property without due process. Asset forfeiture laws are used by DEA, IRS, ATF etc...).

5. *Centralization of credit in the hands of the state, by means of a national bank with State capital and an exclusive monopoly.*

Americans call it the Federal Reserve which is a privately-owned credit/debt system allowed by the Federal Reserve act of 1913. All local banks are members of the Fed system, and are regulated by the Federal Deposit Insurance Corporation (FDIC) another privately-owned corporation. The Federal Reserve Banks issue Fiat Paper Money and practice economically destructive fractional reserve banking.

6. *Centralization of the means of communications and transportation in the hands of the State.*

Americans call it the Federal Communications Commission (FCC) and Department of Transportation (DOT) mandated through the ICC act of 1887, the Commissions Act of 1934, The Interstate Commerce Commission established in 1938, The Federal Aviation Administration, Federal Communications Commission, and Executive orders 11490, 10999, as well as State mandated driver's licenses and Department of Transportation regulations.

7. *Extension of factories and instruments of production owned by the state, the bringing into cultivation of waste lands, and the improvement of the soil generally in accordance with a common plan.*

Americans call it corporate capacity, The Desert Entry Act and the Department of Agriculture... Thus read "controlled or subsidized" rather than "owned"... This is easily seen in these as well as the Department of Commerce and Labor, Department of Interior, the Environmental Protection Agency, Bureau of Land Management, Bureau of Reclamation, Bureau of Mines, National Park Service, and the IRS control of business through corporate regulations.

8. *Equal liability of all to labor. Establishment of industrial armies, especially for agriculture.*

Americans call it Minimum Wage and slave labor like dealing with our Most Favored Nation trade partner; i.e. Communist China. We see it in practice via the Social Security Administration and the Department of Labor. The National debt and inflation caused by the communal bank has caused the need for a two "income" family. Woman in the workplace since the 1920's, the 19th amendment of the U.S. Constitution, the Civil Rights Act of 1964, assorted Socialist Unions, affirmative action, the Federal Public Works Program and of course Executive order 11000.

9. *Combination of agriculture with manufacturing industries, gradual abolition of the distinction between town and country, by a more equitable distribution of population over the country.*

Americans call it the Planning Reorganization act of 1949, zoning (Title 17 1910-1990) and Super Corporate Farms, as well as Executive orders 11647, 11731 (ten regions) and Public "law" 89-136. These provide for forced relocations and forced sterilization programs, like in China.

10. *Free education for all children in public schools. Abolition of children's factory labor in its present form. Combination of education with industrial production.*

Americans are being taxed to support what we call 'public' schools, but are actually "government force-tax-funded schools". Even private schools are government regulated. The purpose is to train the young to work for the communal debt system. We also call it the Department of Education, the NEA and Outcome Based "Education". These are used so that all children can be indoctrinated and inculcated with the government propaganda, like "majority rules", and "pay your fair share". Where are the words "fair share" in the Constitution, Bill of Rights or the Internal Revenue Code (Title 26)?? NO WHERE is "fair share" even suggested!! The philosophical concept of "fair share" comes from the Communist maxim, "From each according to their ability, to each according to their need! This concept is pure socialism. ... America was made the greatest society by its private initiative WORK ETHIC ... Teaching ourselves and others how to "fish" to be self sufficient and produce plenty of EXTRA commodities to if so desired could be shared with others who might be "needy"... Americans have always voluntarily been the MOST generous and charitable society on the planet.

Did anyone else recognize how many of Marx's principles have been swallowed whole into the body politic of American thinking? How do we educate Americans about the root source of our modern thinking on economic issues? Although communism as a system is dead, the ideas are alive and well in the flow of American consciousness. Is it not ironic (to put it mildly) that the American ideals beat the communist ideals in the ideology war, but at the very moment the former communist countries are attempting to learn free enterprise from us, we have swallowed so much of their poison that we have forgotten what allowed us to win the war in the first place! America is a great nation with great ideals. I am proud to share the ideals our country was founded upon with anyone. We must learn our heritage in order to protect our posterity. I have said and continue to say that, "Ideas have consequences." What we believe as a country today, will be tomorrow's reality. We need a group of people with the hunger to learn the truth and the courageous leadership to share it.

I want everyone to know that I believe in a limited government as the founding fathers did. Limited government means; let the citizens accept responsibility for the greatest sphere of action and only utilize government where no individual or group of individuals can accomplish the task. Government is by nature a monopoly and when government gets involved in an activity, it very rarely withdraws from the field. Everyone knows that it is much easier to start a government program than to end one. The more government is involved, the less money and influence the private sector has in that field. People naturally learn from mistakes due to the pain of failure, but government rarely learns because they do not experience the same pain of failure as individuals and private companies. An example would be General Motors, which ran like a federal government for years, (and had a budget that resembled a small country's) but is now paying the price for failed policies and learning hard lessons. Our federal government when it fails, merely taxes more, increases money supply through inflation or borrows more money. This delays the lessons for our future generations. I am not the type of person to pass the buck to our future generations and I desire a restoration of the government principles that made our country great originally! The founding fathers spelled out their principles of government in the Federalist Papers in three broad categories:

1. Settling disputes according to the Rule of Law between individuals.
2. Protection from criminals attempting to steal, lie or coerce profits vs. earn them by service.
3. Ensure liberty for all by providing protection from foreign invaders.

Historical Example
Captain
Samuel C. Reid

One of the key premises in the art of leadership is that one person can make a difference. In a complicated world, with forces for change coming at us from seemingly all directions, it is easy to feel small and incapable. It is easy to shrug off our highest aspirations and think, "What is the use?" This becomes doubly tempting when meeting challenges, and when our best intentions turn out to be more difficult, and more work than we expected. At that point it is more critical than ever to realize that we as an individual have enormous power to not only influence the course of events around us, but to have a major and lasting effect on the impact of those events.

In the long rich history of the age of fighting sail, when complicated wooden warships plied the oceans, privateers were civilian sailing vessels that had been given governmental approval to make war at will upon enemy shipping. Privateers could thus both claim patriotism and wealth while inflicting pain on an enemy country. Privateering was very popular and very effective; in a way, it was the nautical version of today's guerilla warfare, with a little bit of mercenary flavor thrown in.

In the War of 1812 between Great Britain and the infantile United States, a war many called the second war of independence, American privateers wreaked havoc upon the mighty British. As a matter of fact, their efforts against the crown were far more successful than those of the relatively small American navy. Author John Lehman wrote, "During the War there were 513 registered privateers and they took about 2,300 British merchant ships compared to 165 taken by the Navy." That means that the average American privateer captured or destroyed more than four enemy ships each.

One of these privateers was captained by Samuel C. Reid. His story provides a compelling snapshot from history that supports the premise that one individual can make a difference. In fact, Reid's story makes the case that one man's efforts can have a staggering impact, with ramifications that are unforeseen at the time.

Reid was captain of the *General Armstrong*, a schooner mounting only nine guns and having a crew of about ninety men. Reid and his crew were able to break out of the British blockade of New York in a dead calm by pumping water on the sails to capture all possible wind, and by towing the ship with row boats. He sailed to Fayal harbor in the Azores, and arrived just before a British squadron of three battle ships of varying size and armament. The squadron was on its way to New Orleans with British troops to assist in the attack on the city. First, however, seeing the General Armstrong in Fayal, the squadron decided to violate Portuguese neutrality and attack the American privateer.

The first wave of attack was several small boats from the British squadron. When they failed to take the General Armstrong, the next attack went in at midnight with fourteen boats and 600 men. Many of these attackers were successful in climbing aboard the *General Armstrong*. The battle was fierce hand-to-hand combat and casualties were high, and Reid himself killed the commander of the raid. Once again, the British attack was repulsed. Expecting another attempt, Reid moved his ship closer to the shore so he could use the guns from both sides of his ship on one side. He cut new gun ports in the hull and aimed his full complement of weapons seaward. In the early morning the smallest of the three ships in the British squadron attacked, primarily because it could come in closest to shore without running aground. In a raging battle of the cannon from both ships, the British ship was forced to back off. At this point the British had had enough. They next maneuvered their largest battleship in the squadron, a full seventy-eight gun man-of-war, into position to bombard the tiny American privateer. Reid countered by setting fire to his own ship and sinking her rather than letting the enemy capture her. His men escaped to safety ashore. In the entirety of the engagement, some four distinct skirmishes, the British suffered thirty-four killed and sixty-eight wounded, with the Americans two killed and only seven wounded. The little ship had held out remarkably well against superior fire power and numbers. In a gesture illustrative of the chivalry between officers occasionally found in wars in those times, the British Consulate on shore invited Captain Reid to tea where he was given three cheers by the surviving British officers for his bravery and gallantry in the battle.

Reid was only doing his duty. He took responsibility to command his tiny schooner to the best of his ability and put up a stiff resistance to a fierce enemy under hopeless odds. His crew fought viciously and creatively in a complicated warship under dangerous conditions; proof of good leadership and unity. As a leader, Captain Reid did what was required, when it was required, to the best of his ability.

What Captain Reid could not have foreseen, however, as is true with many in leadership, is the enormous ramifications of his gallant stand at the Battle of Fayal. According to John Lehman, "Reid had delayed the British expedition against New Orleans for ten days." The extra time allowed General Andrew Jackson to arrive on scene in New Orleans, take martial control of the panicked town, assemble his patchwork army of pirates, militia, escaped slaves, and prepare his defenses. What resulted was the most lop-sided battle of the entire war as the British were badly defeated, and a peace that brought the hostility between the United States and her former motherland to an end forever. The Battle of New Orleans could have ended differently. Andrew Jackson later told Captain Reid himself, "If there had been no Battle of Fayal, there would have been no Battle of New Orleans." Had that happened, the tentative treaty that had been signed to end the war most likely would have been revoked or at least amended less favorably to the United States, keeping the door open to future hostility. Instead, it sealed the deal on a lasting peace between the two nations.

The story of Captain Reid and his stand at the Battle of Fayal clearly illustrates the difference that one person can make. How easy would it have been for Reid to simply flee from the enemy in his tiny, much faster ship? How easily could he have fired a few shots in defense, as was customary in hopeless situations, and then "haul down his colors" and surrender? Or, he could have simply abandoned his ship and escaped to shore. But Reid chose to stand and fight, and his men with him. That simple decision, and their gallant execution of it, made a huge difference on the world's stage. That is the kind of far-reaching affect that one person can have. That is the difference leadership makes. If Reid had not stood, if his men had not fought, if they had not delayed the British, then General Jackson might not have been ready, the British may have prevailed in the Battle of New Orleans, and all of Western history would be different. But they stood. Reid led and it made all the difference.

Self Deception

Self perception and reality are often miles apart. The result is what we might call self-deception. Author Jim Collins, in *Good to Great*, discusses the importance of a leader being willing to confront brutal reality and take stock of it as it actually is. Nowhere is this more difficult than when looking at ourselves!

There is a big trend in industry today to try and help executives address this very issue: 360 degree feedback. Basically, it involves getting input from people all around you, whether subordinates, supervisors, or peers. There are some merits to this approach, but there are also some dangers. While it could be eye-opening to find out how people really see us, it can also do irreparable damage to our confidence. While much of the feedback is genuine and sincere, often times it can be cruel, vengeful, or political. Are those giving feedback truly being honest?

The merits of 360 degree feedback aside, it still remains that we must get a clear picture of things in order to make proper decisions. We must be clear about who we are, what we stand for, how we are coming across to people, and where we could improve. I would venture to say that none of us operate without some level of self-deception. But again, we have to be careful. I generally see two types of people out there. The first are quick to see their faults, realize they have got a long way to go, and operate with thin confidence as a result. They are quick to "beat themselves up" over failures or mistakes, and generally do not operate with boldness and daring. Then there is the other camp. This group is bold and forceful, and tends to think that most things they do are just fine. They are slow to see their weaknesses and therefore slow to fix them.

239

A great combination would be to find a way to live in the middle. Somehow we must take stock of where we are, where we could improve, and see clearly our blind spots. At the same time, we must continue to grow in confidence and purpose. I believe that growing spiritually, keeping one's self on a continuous education program, and most of all, submitting to qualified mentor are the answers to skating this middle ground. As a matter of fact, one of the projects my friend and co-author Orrin Woodward and I are working on next is an exposition on mentorship. It is truly one of the lost arts of leadership.

So get your spiritual life straightened out, get on a program of personal growth, and get a mentor. Make these inputs in your life as common as eating good food. We cannot afford to be self-deceived. While we may be okay with ignoring our weaknesses, not many others will be!

Leaders Make Others Feel Important - Not Themselves

Among many things absent from today's culture is the habit of treating others with dignity and respect. I have experienced some egotistical managers on life's journey and am disgusted by the way they view and treat people. We all must serve and encourage others like Matt is displaying wherever he goes. Let me give you a preview before we look at Matt's servant based, leadership behavior.

Allow me share a story I wrote about two great Prime Ministers of Victorian England. The general facts of the personalities of Gladstone and Disraeli are true, but I have taken artistic liberty to add other characters for suspense and development of the points.

There is a 19th century story told about and older British woman who had the rare opportunity to have separate lunches with the two most famous living Englishmen of the era: William Gladstone and Benjamin Disraeli. Both had been Prime Ministers of England several times. Both were men of strong character, convictions and decisive leaders. A young reporter tracked down the fortunate Victorian lady and requested an interview. The reporter asked her questions about her lunches with these two leaders to determine what the legendary prime minister's were like as persons. After asking questions like: "What did you discuss?", "What did he eat?", and "What were his thoughts on the political scene?" the reporter was wrapping up his interview and contemplating his story in tomorrow's paper. He had only one more question for the patient woman, "Which Prime Minister did you enjoy lunch with more?" She thought for a moment and then a bright smile covered her face. "When I went to lunch with William Gladstone," she shared, "I was convinced that I was dining with the greatest living Englishmen!" The reporter quickly scribbled down his thoughts and thinking the lady had finished, got up to leave—not wanting to make her feel uncomfortable that she had chosen William Gladstone over Benjamin Disraeli. As he was thanking her for her time, she politely told him she was not finished. "When I went to lunch with Benjamin Disraeli," she enthused, "I was convinced that he was dining with the greatest living Englishwoman!" As the reporter was leaving, he vowed to never forget the beaming smile that had transformed the elderly ladies presence. "Yes," he thought, "it is nice to feel important and capable of impressing others by discussing eloquently on the many subjects of your choice. But others will remember you on how nice it was to feel important and capable of impressing you by your attentive listening on the many subjects of their choice."

Quote: *"You can tell how "big" the person is by the way they treat the "little" person.*

Now I will share a portion of this fantastic letter I received:

"....This weekend I had an interesting experience that I thought might fit into the title of your lesson especially around responsibilities. It was an experience that I will never forget and something I couldn't wait to share with everyone! It reminded me about my responsibility, as a growing leader, to always be a lifter for other people.

For me...I have a responsibility to develop my God given potential and practice my personal "daily dozen" everyday. Why? I believe that my gifts and abilities are God's gift to me and what I do with those gifts is my gift back to God! One of the practices I try to do daily is add value to people I have never met before. Whether it is opening up doors for others, saying "hi!", or striking up a conversation to learn about them I just want to add value to others. In other words I just follow the

Golden Rule that is taught to all of us in the Bible: "Do unto others as you want them to do unto you."

Of all places, my experience happened at a Wal-Mart with a 70 year old lady who was a cashier. I was checking out in line and just struck up a conversation with this cashier and she worked there because her husband passed away. She needed to earn an income since her retirement was not very good. Anyway, to make a long story short, among the items I purchased were two packages of chewing gum. When she was done tallying up what I owed she said, "I charged you for three packages of gum instead of two." Then she burst into tears! I asked her, "What is wrong? Is there anything I can help you with?" She said, "About five minutes ago I did the same thing to someone else and he told me I was so ignorant that I should not even work at Wal-Mart. I am sorry if I made you upset." I told her, "Ma'am I have shopped at many Wal-Mart's during my lifetime, but I have never met someone as kind as you. You are a person of worth! I have watched you serve the previous customers and I wish every store I went into had someone like you working the register!" I was in awe that a $1.99 mistake made this experience happen! She said, "The only person that ever said that to me was my husband, but since he died no one has paid me a compliment like that." Can you believe that someone made this woman feel so low over a pack of gum? I went and got another package off the shelf since I paid for it, and came back to show this wonderful cashier that everything was OK. She held my bags and gave them back to me before I walked out the door. Then she did something that I will never forget. She gave me a hug and said, "I know God has great things in store for you. Thank you for valuing me as a person and not seeing me as 'just' a cashier." I walked out to my car and just sat there, stunned. I could hardly believe that had just happened. It was something I will never forget. I know now how important it is to carry out the responsibility of treating everyone with love and respect....

That is why the stakes of leadership are so high! You see when opportunity comes, as we all know, it is too late to prepare. I am very thankful that, because of my continued learning through leadership media, I was prepared to add value to someone that had just been "de-valued" by someone else. This experience teaches me that no matter who we talk to or run across in our daily lives, God brings us to that moment for a specific reason. It is our responsibility to be lifters of all people not just a select few! In order to be lifters, though, we will have to check our ego at the door. Back off and stop taking yourself too seriously, because you cannot help anyone if you are only concerned with helping yourself! I must say, though, if I would have seen that man before me treat the cashier the way he did, I might have been asking for forgiveness!

There are so many people that are de-valued or de-edified everyday, and our job as a leader is to see that person not as they are, but as they could become. It is our responsibility to see the good in other people and tell them how those great qualities will serve others well.

Assignment: Are you making others feel important? In what specific ways do you make others feel accepted, approved and appreciated?

Struggle

Most everyone has heard the phrase, "Dream, Struggle, Victory." And it seems that there is a lot of literature out there addressing the first and the last of those three terms. But is it not it interesting how little coverage is given to the struggle part?

Obviously, if we undertake some great endeavor we are going to struggle to accomplish it. What most people might not realize, however, is that the struggle is probably the most important part. It is the struggle that makes us grow. It is the struggle that reveals the character we have deep inside for continuing onward in the face of adversity. And it is the struggle that makes for any good movie or story of achievement.

One author I have read actually referred to it as the "gift of struggle." Perhaps some would think it was going too far to call struggle a gift, but I believe it to be one. If you stop and think about it, the struggle is the only place in which we grow. It is the struggle that makes us stronger. No body-builder would be able to build muscle mass without weights or resistance. The pushing against or raising of the weight strains and pulls at the muscle fibers, which then need to repair themselves. Only in this repair process are the muscles made a little stronger than they were before. More lifting causes the cycle to start over again, until the muscles are bigger and stronger than ever before - all because of the "damage" of the struggle and the repair that was necessary afterward. Struggles in our lives work the same way. Just like lifting weights, they do not necessarily feel good. And they can and often do cause pain. But how we handle those struggles, and what we do to overcome them and "repair" our commitment to the dream, will build us stronger than we were before the struggle occurred.

In *Launching a Leadership Revolution*, co-author Orrin Woodward and I even give special consideration to the topic of struggle in the section on mentorship. A good mentor knows that his protégés must struggle to become great, to grow, and to maximize, so he allows the struggles while teaching the protégé how to handle them, overcome them, and learn from them. Some might call this callous or cold; some might call it a lack of caring on the part of the mentor. After all, who would let someone struggle? Why would one not want to swoop in and eliminate the struggle for the protégé and make his or her way easier? It is the same as teaching our child to walk. If every time she started to bobble we grabbed her and kept her from falling, we would appear to be helping her. We would appear to be caring. But actually, we would be hurting our child by trying to help her too much. One of the greatest things my parents and mentors have done for me is to give me the encouragement to try, and then allowed me to make my own mistakes and learn from them. By creating my own messes, and knowing full well that I had the responsibility alone for my actions and cleaning them up, so to speak, I was allowed to struggle and grow through those adversities. When I look back over my life, the times I've struggled have not been fun. But they appear in broad relief, now, as the greatest moments of change and personal growth. I would not be who I am today without those trials and struggles that made me stronger and better.

So embrace struggle. It is not a bad word. It is not to be avoided. And when you see it in the life of those you love and mentor, of course, do what you can to keep them from actual harm. But in the course of events, allow them to take responsibility for their own lives, allow them to struggle against the resistance, and therefore build their mental muscles stronger. For out of the greatest adversity comes the greatest opportunity, and in those moments the greatest leaders are made.

Ships may be safe at harbor, but they were not made for the harbor, they were made for the dangerous high seas. And leaders may be safe on the couch, but they were not born for the couch, they were born for the tumultuous waters of engagement.

Have a dream. Embrace the struggle. Capture the victory!

The Right Information

Author Andy Stanley wrote, "It is not the acquisition of information that properly prepares a leader to lead; rather, it is the application of the right information. People need to be trained around the core principles they need to know, not an endless amount of information that is nice for them to know."

In today's Information Age, information is all around us. It is almost too plentiful. We can get information about almost any subject effortlessly. But an increase in information does not necessarily lead to an increase in knowledge, and certainly not so for wisdom. We must become adept at tuning out the noise, figuring out quickly and effectively what information is relevant and principle-based, and disregarding the rest. The most successful people are those who can differentiate the important from the almost-important as a matter of habit. In all the noise of our modern world, what is important? What is fruitful for study? What is worth my time to learn? What is principle-based? What is core?

This is where it is helpful for a developing leader to have a mentor who can recommend great books that will focus on the right information. A strategic leadership development plan and system are also very important. The short-cut through the noise is to follow someone who has successfully navigated the same waters successfully. To lead, one has to be a student. To grow quickly and effectively as a leader, one must become an astute student. Get good at getting the right information. You can't learn everything, so focus on learning the most important things!

Standing on Conviction

Polycarp was the Bishop of Smyrna in the mid-second century. As an outspoken Christian, his position became tenuous with the Roman authorities. Christians in the Roman Empire at that time were under heavy persecution because they refused to worship Caesar as God. Justice in the Roman Empire regarding the "crime" of believing in Jesus as the Son of God was a strange affair: Christians were spared persecution if they would only renounce their allegiance to Christ and acknowledge Caesar as God.

Polycarp, as a man in his late eighties, was taken to a country house for safety by a group of his friends. When it became known that the authorities were after him, his friends helped him move to an even safer location. The soldiers found two servant boys at the original house, however, and immediately set upon torturing them to determine the whereabouts of Polycarp. One of them divulged his location. Receiving word of this, Polycarp chose not to flee any further, deciding instead to face his foes, saying simply, "The will of God be done." When they arrived, instead of resistance or flight, the Roman soldiers found Polycarp and his many friends in preparation of a feast prepared in their honor. In near disbelief, the Roman soldiers partook of the feast, and were therefore inclined to listen to the prayers of Polycarp and his followers. These prayers reportedly lasted for almost two hours, and focused upon the wellbeing and salvation of the soldiers and their superiors. It was said that many were moved by this, and, seeing the condition of the old man Polycarp, wondered at the justice of capturing the man. Eventually, Polycarp was taken.

When he was brought into town, the officials, Irenarch Herod and his father Nicetes, both joined him on the last leg of the journey to the stadium. Riding with Polycarp, they implored him to simply speak a few words to save his own life. As was told by his friends who were eye-witnesses, the officials said to Polycarp, "What harm is there in saying, Lord Caesar, and in sacrificing, with the other ceremonies observed on such occasions, and so make sure of safety?" But Polycarp said he would not do as they recommended. Eventually the officials got mad at him because he would not speak a few simple words and spare his life.

Arriving at the stadium, Polycarp was greeted with a crowd of bloodthirsty pagans, anxious for his death. The proconsul in charge of the affair, noticing his feebleness and advanced age, again implored him to speak words of "safety." "Swear, and I will set you at liberty, renounce Christ," said the proconsul. But Polycarp was resolute, replying, "Eighty and six years have I served Him, and He never did me any injury: how then can I blaspheme my King and my Savior?"

Polycarp's refusal to acknowledge Caesar as Lord, and his refusal to deny Christ as the risen Savior, sealed his fate. With the crowd loud and cheering, an attempt was made to burn him at the stake. This, however, failed to kill him. To finish the job, Polycarp was stabbed to death.

I would like to thank Pastor Tom Ascoll for sharing this story during his sermon this morning. It is a beautiful picture of the ability of the Holy Spirit to sustain one in times of horrendous circumstances, the love of Christ that transcends earthly sufferings, and the extent to which Christians throughout the ages have been willing to go to prove and uphold their faith in Christ.

This story, and so many others like it throughout history, is so inspiring simply because men like Polycarp are so few. Most men, when confronted with difficulty and tough choices, sadly do not stand on their beliefs and principles. Counting the cost to themselves, saying anything to save their own skin, taking expedience and pragmatism over principle and absolutes, they sell out for a price. Some men sell out for comfort, some for wealth. Some sell out for reputation and status, others for power. But when confronted by evil, by wrong circumstances, by injustice, by threat to personal peace and affluence, heroes stand on principle. Regardless of cost to self, heroes do what is right, simply because it is right.

I have seen both examples on display in my life. I have seen men beat their chest and "talk a good game" but choose ease, comfort, and the almighty dollar over principle. This is always followed by flowery explanations and justifications of "need" and expediency. On the contrary, I have witnessed men who take stands because they believe in what they are doing and will pay whatever price necessary to maintain the courage of their convictions. It is those in this second category to whom I give my admiration, loyalty, and encouragement.

Every couple of years there is a lot of talk and interest in the candidates running for political office. To me, one of the greatest points of analysis concerning who may or may not be worthy to hold high offices in our land should be to determine how they have behaved in times of crises. Did they take the easy or most expedient road? Did they decide for personal power, prestige, or wealth? Or did they stand for what was right regardless of cost or personal risk? Remembering that the Polycarp's of the world are few, and the pragmatics are many, I will always make my selections of whom to vote for very carefully.

When it comes to leadership and the principles that make a great leader, I will be looking to follow those who choose the high road regardless of risk or cost, simply because it is the right road. Those who decide for the sake of personal considerations, comforts, or income will also be going without my vote. I may like them, but I will never follow them.

Finally, and not least of all, I hope that every Christian reading this page is inspired by the example of Polycarp and his love and devotion to his Lord and Savior Jesus Christ. We Christians should be just as willing to renounce all for the sake of our testimony in Christ. And for those unfamiliar with God's grace and his finished work of redemption through Christ on the cross, I hope, as Pastor Dickie often prays, that the eyes of your soul will be opened to your need of Christ.

Ronald Reagan:
A Great American

Here is one of my favorite stories about Ronald Reagan. I am not impressed as much by a person's achievements as I am by a person's life. Jesus said it best, "What good is it to gain the whole world, but lose your own soul." Ronald Reagan was not merely a great politician, he was also a great man. If you asked Mr. Reagan he would tell you he was not a great man, he just dealt in great ideas. I believe he was a great man because not only did he associate with great ideas, but he never forgot that he was just a person with faults and foibles like the rest of us. It is very rare to see someone who can achieve great results and still maintain personal humility. This is something I believe Reagan exemplified in his life. Reagan loved people in the particular as well as in the mass. So many would-be leaders love the masses as long as they do not have to know and serve them personally. The "people" becomes a slogan to use and the leader often forgets that those people are flesh and blood with hopes and dreams. The great leaders know they are called to serve people in the particular as well as the general. In fact, only when we serve people personally are we qualified to serve them generally. Here is a story from Dick Wirthlin's excellent book, *The Great Communicator*, that I think will tie this all together:

On February 23, 1984, I walked into the Oval Office and found the president standing beside his desk holding what appeared to be a photograph.

"Mr. President, what's that you've got there?" I asked.

"Well, Dick, I just got off the phone with this young man."

As the president turned the photograph around for

me to view, I winced at the haunting image staring me in the face. It was the picture of a twelve-year-old boy who had been severely burned while attempting to rescue his two younger brothers when their family's trailer caught fire. The first brother he found easily, and simply passed through the window. Saving the second brother, however, proved much more difficult. While frantically searching through the flaming trailer, the young man sustained severe burns before carrying his sibling to safety. As a result, the president explained, the boy's face and body had been seriously scarred and disfigured.

"I called this little fella to see how he was doing and to tell him how proud I was of his heroism," Reagan said.

Still shaken by the image, I struggled to get something out. "I'm sure he appreciated your call, Mr. President."

As he looked back down at the little boy's visage, a smile spread slowly across the president's face.

"Dick, at the end of our conversation the youngster said, 'President Reagan, I sure wish I would have had my tape recorder on so I could remember our call together.' So I said, 'Well, son, turn it on and let's chat some more.'"

Now that is character in motion, which is another name for leadership! The president of the United States takes the time to encourage a young boy's heroic actions. Never forget the tasks are secondary to the relationships. As leaders, we many times get so focused on getting something done, that we forget to build those around us. In fact, I would say this is the number one task of the leader is to build those around him. Ronald Reagan knew and practiced this principle. A principle for every leader to remember is, "Never be too big for the little person, because we are all little people!" I believe Ronald Reagan's prayer life kept him humble as he approached an Almighty God. It is hard to think of yourself as too big when you face the Infinite.

Look at your life. Are you taking the time to nurture relationships and encourage the discouraged? Are you too busy to point out other people's gifts? Worse yet, are you too self-occupied to even notice their gifts? If the President found time to recognize heroic actions and encourage a young boy (and non-voter) then how much time can we find to do the same?

When All Is Said and Done...

I read a quote recently, "And remember, when all is said and done, much more is said than is ever done." This quote resonated with me because it describes so many organizations, committees, families, and countries. I believe strongly in discussion and gathering all the facts, but all the facts in the world will not amount to anything until someone makes a decision and follows through. Think back to organizations that you have been a part of that discuss great ideas and never seem to implement them. It has been said that there are enough great ideas in Washington, D.C. to solve many of our countries pressing problems. What our world needs more than great ideas are great implementers of these ideas. Why is there so much talk and so little action? I have come up with at least three possible reasons:

First, many people fall into analysis paralysis. With so many options to choose from it is difficult to decide. To decide means to close off all other options but the one chosen. This can mean that others will be upset because you did not choose what they wanted. It can cause fear that maybe the wrong option was chosen. Analysis paralysis is caused by looking at too many options without a sufficient way of breaking down options into the most logical choice. It has been said that the number one tool for a lion trainer is the stool and not the whip. When the lion begins to act up the trainer sticks the stool in the lion's face. The lion cannot focus on one attack point because the four legs of stool are all options. This causes analysis paralysis in the lion and he becomes docile from indecision. If you are going to be a leader you must determine options and then decide on a path and move. The worst decision is

> *The point of analysis is to come to a decision.*
> –Orrin Woodward

the one you do not make. If you decide wrong you still get feedback which will help you decide better next time. Most decisions are not fatal and every decision increases your ability to decide the next time.

Second, few people want to be held responsible for implementing any change. They know if they push for any change and it goes wrong the crowd of Monday morning quarterbacks will state why they knew this was a bad move. People can become so jaded by the criticisms of others that they will become fearful to make the tough decisions. Leaders have to have courage to make the tough decisions. Do not let the criticisms of the non-achievers allow you to become a non-achiever through fear of failure. I do not know any great leaders who have not failed a few times and had to listen to the critics. In fact this is one of the major factors credited to leaders in general. If you do not have the guts to make the tough decisions, then call yourself anything you want, but you are not a leader. Harry Truman on his way to Potsdam at the end of the European portion of World War II said, "I did not come here just to discuss, I came here to decide." Harry constantly talked about the ability to decide is what separates the leader from the follower.

I can remember an incident in my own life as an engineer. We had a machine that ran only eighty-seven percent quality first time through. This is terrible and we were throwing away over three dollars every failed part. I spent over three months developing new tooling to hold the assemblies in place. Everyone told me not to mess with this machine because if it did not work—we would shut down car lines that needed this part. I weighed the potential upside and downsides involved and felt a million dollar plus scrap issue was worth

taking a calculated risk. The first night the new tooling was in place we had designed a new pin that failed to center the part properly. This led to a near forty percent scrap rate the first day. I had the supervisor, general supervisor, superintendent and plant manager in the building yelling and criticizing the new tooling. The criticism was so great that I nearly gave up the design entirely and contemplated retooling the old design. After watching the machine run for a couple of hours I realized the design engineer had inadvertently used the wrong pin to guide the bearing into position. By quickly replacing the new pins with the old pins from old tooling and keeping the rest of our new tooling the scrap rate dropped to less than one percent. The machine ran for less than twenty-four hours with the incorrect pin and ran for the next year plus at over ninety-nine percent first time through quality. Why do I tell you all this exciting engineering detail? The main point is how easy it would have been to draw the wrong conclusion here and never attempt anything great again. I could have easily let the machine run with poor quality like the five engineers before me did and have no problems. In fact, deciding to make a change caused me to be criticized by every major leader in the facility. Not one of the managers ever came back and thanked me for the machine running so effectively after twenty-four hours. This is a perfect example of why everyone talks and few decide because they know when they decide as Harry Truman said, "The buck stops here." I decided a long time ago to strive for excellence in all I do. If that means others without the same drive will not like my decisions then so be it. I am ultimately accountable to God, not man.

> *Procrastination makes easy things hard, hard things harder.*
> –Mason Cooley

Thirdly, many people delay decisions waiting for perfect information before deciding. This is an excellent way to fail in business. By the time you would have perfect information your opportunity has passed you by. When I started in business many told me they would wait to see how I did. I told them if they waited it would only place them years behind. The interesting point is that none of the people who said come back when you make it ever chose to start the leadership journey of success. Procrastination is the assassination of motivation and many people are suffering from this disease. They feel if they have good information today that they will have better information tomorrow. This may be true, but the competition has already decided and has moved ahead by making the tough decisions. There is no such thing as perfect information. This is why it requires guts to succeed. Jack Welch has come up with a fancier term and calls it "Edge." Call it what you want, but it boils down to intestinal fortitude and the willingness to make the tough calls. If you know you cannot accomplish your destiny with path A, then make the tough call. So many people give up their destiny and true dreams for the convenience of what they already have. I refuse to be part of the "settle for" club and I refuse to wait for perfect information to decide. Confront the facts, analyze the options, and make the call. Remember, the ability to learn and decide faster is a major competitive advantage. Slow organizations to not last in today's market environment.

When your life is said and done, will people talk about what you said or what you have done? Make your life count! I heard a speaker say, "If you are going to run with the big dogs—you need to get off the porch!" It is time to get out of the stands and on to the field. The game of life is being played! Are you a participant or a spectator?

Social Capital and Leadership

Definitions of Social Capital:

Social Capital - The degree to which a community or society collaborates and cooperates (through such mechanisms as networks, shared trust, norms and values) to achieve mutual benefits.

Social Capital - The value of a social network is that people can draw others to solve common problems. The benefits of social capital flow from the trust, reciprocity, information, and cooperation associated with social networks.

Social Capital - Skills and infrastructure that aid in social progress.

Social Capital - A "composite measure" which reflects both the breadth and depth of civic community (staying informed about community life and participating in its associations) as well as the public's participation in political life. It is characterized by a sense of social trust and mutual interconnectedness, which is enhanced over time though positive interaction and collaboration in shared interests.

Social Capital - represents the degree of social cohesion which exists in communities. It refers to the processes between people which establish networks, norms, and social trust, and facilitate coordination and cooperation for mutual benefit.

Social Capital -The relationships, human networks, language, etc., possessed by the individuals in the organization.

You guessed it. Our subject is Social capital. Social capital, Economic capital and Cultural capital make up the three types of capital in the world. Economic capital is monetary and is the common form of wealth. Cultural capital is the accumulated wisdom of a society like: engineering, music, architecture etc. Social capital is the wealth created by tight interconnected relationships. Today's society is becoming more and more autonomous and less involved in their communities. An effective community gets people involved and not sitting at home in front of the TV. Even if you are with your family watching TV, you are still alone as everyone is passively being entertained. I believe Social capital provides at least three major benefits:

The first benefit is that a large community has people with skills in nearly every area of life. This is a form of Metcalfe's law, which is defined in wikipedia in the following way:

Metcalfe's law states that the value of a telecommunications network is proportional to the square of the number of users of the system (n2). First formulated by Robert Metcalfe in regard to Ethernet, Metcalfe's law explains many of the network effects of communication technologies and networks such as the Internet, social networking, and the World Wide Web. It is related to the fact that the number of unique connections in a network of a number of nodes (n) can be expressed mathematically as n * (n − 1) / 2, which follows n2 asymptotically. The law has often been illustrated using the example of fax machines: a single fax machine is useless, but the value of every fax machine increases with the total number of fax machines in the network, because the total number of people with whom each user may send and receive documents increases. In fact, Metcalf's law measures the potential number of contacts, i.e. the technological side of a network. However the social utility of a network depends upon the number of nodes in contact. For instance, if Chinese and Non-Chinese do not understand each other the utility of network of users that speak the other language is at zero, and the law has to be calculated for the two networks separately.

It may sound confusing, but actually it is fairly simple. One fax machine has no value because you cannot send or receive anything. With an addition of one machine, now you have a value of $2*(2-1)/2 = 1$. Add one more fax machine and now you have $3*(3-1)/2 = 3$. Let us do one more to show you the compounding effect. Let us increase to 100 fax machines interconnected. $100*(100-1)/2 = 4950$. Two fax machines produced a connectivity value of 1 and 100 fax machines produced a value of 4950. If you are following me, this means a 50 increase in machines produced a 4950 increase in connectivity value. The value of the community compounds exponentially with every person or item added. A truly dynamic community will increase at a similar exponential rate. There is a huge social capital value difference between a 100 person team and a 200 person team. Run Metcalfe's law and see for yourself. Now you see why in the Information Age, leadership is the highest paid profession. Those who will invest in their leadership ability and build communities will have company after company pleading with them to market their products. Leadership is clearly the major competitive advantage in today's connected economy.

Laurie and I had a leaking faucet and instead of looking in the yellow pages, we called a friend of ours. This friend is a former plumber and he gave us a recommendation on a good plumber to use. The plumber did a great job and we were stress free because we knew they would do a great job at a reasonable price. It is hard to put a price tag on the security of knowing that any challenge you have, someone in your community is an expert in that field. When you join a community, you automatically begin to enjoy the benefits of Metcalfe's law in the accumulated Social capital of that community. How much would you pay for that kind of security? This is one major benefit of social capital.

The second benefit is; when life knocks you down, you have people there to encourage you through the pain. The increase in prescribed drugs and counseling for depression is a national dilemma. Why are people wealthier and enjoying more material blessings than ever before, yet more depressed than ever? Aristotle said that human beings were political beings and needed interaction with other humans. Our society is losing the ability for people to empathize with one another. I read a study where people could endure twice the level of pain, while immersing their arm in an ice bucket, if they had someone there to comfort them. Life can be tough at times and it sure is nice to have a group of friends to encourage and uplift you when you get knocked down. This is another aspect of social capital that is priceless to me and worth more than all the material rewards Laurie and I have been blessed with.

The third major benefit of a social community is the modeling and mentoring of people who have more success in specific areas than we do. There are so many conflicting opinions in life about what to do and how to succeed. What I love about a tight community and the social capital developed therein, is the ability to check the fruit on the tree. Anyone can offer advice, but a community allows you to see the results of a particular way of thinking in their lives. There are so many talented people involved with the community that account for the social capital. In nearly every area of life from: faith, finances, fitness, friends, and family, someone in the community has a system that is working in that area. The beautiful part is, they are ready and willing to share anything they have learned with you. This is why Laurie and I listen to CDs and recommend specific books for all areas of life. I love the statement, "Learn from experience, preferably someone else's." The books and CDs have proven to be effective in providing the right information for people to change their thinking and behaviors. What would it be worth to mentor with someone with the results in life you are looking for?

I have just scratched the surface on the value of social capital. I would say hands down that social capital is worth more than financial capital and can be converted to financial capital a lot easier than financial capital converts to social capital. A billionaire with no social capital is not worth as much as a leader who has it. The future leaders of society will be the connectors who build social capital. I hope this helps explain the value of community and the value in developing your personal leadership skills. Bring your talents and abilities to the table and you will exponentially increase the social capital of your team.

What abilities and talents do you bring to your community?

Are you connecting your skills with others to create a team and bring Metcalfe's law to fruition?

What other benefits of a community creating social capital can you think of?

Billy Durant - Creator of General Motors

As a student, I attended GMI-EMI (now Kettering University) and learned about the standard history of General Motors in the library. Alfred Sloan and a litany of other top leaders are referred to, but the founder was mentioned only in passing. A name that has been relegated to a footnote of history is Billy Durant the founder of General Motors. Why would the name of the founder of the largest corporation in the world for many years be hardly recognized? How many of you have never heard of Billy Durant?

Billy Durant grew up in Flint, Michigan and attended the local Flint High School. From humble beginnings, he accomplished incredible things. I feel it is my responsibility to remind people of the incredible visionary leader, who was responsible for much of the growth of Flint. You want to talk about vision? Billy founded Buick, Chevrolet, General Motors, and Durant Motors. Billy Durant stated in the early 1900's that highways would stretch across the United States. J.P. Morgan, the wealthy financier, thought Billy and his dream for the automobile were insane and refused to give him money. As a visionary you must expect the criticism of smaller minds that cannot see as far. It is a given in any large undertaking. It has been said, "The biggest minds with the biggest ideas will be criticized by the smallest minds with the smallest ideas." Billy received this critical treatment in spades.

Henry Ford twice sold Ford to Billy Durant and it was only Henry's refusal to accept anything but cash that nixed the deals at the last minute. Think about how different the story would have turned out if Billy would have bought Ford and joined it to General Motors. Henry Ford's willingness to sell to Billy Durant displays who had the real vision for the automobile. The Big Three automobile firms for years were GM, Ford and Chrysler. Billy founded GM, nearly bought out Ford twice, and hired Walter Chrysler at Buick. All three major US firms were affected by the entrepreneurship of Mr. Durant. Billy made and lost his fortune three times in his life. He died near penniless in Flint Michigan during World War II. Approaching death, he stated in the early 1940's that fast food restaurants and bowling alleys would be big and began developing them! Billy's vision has always inspired me personally. I will not tell you the whole story, but you can read it for yourself in a couple of books finally written about Billy Durant.

The following article is an epilogue from Lawrence Gustin's phenomenal book on Billy Durant. The epilogue was written by Clarence H. Young who was the assistant director of the Manufacturers Association of Flint. He has been cited as a leading authority on Billy Durant and his tribute to Billy Durant is one of the best I have ever read.

In the creation of the Mass Production Age, Durant was not only the presiding genius; he was, indeed, the Titan and, as was the fate of the original Titans, he was destroyed by the Olympians whom he had created.

It is almost poignant now to tell the beads of carping criticism reiterated against Durant: he lacked or ignored technical mastery . . . he was a good promoter, but no administrator. . . He had no organization. . . . He could not delegate authority. . . He made poor choices of executives. . . He was a promoter, a gambler. . . He was wrong in believing in himself. . . .

It is completely true that W. C. Durant had a weakness: he was human. His humanity included love and trust of his associates and the not-always-correct assumption that they were as honorable as he. He gave a degree and quality of loyalty to "his people" beyond any measurement; he expected the same magnitude of loyalty from them.

He surrendered the control of General Motors in 1910 to preserve the company for its investors. In 1920, his loyalty to his company and its stockholders drove him to spend more money than he had preserving the value of the company's name, reputation, and stock. As for his feckless choice of executives, he hired and developed Charles W. Nash, Charles F. Kettering, Alfred P. Sloan, (also Walter Chrysler and almost Henry Ford) and a few thousand others.

Who was Durant? A small-town boy from a broken home who had no advantages at all except his own character. With a borrowed $2000 he built up the largest carriage company in the world. With a debt-ridden, faltering motor company, he created the world's largest corporation, providing millions of jobs all over the world in the past 65 years. (Over 100 years now!)

Small in stature, W. C. Durant was larger than life in every aspect of his thought, spirit, and practice. He was, indeed, so much larger in concept that he made the lesser men who surrounded him uncomfortable. He was unpredictable as an elemental force of nature.

Durant was an original genius who escapes classification and definition; he had an almost godlike prescience; he had the creativity to translate his vision to reality, not only for himself but for his fellow men. He was compassionate, gentle, charming, delightful, considerate, brilliant, generous, ingenious, and infinitely loyal.

Mass production, the greatest servant ever tamed to the uses of mankind, was still only an idea when Durant grasped it. He more than any other man, implemented this great multiplier of goods and good for mankind. He was, indeed, what Dickens called, "The Founder of the Feast" and we are still eating at his bountiful table, although we have forgotten his name.

Is that not a moving tribute? Durant and his team started the mass production explosion of the automobile. Today we are in the Information Age and need a new group of entrepreneurs. This group must tame another great multiplier for the good of mankind: Leadership. The greatest enhancement of productivity today will be the leadership capabilities of the teams in the companies. Everyone has mass production, but not everyone has an understanding of building united teams. Leadership is the new competitive advantage! We stand on the edge of a new era and we need a generation of visionaries like Billy Durant to fulfill the promise of the Information Age.

Are you one of those visionaries?

**Top 10 influencers in History
(As compiled by Chris Brady)**

10. William Wilberforce

9. Winston Churchill

8. Alexander The Great

7 Queen Elizabeth I

6. Ronald Reagan

5. George Washington

4. Moses

3. Emperor Constantine

2. The Apostle Paul

1. Jesus Christ

Separation of Religion and State

Ok! I have to get this off my chest. I cannot remain silent any longer! I am imploring people to get the real facts on the meaning of "The Separation of Church and State". In my opinion, this one of the frontline issues in the media war and as this issue goes, so goes the country. The original definition of Separation of Church and State was based on protecting the local churches from a government sponsored national church. This separation has been turned upside down to mean separation of any religious values from the state. Can a society honestly survive while rejecting all religious values? How far we have wandered from the founding principles on separation, based upon John Locke's writings. Just a cursory look at the history of Separation of Church and State will produce a major conflict from the interpretation that is used today. Here is the wikipedia entry on Separation of Church and State.

The idea of separating the church and state is often credited to the writings of the British philosopher John Locke, which deeply influenced the drafting of the United States Constitution. According to his principle of the social contract, Locke argued that the government lacked authority in the realm of individual conscience, as this was something rational people could not cede to the government for it or others to control. For Locke, this created a natural right in the liberty of conscience, which he argued must therefore remain inviolable by any government authority. These views on religious tolerance and the importance of individual conscience, along with his social contract, became influential in the American colonies.

The concept was implicit in the flight of Roger Williams

from religious oppression in Massachusetts to found what became Rhode Island on the principle of state neutrality in matters of faith.

The phrase "separation of church and state" is derived from a letter written by Thomas Jefferson in 1802 to a group identifying themselves as the Danbury Baptists. In that letter, referencing the First Amendment of the United States Constitution, Jefferson writes:

> "Believing with you that religion is a matter which lies solely between Man & his God, that he owes account to none other for his faith or his worship, that the legitimate powers of government reach actions only, & not opinions, I contemplate with sovereign reverence that act of the whole American people which declared that their legislature should "make no law respecting an establishment of religion, or prohibiting the free exercise thereof," thus building a wall of separation between Church & State."

Another early user of the term was James Madison, the principal drafter of the United States Bill of Rights, who often wrote of "total separation of the church from the state." "Strongly guarded . . . is the separation between religion and government in the Constitution of the United States," Madison wrote, and he declared, "practical distinction between Religion and Civil Government is essential to the purity of both, and as guaranteed by the Constitution of the United States." This attitude is further reflected in the Virginia Statute for Religious Freedom, originally authored by Thomas Jefferson, but championed by Madison, and guaranteeing that no one may be compelled to finance any religion or denomination.

"... no man shall be compelled to frequent or support any religious worship, place, or ministry whatsoever, nor shall be enforced, restrained, molested, or burthened in his body or goods, nor shall otherwise suffer on account of his religious opinions or belief; but that all men shall be free to profess, and by argument to maintain, their opinion in matters of religion, and that the same shall in no wise diminish enlarge, or affect their civil capacities."

I believe the original documents of the Founding Fathers and John Locke's writings are very clear as to their meaning. Religious toleration meant giving all the Christian denominations the right to worship God in the way they deemed fit. There was a strong under girding of Judeo-Christian principles that supported our laws, communities, and leaders. No founding father imagined a separation of religious values from the operation of government. I could prove this point in many areas, but let me stay focused and just pick the Ten Commandments given from God to Moses on Mt. Sinai.

Why should we be shocked when a politician accepts bribes or embezzles? Should not their defense be; "I separated my religious values from my political assignment."? If he was a Christian and brought his values to his job, then he would not steal, lie, commit adultery, etc. Only an inconsistent Christian would do what a consistent person would do who rejected Judeo-Christian values. But if these religious values are rejected from government, then what values are left? I can see the politician who consistently follows through on Separation of Religion and State. They could state, "I will lie, cheat, steal, disrespect my parents, and fornicate with other people's spouses and this is just the beginning of my value system for government work." Would anyone legitimately vote for this person? If not, why would anyone honestly argue for separation of religious values from government positions? The wall of separation should ensure government does not create rules of faith for religious groups. If a religious faith violates the basic ten commandment rules, our judicial system will intervene, because our judicial system is based upon the traditional Judeo-Christian faith.

Let me give an analogy of how people have turned the Separation of Church and State on its head and are applying the principle backwards to its original intentions. The Dutch nation in the 13th century was a hardworking, future focused group who built dams, dykes, and other barriers to separate the ocean from the low lying land. The Dutch created this separation to allow them to reclaim the land and have farms where the ocean water previously had been. The separation was designed to keep the ocean out of the farms—not the farmers out of the ocean. Can you imagine if a century later the government argued against the Dutch

sailing on the ocean? The government would argue, "Our forefathers separated the ocean from the Dutch people and we cannot have any sailors sailing on the oceans. This would violate the principle of Separation of Ocean and Dutch. The Dutch people would rise in outrage against this disingenuous interpretation. They would argue the separation was designed one way, to keep the ocean from the Dutch people, but not the Dutch from the ocean. The Dutch have always been an ocean going people and would not tolerate this unconscionable interpretation. Is this not exactly what happened to the Separation of Church and State? It was designed to keep the State (ocean) out of the Church (Dutch people), but now keeps the Church and its values out of the State.

In the same way Americans have always been a religious people and should protest the wrong interpretation of Church and State. I am disappointed that someone would argue such twisted logic, but I am more disappointed that the vast majority of the American people will swallow this confused thinking with hardly a word of protest. I fear for our country if we reject the underlying principles of a good society. What society can last long term—if the people elected are liars, stealers, adulterers, etc? Our first president, George Washington said,

> "Where is the security for property, for reputation, for life, if the sense of religious obligation desert the oaths, which are the instruments of investigation in Courts of Justice? And let us with caution indulge the supposition, that morality can be maintained without religion. Whatever may be conceded to the influence of refined education on minds of peculiar structure, reason and experience both forbid us to expect, that national morality can prevail in exclusion of religious principle."

I could not say it better than Mr. Washington. He understood that a government would only be as good as the people it represents. I believe the people elected are only mirrors of the people in total. We must educate Americans as to the true meaning of the issues or we will become victims of revisionist spin. It would have been inconceivable for anyone to spout the current views of separation only fifty years ago. I love the yarn about the man asked; are you more concerned about the ignorance or the apathy of our current culture? "I don't know and I don't care" was his answer. The historical revisionist relies on the apathy and ignorance of the people in order to sell their inverted views of historical events. It is time for the people to get convicted and educated.

I certainly am not proposing a national church and strongly support the true interpretation of Separation of Church and State. I am not proposing mass elections of Christians as they will only have the support if the people are behind their actions. But I am proposing the individual responsibility of Americans to educate themselves on the historical issues. How can we possibly vote without an understanding of the underlying issues accepted or rejected by the candidates? I strongly believe if we get the American people right, the politicians will miraculously get it right! I do not believe in one person telling everyone else how to think. This would not be freedom, but demagoguery. I am encouraging everyone to read and think through the issues themselves. Our republic will not survive without a literate and educated citizenship.

Only a person, that does not know their history can fall prey to a charlatan selling a false interpretation of its history. Please share this article with others and be part of the solution and not part of the problem. We are a blessed nation and we must accept responsibility to carry on this blessed tradition.

Were you aware of the true history of the Separation of Church and State doctrine? Have you heard a twisted version espoused by the media? What are you doing to separate the truth from fiction? Pass this book on to others and encourage everyone to read the history for themselves.

Level Four Leadership -
"Every Captain Was a Nelson"

The Battle of Trafalgar was really the zenith of the fascinating age of fighting sail. Admiral Viscount Lord Horatio Nelson completed one of his most astonishing annihilations of his French and Spanish adversaries, and was killed in the process.

What Orrin Woodward and I wrote in the book *Launching a Leadership Revolution* about Nelson's victory at the Battle of the Nile a few years prior was also true of his conduct at Trafalgar. Nelson spent considerable time developing his ship's captains. He met with them every chance he got to impart his fighting philosophy unto them. He held special dinners to get them acquainted with each other to foster better team work. Most importantly, when the battle had commenced, he turned them loose to fight on their own. Since battle was confusing and communication was nearly impossible across the smoky water, with the loud cannons roaring almost non-stop, trying to coordinate fleet movements was nearly impossible, anyway. Nelson's preference was to rely on the ability of his fighting captains to make their own decisions in the heat of battle and to act on the philosophy he had so painstakingly taught them beforehand. As his fleet sailed into battle, Nelson's flag ship made a few signals to coordinate the fleet's movements as it came into battle. But once the fighting began, Nelson's signals changed to those of encouragement to "engage the enemy more closely," and famously, "England expects every man will do his duty."

This style of fighting, a significant departure from the standard method of engagement at that time in the Royal Navy, was what Nelson called the "Nelson touch." Uniquely,

Nelson was the only fleet commander in British history that purposely brought on a "pell-mell" battle and succeeded at it time and again. The reasons were many. Primary among them was the fighting initiative of his individual captains. They clearly knew what Nelson expected of them and they performed accordingly. Nelson had the master touch of decentralizing his leadership style at the right moment to wreak the most possible destruction on his enemy.

Perhaps no one summed up the results of the "Nelson touch" quite as well as Vice-Admiral Villeneuve, the French fleet commander that was defeated at Trafalgar. He was said to have made the following comment after learning of Lord Nelson's death at the battle:

"To any other Nation the loss of a Nelson would have been irreparable, but in the British Fleet off Cadiz, every Captain was a Nelson."

The Battle of Trafalgar is a prime example of the power of the Fourth Level of Influence.

The Only Way to Be Happy is to Give Happy

It is common to hear people say, "I just want to be happy." And who does not? It's certainly much better to be happy than sad. Good times are better to experience than bad. But pursuing happy is a little off the mark. It is like trying to grab smoke.

Whenever we make happiness our goal, we set ourselves up for a futile chase. First, we do something that we think will make us happy. Then, once that pleasure is through, we move on to the next. Usually, the pleasures have to escalate to continue to satisfy, and we find ourselves in an endless climb. From pleasure to pleasure we go, never really finding happiness.

The paradox is that happiness comes from living according to the highest picture we have of ourselves, not from pursuing and receiving pleasure. Everybody has an image in their mind of who they are and what they stand for. Sometimes our actions verify this inner image, and sometimes they run counter to it. This is where our spirituality comes in. The proper picture of ourselves is from God's perspective. Our perspective will always be a little flawed, skewed, and biased. We either tend to think we are better than we are, or we think horribly of ourselves; but our Creator has the true picture, and the closer we get to understanding what the Bible says about who we are, about "who's" we are, and about what we are here to do, the more we can understand what the correct picture of ourselves should be. Happiness then comes from living according to this accurate and true picture of our self.

Interestingly, the result is service to God and to others. When we are faithful in this service, in which we may or may not find "pleasure", we will, however, discover happiness! It is such a strange paradox, but I believe you'll find it to be true. It's one of the reasons that serving other people works so well to lift your spirits when you are down. Tis much better to give than to receive. But every time we give, we actually receive at the same time. It cannot be helped. Happiness will find you there!

Leadership ultimately ends up being about service to others. That is why most leaders, even in the middle of strife and surrounded by obstacles, are actually very happy. They might not be the biggest consumers of pleasure in our society, but they generally have a corner on the market of happiness! I guess it is one of God's rewards to those of you who give of yourself in the service of others. God bless those of you who are out there learning and growing, seeking to expand in your leadership ability, and looking for ways to make your gifts count in the lives of others! May you experience all the happiness your pursuit earns you!

Character Under Fire

The American Revolutionary War, which likely had not been called that yet, was not going well for the colonials at the end of 1776. George Washington and his volunteer army had been battered all across the islands of New York by the British. The combined forces of the Royal Navy and the British regular infantry and cavalry had made a mockery of the colonial resistance. A nighttime escape in fog was all that preserved Washington's forces. Forced to retreat into New Jersey, the colonials were then pushed all the way across the Delaware River into Pennsylvania. Fortunately for them, the British decided to hunker down for the winter, and pulled most of their forces back to New York. Detachments were left throughout New Jersey to keep an eye on the miniscule colonial force.

With enlistments running out, and the confidence in the cause of independence at an all time low, Washington made a daring move to cross the Delaware on Christmas night and surprise-attack the garrison at Trenton. In the annals of military history, it was a small engagement, but in the morale of the colonies it was a master stroke. Washington's attack succeeded perfectly, capturing the entire detachment at Trenton. Instead of going from defeat to defeat, retreating across state after state, the little band of revolutionaries had proven that they were not yet beaten.

The commander in chief of British and Hessian forces in America, Major General Howe, was furious. He immediately ordered General Cornwallis and his army to march on Washington in New Jersey with full force. Over five thousand professional soldiers, including artillery, set out immediately for New Jersey.

George Washington, managing his prisoners and captured stores in Trenton, received word of Cornwallis's advancing army. He quickly dispatched 600 men to slow the British advance so he could arrange yet another of his last-minute escapes. Without sufficient time to depart on his terms, his little army would be crushed.

Washington placed the French aristocrat General Roche de Fermoy in command of the small force. de Fermoy was one of a long line of adventurers from Europe who had come to America seeking military honors and fame. Many of these men made claims concerning their past leadership experiences and titles that may or may not have been true. Forced to keep good relations with foreign countries supporting the cause, Washington was often given no choice but to award command positions to many such adventurers. Some proved capable, others did not. Second to de Fermoy, with his 200 Pennsylvania rifleman, Washington placed Edward Hand. Hand's men, accustomed to hunting in the hills of Pennsylvania, were famous for their marksmanship. They were deadly accurate with their long, rifled guns.

It would be 600 men against 5,000, but the colonials only had to slow the advance of the mighty British. Placing themselves in the woods on either side of the road, and splitting the Pennsylvania riflemen into two groups, 100 for each side of the road, the colonials got into position.

The sight of 5,000 men in brilliant military discipline marching boldly down the road was apparently too much for

de Fermoy. At the first shot fired he was seen riding at a full gallop toward the rear of the colonial lines.

Then he continued riding and left the scene altogether. Confused and stunned, Edward Hand calmly assumed overall command.

Hand directed the colonials to wait until the British were extremely close before firing. Then suddenly the woods around the British force erupted in smoke and noise and clumps of British soldiers fell wounded and dead. The British scrambled to form battle lines, and then fired in rapid succession. The colonials had already pulled back through the woods. Now the Pennsylvania riflemen had their turn from a greater distance. Again, the incoming fire into the exposed British was deadly. Not to be deterred, the British ordered an advance into the woods, but by the time they reached where their enemy had been hiding, the colonials were long gone.

This process of heavy hidden fire, quick retreat, Pennsylvania rifle decimation, and more retreat was repeated throughout the day. At no point did the small colonial force give the British a chance to use their superior numbers or artillery. But continuously the raking fire from multiple angles of woods was deadly for the British. By the time this process was repeated for the fifth time, however, Hand and his brave band of men were being overrun. There was only so much 600 could do against 5,000. Then suddenly loud bursts of artillery shells were heard as plumes of dirt and death soared into the sky among the advancing British ranks. It was Washington's main army joining the resistance. The two armies were beginning to engage as it grew dark.

Cornwallis, weary from pushing through heavier resistance than expected, with enormous casualties on his side, decided not to press the attack at night. He called off his troops and encamped for the night. And of course, this is exactly what Washington needed. He kept campfires burning and charged a small group of men with making enough noise to sound like an entire camp.

Washington's escape was successful that night, as he stole away an entire army from right under the nose of the enemy.

Marching quickly before Cornwallis could figure out what happened, Washington and his force showed up in Princeton, New Jersey and routed and captured the troops Cornwallis had left there in reserve. Ultimately, Washington was able to escape the beleaguered British and winter safely, riding high on the wave of victories he had stolen from the jaws of defeat.

The small victories at the close of 1776 proved critical. Morale was raised, hope in the cause was re-sparked, and the fight for independence survived its' closest brush with extinction. As is usually the case, it all hinged on leadership. Edward Hand and his contrasting example of leadership as opposed to de Fermoy could not be more illustrative of the difference between true and counterfeit leadership. De Fermoy was all bluster; beating his chest, showing his titles and claiming great abilities; but when the first shots were fired, he fled for the hills like a frightened school girl. On the other hand, Edward Hand had no formal training, title or claim to fame; but he was a real leader. When the imposter fled the scene, Hand filled the gap. He very confidently and competently took command and did what needed to be done.

This great example from the founding of a nation and what it shows about leadership should never be forgotten. Imposters in the world of leadership abound. Those who talk the loudest about how great they are, what they are going to do, and how great their abilities are, are often the first to flee the scene when the going gets tough. Real leaders, on the other hand, quietly go about the business of doing what needs to be done; often without fanfare, title or official position. Orrin Woodward has often said, "When the going gets tough, the tough get going." Indeed, you can learn a lot about someone by how they act when the shots are fired, when the 5,000 are advancing on 600, when it is time to put up or shut up. In motocross racing there is a saying that, "When the gate drops, the talk stops."

Further, it can be seen how much can be accomplished by just one person deciding to lead. Edward Hand was only one man, and he was not even officially in charge of the 600 men who had been abandoned by their commander. However his actions had enormous ramifications on history. Every leader would be wise to remember his example. One person can, and does, make a difference. Often, that difference is too large to be measured.

So when challenges come your way, when the shots being fired are live ammunition, when the going gets tough: you will have a choice. You can be a de Fermoy, or you can be an Edward Hand. That choice, at those moments, will define your legacy. Choose well. Lead.

Edward Deming: Success Process

I have been teaching for the last few years a simple (but not easy) technique to create change in your life and business. It is a process I originally read as an engineer called the Deming Cycle. Edward Deming was a professor and statistics guru who went to Japan and helped rebuild their manufacturing after WWII. His original cycle was Plan, Do, Check and Act. After working for a couple of months on how to teach this concept to developing leaders I made one subtle change. I like; Plan, Do, Check and Adjust (**PDCA**). With this simple process you can identify any area of life you wish to improve and develop a plan to create the change. Check your results and adjust where necessary to accomplish the plan. One can improve any area of life through this process, from losing weight to improving sales, improving relationships to speaking ability, etc. In my opinion, this is the single biggest tool to change the results you are currently obtaining in life. This tool will produce as dramatic an increase in personal effectiveness as the change from horses to automobiles did in travel effectiveness. In fact, I believe that great achievers in every area whether it be sports, business, faith, etc. use some type of feedback loop for personal and professional improvement. Let us break down each step:

Plan – "Those who fail to plan are planning to fail." You must have a plan to accomplish practically anything in a positive direction. It has been said, "Any dead fish can float downstream, but it takes a live one to swim against the current!" To be a live fish you must have a plan; otherwise, you are floating downstream.

Do – "The road to Hell is paved with good intentions." Many would-be leaders were planning on doing something great, but never got around to it. One of my favorite quotes is, "When all is said and done, much more is said than ever done." The best plan in the world will not accomplish anything unless it is implemented. Develop the plan and then have the courage to begin. A job well begun is half done!

Check –Many people fail at this point. They set a plan and begin the work, but never check to see if the plan is moving them in the right direction. Life is more like taking a canoe down a river. There are many course corrections along the way. Factors like the river current, obstacles in the water, and bends and turns will make you constantly seek feedback. Without feedback you will run ashore and wonder why the plan did not work. By checking the results you will know which factors are different than originally assumed and be in a position to make the necessary changes.

Adjust – After checking your results and identifying areas for improvement, the next step is to make the necessary adjustments. This does not mean your plan was bad, but only that we are human and cannot predict all the possible outcomes. By following this PDCA process, the destination will be met by adjusting the plan after you have checked for feedback. If we were all knowing, we could succeed simply by planning and doing. As human beings we must plan our work, do our work, check our work and adjust where necessary.

PDCA is the best way I have learned to accurately assess reality and to make changes to improve. I have used this process for years in my life and it has resulted in great success. Swim against the currents of mediocrity and negativity. You can dream bigger and achieve bigger with the PDCA process! Ask yourself do you have a plan in this area or are you merely floating downstream?

Developiŋg Heroic Virtue

I am reading a great book for the second time! It is titled, *"The Closing of the American Mind"* by Allan Bloom. There is a chapter on books that will make you think about the importance of reading in a person's life. Mr. Bloom has watched a decline in good reading from his students. His thesis states that without good reading the soul is shallow and has a reduced capacity to process heroic virtues. The pop culture does not recognize virtuous behavior, but instead recognizes bizarre behaviors. Classic books give people examples of heroic virtue and help us draw on the strength of our past when we go through our own struggles. When you have a friend that is hurting you can draw on the loyalty of Achilles to his friend. When you need to make a moral stand, you can draw on Daniel willing to be thrown to the lions for what he believed. When you are oppressed by tyranny you can read about Patrick Henry, "Give me liberty or give me death!" How would you process your own trials without reference to the great men and women of the past? I encourage everyone to read more and read better books. Just as there is junk food there is also junk reading. To be virtuous you need to have examples of virtuous behavior and model this behavior in your own life. No excuses about your past or how you were raised will do! It is your life and you have the power to choose to read, listen and grow. Leadership is a choice and a life well lived is the reward! Let me give you a couple of Mr. Bloom's thoughts:

"I began to ask students who their heroes are. Again, there is usually silence, and most frequently nothing follows. Why should anyone have heroes?"

"In us the contempt for the heroic is only an extension

of the perversion of the democratic principle that denies greatness and wants everyone to feel comfortable in his skin without having to suffer unpleasant comparisons."

"One can only pity young people without admirations they can respect or avow, who are artificially restrained from the enthusiasm for great virtue."

"Idealism as it is commonly conceived should have primacy in an education, for man is a being who must take his orientation by his possible perfection. To attempt to suppress this most natural of all inclinations because of possible abuses is, almost literally, to throw out the baby with the bath."

"But deprived of literary guidance, they no longer have any image of a perfect soul, and hence do not long to have one. They do not even imagine that there is such a thing...... Thus the most common student view lacks an awareness of the depths as well of the heights, and lacks gravity."

Drink deeply of the classics and watch your perspective choices widen as you draw on the knowledge gained from great books. You will enjoy Mr. Bloom's thought provoking book.

The Leadership of Proverbs: Part Five

Proverbs 1:20-22 *Wisdom crieth without; she uttereth her voice in the streets:*

> *She crieth in the chief place of concourse, in the openings of the gates: in the city she uttereth her words, saying, How long, ye simple ones, will ye love simplicity? And the scorners delight in their scorning, and fools hate knowledge?*

Christians all over America will attend church this Sunday and hopefully learn more wisdom from the preaching of God's word. Next to the message of salvation through Jesus Christ—I would state wisdom as the greatest value to gain from reading the Bible. Wisdom encompasses so many areas; wisdom with people, money, family, community, government etc. I look back on my own life and realize what a fool I was in the area of wisdom. I was hungry to learn, but to paraphrase an old song; I was looking for wisdom in all the wrong places. I had read over 500 books by my mid twenties and had never read the Bible. Imagine a young man wanting to learn about the world and reading all these books, but never bothering to read the one by God himself? If you would have asked me if I was wise; I would have told you about all the books I had read; but deep down, I knew I was unhappy and incomplete and yearned for inner peace. Augustine stated, "Our hearts are not at rest until they find their rest in you my Lord and my God." God had watched me break myself against the rocks of life and in His mercy rescued me from my foolish thinking. The wonderful thing about Christ is he is no respecters of persons. All of us must humble ourselves to receive the free gift of peace and mercy Jesus has bought for us.

286

According to verse 20 and 21, wisdom is crying out to be heard in the streets, concourses, gates and city. I stopped attending church at eighteen and did not attend for the next eight years. I think about how many Godly messages that faithful pastors shared during this period of time. Wisdom was crying out in these churches and yet I was too prideful to humble myself to seek answers there. How many churches did I drive by on a Sunday morning on my way to fish or watch football games? I was looking for answers; frustrated about the lack of peace in my life; yet refused to seek Wisdom from the source of all true peace. Think about your life. Are you attending a place of worship where God's word is proclaimed? Do you attend church at all? If you do attend a church, what is the specific reason that you attend? Is it because they have great music? Because of the children's program? Because they have skits and plays to entertain people? My only question is: Are they teaching God's word to you so you can develop a hunger for wisdom? We have always taught in our leadership business to keep the main thing the main thing. The main thing in a church should be its faithful exposition of God's word. All the others issues are just icing on the cake. If there is no cake, then the icing is worthless.

But what is liberty without wisdom, and without virtue? It is the greatest of all possible evils; for it is folly, vice, and madness, without tuition or restraint.
– Edmund Burke

Wisdom is crying to be heard. Are you attending a church to gain this wisdom or to be entertained? Our culture has bought into the entertainment trap and must return to the discipline of Bible study and Bible exposition. Wisdom is gained through applying Biblical principles to life's situations. The wisest man is the one who knows and applies the Bible consistently to his life. This is why I respect Pastor Robert Dickie so much. I have watched his life for over a decade and have been inspired by his consistent application of Biblical principles to life. Do you live your life by Biblical principles or the latest: Oprah show, radio shock jock, agnostic professor, pragmatic boss, self-made philosophy?

This Sunday, somewhere in your area there will be a faithful minister expositing God's word. It does not have to be a big church to be teaching truth, but it does have to be teaching faithfully from the Bible. Find a Bible believing church and hunger for the wisdom that only the Bible and Holy Spirit can teach you.

Verse 21, ask how long will you love simplicity, or scorn or be a fool? The simple ones never ask the deeper questions: What is my purpose and why was I created? The simple are ignorant and even ignorant of their ignorance. The scorners are hardened in their sins. They mock the truth because they wish to live their life independent of God's law. Although they can choose to reject God, they cannot choose the consequences of this rejection. How many broken lives have I seen from this sinful rejection of truth and wisdom? The fools know they are ignorant, but choose to remain so. They continually keep themselves occupied through entertainment, sports, music and association with other fools. Fools will purposely avoid asking the deeper questions because they choose to remain fools rather than be accountable to an Almighty God. The problem is that fools lead empty lives, devoid of purpose and direction. If you are in any of these three groups, then today is the day to change! Turn from your ignorance, scorning or foolishness and seek wisdom! Pick up your Bible and read today. Find a local Bible believing church and attend. Living a life without wisdom is like playing in the NFL without pads; you are bound to get hurt, it is just a matter of time. The wisdom is available, but you must discipline yourself to read, associate and pray for God's guidance. Wisdom is a major for anyone aspiring to be a leader. We have much to do and we need leaders with wisdom to accomplish the Launching of a Leadership Revolution! God Bless you on your journey to wisdom.

Initiative: The Not-So-Secret, Secret to Leadership

You may have heard the old line that there are three types of people in the world:

1. Those that make things happen.
2. Those that watch things happen, and
3. Those that wonder..."What happened?"

I think it might be time to talk about the role that initiative plays in the world of leadership. One trait common to all leaders is the initiative they show toward their vision.

Leaders do not have to be told to do something. Leaders do not need managers above them. Leaders do not wait for the lights to all turn green before taking off on a trip. Leaders take action, they take responsibility, and they do not take their time waiting and wondering if they should act. At the end of the day, it is the go-getters that seem to become the biggest leaders. Time after time I have seen people with less talent, less of a head start, less connections, and less information absolutely outperform others simply because they got moving! Even if a person is not effective, the very fact that he or she is taking action usually forces an improvement in effectiveness. Even if a person heads in the wrong direction, sooner or later he or she will get on track.

> *Without initiative, leaders are simply workers in leadership positions.*
> –Bo Bennett

Conversely, those who deliberate, dilly-dally, hesitate, ponder, get bogged down in analysis, or have to be sure everything is perfect before taking action generally do a very good job at what they do, they just don't get much of it accomplished. They have beautifully detailed goals printed out in multi-colors but do not ever seem to hit them, and they have all kinds of theoretical knowledge about how things are going to work out for them once everything is perfectly situated for them to make an attempt.

Over time, there is no comparison between the results of the "active" people and the "pondering" people. The active people almost always win out. While one group is busy wondering how things are going to be, the other group is busy making them that way! Often sharp, talented, and smart people wonder why the guy who used to have poor people skills, with a limited education, and no connections blew right by them in life. Usually, personal initiative was a big component in the success story.

Wondering who the next leader is going to be? Curious about who is going to grow the most personally in the next couple of years? Look for the person showing initiative. Look for the person taking action. They may not be the most likely candidate at the moment, but all that action will lead to greatness. And you will see that the old saying has come true. They will be the ones who make things happen, while the deliberators watch it happen, and a few will deliberate too long and wonder what happened! So get started today. Get a goal and go after it. Do not worry about looking good along the way or about your qualifications. Just show some initiative and get started. You will be shocked at the power of action!!!!

Taking Stock of Accomplishments

There is always a lot of talk around the New Year's celebration about resolutions and things people are going to change in the year to come. I find this a bit curious, however, in the absence of a scoreboard to reflect the performance for the year that is passing.

A habit that is becoming a tradition for me is to take a moment at the end of each year and write out a list of all major accomplishments, events, and outstanding moments from that year. This has proven to be both enlightening and rewarding. It lets me see that in some cases and certain areas, I am not accomplishing nearly as much as I might have thought, while in others I am perhaps doing better than I might have imagined. Without taking stock of these things specifically, however, we only have a fuzzy feeling for what we have accomplished in the previous year. Pessimists will be likely, in the absence of such data, to assume the worst and think that they have not done much at all. While the confident types will be a little self-deceived and think they have done better than they actually have.

As the saying goes, In God We Trust, all others must bring data. I guess it only makes sense to include ourselves in "all others." Should not we take stock and produce data on our own performance? If not, how can we make accurate assessments of where we are and what changes need to be made? It is the difference between living approximately and living accurately. Remember, it is easy to become self-deceived; we must fight the tendency with facts.

For instance, as I write this I am looking at my "year in review". I see that I could still find a way to read more, write more, and hit several other key areas for myself. In some categories, like lawsuits, for instance, I am overachieving! In physical fitness, I have had a year of advancement. Knowing where I was a year ago helps me see that I have, in fact, improved in this category. However, I can readily identify areas of health and physical fitness in which I would like to push harder.

These are just some examples from my current year. Obviously, there are many more. We can and should all do this in other categories, as well. Finance, friends, family, business, career, spiritual, biblical study, etc. are all areas that should be considered. Just how many books did we read? How many uplifting, educational CDs did we listen to? How many leadership development meetings did we attend? How much money did we give to charities? Which ones? How much time did we spend with family and friends? How many specific steps did we take to express love and encouragement to others?

This may all seem a bit much, but I assure you, it only takes an hour or so to look back through calendars and records and benefit from this process. As with most of these types of things, it turns out to be a bit of fun, too. However, as I stated, the value of doing this keeps us from operating on assumptions and puts real, actual data at our finger tips. Now, I ask you: what could be better for a leader looking to improve his or her life than accurate data from which to make new resolutions?

May this next year, be a year for your record books!

ANSWERS TO FISH TRIVIA:

1) B: 27,000

There are approximately 27,000 known species of fish, easily making them the most diverse group of vertebrates, and scientists estimate that there are still thousands of fish species yet to be discovered!

2) A: Ocean sunfish

The ocean sunfish (Mola mola) produces more eggs than any other species of fish. In fact, it produces more eggs than any other vertebrate on the planet. A single female can produce up to 300 million eggs at a single spawning, each measuring about 1.3 mm (0.05 in) in diameter! Considered a delicacy in Asia, a single mola can fetch prices as high as $600 (U.S.).

3) C: 100

There are over a hundred different varieties of goldfish, classified by color, body shape, finnage and outgrowth of the eyes. Some common varieties of goldfish include the Comet, the Fantail, the Oranda, the Shubunkin, and the Black Moor. Perhaps the most popular of all aquarium fish, goldfish have been known to live up to 25 years!

4) D: Sailfish

Although it is, of course, extremely difficult to measure the swimming speed of large fish in the wild, the cosmopolitan sailfish (Istiophorus platypterus) is considered by many experts to be the fastest fish in the world. It has been clocked at speeds of 110 km/h (68 mph). The average fish would be hard-pressed to reach 20 km/h (12 mph).

5) C: Puffer fish

The most poisonous fish (to eat) is the puffer fish whose ovaries, eggs, blood, liver, intestines and skin contain a fatally poisonous toxin called tetrodotoxin. Less than 0.1 g (0.004 oz) of this toxin is enough to kill an adult in as little as 20 minutes. Ironically, the poisonous puffer fish is considered a delicacy in Japan. Although the poison is generally removed before they are served, eating puffer fish can still be fatal if the fish was improperly prepared. In some countries, a chef must be certified in order to serve puffer fish because the poisonous parts of the puffer differ slightly from species to species (there are about 120 different species of puffer fish). About 100 diners die each year after eating puffer fish.

6) C: Whale Shark

Reaching an average length of 45 feet and weighing up to 15 tons, the Whale Shark (Rhincodon typus) is generally considered the largest species of fish in the world. One specimen captured in the Gulf of Thailand in 1919 measured an incredible 59 feet! Not related to whales (which are mammals, not fish), the Whale Shark probably earned its name because of its abnormally large size as well as the fact that, like whales, it is a filter feeder, swimming with its mouth open in order to suck up plankton and small sea creatures.

7) B: Stout infantfish,

Measuring only 7mm (about the width of a pencil), the stout infantfish holds the record for world's smallest fish. It lives around Australia's Great Barrier Reef and is thought to have a lifespan of only two months. Prior to the discovery of the stout infantfish, the dwarf goby fish was generally considered the world's smallest fish.

8) C: 50,000

When a shark loses a tooth, a new tooth grows in to replace it. In fact, below each tooth (inside the gums) are up to 7 layers of replacement teeth, just waiting to grow in. Some species of sharks have been known to shed as many as 50,000 teeth during their lifetime!

Bestselling Author and leadership consultant Orrin Woodward invites you to check out his award-winning leadership blog. On a weekly basis, Orrin posts entries on subjects ranging from leadership example to relevant business topics, from religious issues to current events affecting the culture war. Mr. Woodward has a bachelor of science degree in manufacturing engineering from Kettering University (formerly GMI) and business administration training from the University of Michigan. He holds four United States patents, an exclusive National Benchmarking Award for product analysis, and has been recognized in national trade journals. Mr. Woodward enjoys ocean fishing, physical fitness, and adding to his extensive library.

Orrinwoodward.blogharbor.com

Here is a sample of what the readers in Mr. Woodward's blogging community are saying:

"Orrin, thanks for a great history lesson!…"
   -Matt

"This post reminds me of two things, first, your commitment to GOD, and second your   unwavering commitment to leadership…."
   -Brian and Sherry

"Orrin, each day you help us to understand more of your thinking and also help us to understand ourselves better…."
   -Ben

"I read your blog everyday…Thank you for your encouraging words everyday, they mean so much to me. As I go about my day, I often think to myself….what would Orrin do?…"
   -Ally

"Another great post - I don't know how you do it, but you just keep coming up with more and more great articles that get the wheels turning in my head!…."
   -Ann

All Grace Outreach

All Grace Outreach originally began in 1993 in Maine as "Christian Mission Services". In March of 2007, the charity organization was transferred to Michigan and the name was changed to All Grace Outreach. All Grace Outreach is a 501c3 organization committed to providing assistance to those in need. Our main focuses include helping abused, abandoned, and distressed children, supporting U.S. military families that have lost loved ones in war, and spreading the gospel of Jesus Christ throughout the world.

Mission and Vision - To impact and improve the lives of others by contributing to charitable organizations which are committed to making a difference both locally and globally.

Here is a partial list of the organizations your donation supports:
Whaley Children's Center
Kindred Spirit
Here's Life Inner City
Evangelical Press
Angelman Syndrome Foundation
St. Jude's Hospital
The Marine Corp League ROTC
US Air Force Center for Character and Leadership

www.allgraceoutreach.com